BUILDING A MYSTERY

Live and Interactive at the MuchMusic
Debut of SURFACING *26 June 1997.*

BUILDING A MYSTERY

The Story of
Sarah McLachlan
& Lilith Fair

JUDITH FITZGERALD

QUARRY MUSIC BOOKS

To Walt Grealis, O.C. and Stan Klees:
Your guidance is unfailing
and your advice unflinching.
Your contribution to Canadian music
is inestimable.
Thank you.

In Memoriam
Uwe Vandrei
(28 February 1960 — 14 September 1994)

The publisher gratefully acknowledges the support of
The Canada Council for the Arts and the
Department of Canadian Heritage for
the arts of writing and publishing in Canada.

Building a Mystery: The Story of Sarah McLachlan and Lilith Fair is a serious biographical study of Sarah McLachlan's life and career. The quotation of lyrics from songs composed by Sarah McLachlan and copyright by her publishers is intended to illustrate the biographical information and criticism presented by the author and thus constitutes fair use under existing copyright conventions.

ISBN 1-55082-190-3

Design by Susan Hannah.

Printed and bound in Canada by
AGMV/Marquis,
Cap-Ste-Ignace, Quebec.

Published by Quarry Press Inc.,
P.O. Box 1061, Kingston, Ontario
www.quarrypress.com

CONTENTS

If you love large, you've got to hurt large. If you've got a lot of light, you've probably got an equal amount of darkness.

— Sarah McLachlan

Nothing touches a work of art so little as words of criticism. They always result in more or less fortunate misunderstandings. Things aren't all so tangible and sayable as people would have us believe; most experiences are unsayable, they happen in a space that no word has ever entered, and more unsayable than all other things are works of art, those mysterious existences whose life endures beside our own small transitory life.

— Rainer Maria Rilke, *Letters to a Young Poet*

I hang my laundry on the line when I write.

— Joni Mitchell

one

JUDITH'S DAUGHTER

or The Path Of Thorns (Terms)

On my way to Halifax, I pick up J.P., a young man around Sarah McLachlan's age who, for lack of anything better to do, consents to this share-the-driving jaunt because Windsor's clotted with tourists losing their money *and* he's never seen either the Atlantic *or* the Pacific *and* he figures he'll make an excellent all-round gopher, snap-shooter, chaperone, *etc.*, *and* he snares a captive audience for the convoluted never-ending story of his life.

You get the yakkative idea.

The kid does *oozée à la bouche*. Grad-school this, grade-nine that and daycare the other on top of some circuitously logo-maniacal segue concerning a dame named Eve who'd recently moved on to greener victims and blah, blah, blah, blah, BLAH!

Only when we stop at Hymns — our twisted moniker for a certain hockeyist's doughnut chain — do I get my turn at the table. Then, I squeeze in synopses of the ongoing Sarah Saga in which he unknowingly participates. Of course, we scarf down the extra-large pick-us-uppers, visit the on-site facilities, and gear up for the next verbicidally prolix instalment of The Excruciatingly Long-Winded and Oft-Wandering Life of J.P., told in multiloquious detail in the close-quartered cab of A-M-T (Adam My Truck).

Until Longueuil. At Longueuil, we get lost *and* I lose it.

We do not get lost because I give amazingly accurate co-pilot directions, *nor* do we get lost because he's never driven through Montreal before, *nor* because he's a little weary after all this non-stop loquacity, *nor* because he forgets to tell me he can't read signs in French. Nope. We get lost because, as the garrulous and gabacious J.P. avers, he thought he'd seen a Hymns and forgot he was not to leave the Trans-Canada Highway.

Naturally, I get behind the wheel and tell him to shut up. Forever. (Or, at least until Quebec City.) Naturally, I tell him this in the bluntest way possible: "Shut up or ship off. Ixnay on the *luxfay de mots*. This is not the story of J.P. This is the story of Sarah McLachlan, the one you're going to witness for me."

"Kew-l-l-l-l! I've never been a witness before. I've been a student, a factory worker, a Trivia champ, a research assistant, a computer-resource person, an executive . . .

"Fitz! You're doing 145 in a 90! *Sweet Jesus . . .*"

"Yup. Good of you to notice. It's like this: The more you talk, the faster I drive. Adam might have 198,722 kilometers on him; but, believe me, I've pushed him to flat-out 170, no sweat. Keep talking. At the rate you're varnishing nonsense with the charms of sound, we'll hit Halifax in one hell of a hurry."

"I'm all ears."

"Well, you and yours truly are going to Halifax for one reason and one reason only: I need corroborating evidence a certain person exists. Her name is Judy (Kaines) James. I can tell you that much. I'm sworn to an oath not to reveal her address or telephone number. So, I won't. But, the woman's name is Judy and I have to prove she exists so I can prove she is who she says she is."

"Who does she say she is?"

"She says she's McLachlan's birth mother. A lot of other people — reliable and trustable people — I've interviewed also say McLachlan's got a birth mother."

"So what? Everybody's got a birth mother."

"Yeah, but not everybody's got a birth mother *and* an adopted mother, right? Look at me, for instance. I've got two mothers."

"Sarah McLachlan's adopted? Holy shit! That's awesome. Like, Joni Mitchell in reverse, eh?"

"Yeah, I guess you could put it that way. Anyway, I think McLachlan's adopted and I think I found her birth mother. In Halifax. Don't think she'll see me; but, I've talked with her a couple of times on the 'phone."

"If you don't think she'll see you, then why are we going to Halifax?"

"To see *her*. To prove she exists and, if she does exist, to make sure it's properly documented in order to prove she exists."

"Oh, like *Due South*?"

"Do what?"

"*Due South*. The best show on TV. Like, you're the hard-boiled American cop and I'm your good Canadian Mountie sidekick?"

"Sorry, Kid. Don't own a TV"

"Well, this guy's been sent to Chicago and he's a Mountie and it's a great show and it's one of my all-time faves. Fitz, you'd love it. It makes fun of absolutely everything. It turns every cliché in the book on its head, right? Like, there's this one episode ... Holy shit! Slow down!"

"Yeah, you're my witness. Better not lose you, eh?"

I begin to appreciate Adam's pings, pangs, squeaks and rattles from an entirely different perspective. J.P. begins to appreciate his part in our promptly dubbed "excellent easterly adventure." Right around Lévis, he begins to take a genuine interest in his role as witness and, accordingly, demands the specs on the story.

I preface said story by explaining I'd planned to write a celebration of a Canadian artist who had made a refreshing contribution to the global soundscape as well as subtly demonstrating that, in the bimbo-driven cock-rock world of pop, women could command the attention and respect habitually slathered all over men in the field.

To that end, I'd sent an e-mail to McLachlan's manager in

Vancouver, Nettwerk Production's Terry McBride. In it, I'd request-ed an interview and plus-one (Read: A pair of tickets including a photographer's pass) for the Lilith Fair show in Toronto. I'd sent the e-mail to info@nettwerk.com because I didn't know McBride's personal address, and, knowing a little about both McBride and the way these things generally work, I knew he'd see the e-mail.

Also, I pointed out to J.P., since I'd long ago learned to swim with the sharks in the muddied waters of the music industry, I hadn't expected McBride would even bother to respond to me, especially after I'd queried a few of my key contacts in the biz (who'd told me this, that, and the other about the kind of guy McBride might be).

So, for the record, I'd sent this really positive, perky, and downright drivelly e-mail on the off chance my ballsical braggadocio would at least merit an interview with you know who. I thought I'd give it a week before I contacted McBride tele-phonically (which I did).

The day I called Nettwerk, I asked the phone-answer person if I could speak with Mr. Terry McBride.

"Who are you?" she wanted to know, naturally.

"Judith Fitzgerald," I replied, naturally.

"Does he know you? Can I say what it's about?"

"Oh," I said, "I think he'll want to speak with me. Tell him I'm the woman writing the biography of Sarah McLachlan."

"Terry, here, what can I do for you?"

McBride and yours truly enjoy a delightful conversation in which he jocularly informs me he'd like to see something in writing before he'll agree to anything. I offer to re-send my e-mail he says he's never received. When he asks me if I'm aware that a book about Sarah is already being written, I ask by whom.

McBride explains he's hired a reporter/photographer to fol-low Lilith Fair and write his own book about it. I explain I'm writing a pop biography — not a tour book — and, in my hum-ble opinion, there was room for more than one fish in this sea.

Well, McBride wants to know, do I know how tightly con-trolled photographs and representations of Sarah McLachlan are? Actually, I counter, I do. McBride says he can't respond to my request until I put it in writing and e-mail it to him personally at terry@nettwerk.com (which I do).

By the way, I also say, nice makeover on your girl. She looks like a million *Buicks* in *Elle*, eh? McBride actually veers off the message-track and confesses he's tried to talk Sarah out of regrowing her tresses. He really likes the close-cropped look for her. Well, I say, women, eh? What can you do? Mr. Avuncular concludes our conversation by informing me he'll give my request "serious thought" before he gets back to me.

Must be some deeply seriously thoughts going on with McBride, I figure. I have yet to hear from him. Instead, I hear from his lawyer in Los Angeles who warns me and my publisher not to infringe upon any of Ms McLachlan's rights while writing the book, a warning that biographers and publishers have come to expect when managers refuse to cooperate. I can't quite figure why McBride feels threatened by this innocent request. After all, I'd sent him an outline of my accomplishments and I thought he'd at least deliver a more personal TNT — Thanks, no thanks! — and besides, as I'd explained in my e-message, this book would celebrate the accomplishments of one of North America's ascending stars.

Nothing doing. Not only could I not interview McLachlan, I could also not contact her this, that and the other, either. (Fortunately, I'd done all my contacting prior to contacting *him*.) Of course, McBride could not possibly threaten me with legal calamities if I talked to McLachlan's friends, McLachlan's family, my friends, my family, people in the street and such like. You get the idea. The way I'd heard it, the guy's litigious streak ran several stories high. That's the way Stein and Saltzberg both see him, anyhoo . . ."

"Who?"

"Norman Stein and Brad Saltzberg, two guys on the West Coast. Chatted with them both. One wanted to sing; the other wanted to sing the blues . . .

"*Hmm-mm . . .*"

"*Hmm-mm*, what?"

"Well, Stein, it seems, gave McBride his start in business, way back in the early '80s. And, Saltzberg? Poor fellow. He moans and groans about bailing out of the earliest incarnation of the Nettwerk partnership with McBride — when the soon-to-be company was called Noetix — like it was his OGSD (One Great Stupid Decision) or something. Anyway, that's another story in the book, eh?"

"Kewl-l-l. Which one am I gonna be in?"

"Judith's, so far as I can tell."

"Actually, Fitz, I'm not sure what all you're talking about."

"Well," I say in my very nicest *it's-been-a-long-time-coming* voice, "when you work in the trenches of popular music, you hear things. Comes with the turf. I'd heard a few things about McLachlan during my stint as *The Toronto Star*'s country-music columnist. Stuff I'd heard involved her admirable proclivity for what the superior satirical *FRANK* calls 'libidinous legovers' alongside rumors she had, as *FRANK* says, 'a taste for sushi.' "

I also tell him about Uwe Vandrei, the obsessed fan allegedly of the stalking persuasion who'd wound up dead in his black Mazda pickup after he'd publicly claimed co-write status on McLachlan's break-out single, *Possession*.

Plus, he gets an earful on an array of lawsuits in Vancouver over song rights, copyright infringement, royalties and something to do with a couple of guys who'd been outsized of the partnership by McBride alongside an item of a personal nature, one which spoke keenly to me, given the fact Sarah Ann McLachlan was, as they say, somebody else's baby.

So, I explain:

Shortly after the Hollywood lawyer missive, I become the owner of a photograph of Judy, McLachlan's birth mother. I cannot disclose the way in which I come to own said item; however, it comes complete with a telephone number where I can speak person-to-personally with the woman known as "Judy."

Speak with her I do. McLachlan's birth mother relates a heartbreakingly chilling story, a story far too similar to my own for comfort, a story that slashes through every last thread of professional composure in me.

However, this is not my story; it is Judy's (and that's the way it must be).

The first time we speak, Judy immediately asks me if I'm "looking to do some work on Sarah" and, when I reply in the affirmative, she states flatly: "Well, see, the problem is I'm her natural mother and she hasn't really acknowledged publicly that she has found me."

According to Judy, McLachlan has not done so because her adopted parents do not know that Judy and Sarah maintain an active friendship; however, the McLachlans do know their youngest and only daughter of three found Judy by a serendipitous set of flukes when she was 18.

Born in September 1947 in St. John's, Newfoundland, Judy (who describes herself as "a black Anglican") attended Halifax's Nova Scotia College of Art and Design in the latter half of the 1960s. Sometime during the late spring of the celebration of Canada's centenary, she became pregnant with Sarah (and, according to a source close to the family, the identity of the birth father has never been revealed, a fact which Judy politely refuses to share with me).

"Well, you see," admits Judy, "I had her when I was in college, and she was put up for adoption. We found each other by accident. She has other parents, and that's why we have to be careful, and not hurt them. . . . You know what I mean? I love her. She's my daughter; and, whatever goes for her . . .

"Sarah was my only one. I never wanted babies. I'm just not that kind of person. Babies are too demanding. I just don't have the makeup to want to look after babies. They're too needy. And, I don't have the tolerance for small children. Children are fine, so long as people take them home with them when they go. I have no balls about saying that. That's the way I am. I have always had cats. I do have some sense of obligation. I have a cat in front of me right now, flat on his back, belly spread, looking at me, wanting some attention . . .

"I think I did the right thing for Sarah. I mean, I was an art-college student in the '60s and, what could I do? This was the '60s, you know? In the '60s, you just didn't . . . I mean, especially on the East Coast. I would have had to take her home to Newfoundland and raise her. (Sarah thanked me for not doing that!)

"The only thing I could have done was to have her. I couldn't have an abortion. I had to put her up for adoption and, these people she had a family with, they did her all kinds of great stuff; they gave her all kinds of wonderful opportunities to pursue her musical career; and, they gave her three years in a musical academy. I could never have done that for her.

"Well, these people were the people who raised her and, you know, the woman that raises you, cleans your diapers, and wipes your nose, and all that stuff? That's your mother, you know? I didn't do all that stuff . . . She came to me when she was 18. I just came in then. We're friends. She was born on January 28, 1968 and I put her up for adoption shortly after that. That's it. That's all of it. I don't know any of the stuff about how she grew up. I didn't know her, then.

"I don't even know her adopted parents. They know she's found me. Her friend told me. Her parents don't know we're friends. We met because I was working at the same store as her girlfriend, Robin, who was living with her then.

" No, I don't want to tell you the name of the store."

"I'm always concerned about [Sarah's] feelings and stuff, that's all; so, I'm not interested in having any kind of notoriety, at all, period.

"That's why I want to support her now; and, I don't want to do anything that she might frown on, so, I'll have to cover it with her before I talk about her to you. It might take me a few weeks before I even talk to her. The last time I talked to her was at Easter. We don't talk every week. She's a busy girl. And we have a different relationship.

"I mean, we talk probably three-four times a year — and, it might be a while before I talk to her because she's going on tour with all those girls — and, probably, I won't talk to her until the fall. But, if I do talk to her — there might come an occasion when she might call me — I will bring it up to her. . . .

"Yeah, of course, I am [so proud of her]. And, yeah, I think, well, yeah I sing. I've got a decent voice. I don't play an instrument, no. Sarah's just very talented in that respect. She can just play and record music and write music for anything. And, I respect that.

"Listen, all I can tell you is that I had her when I was 20 years old and I put her up for adoption. I was at the Nova Scotia College of Art and Design. There's nothing I can give you besides what I've told you. I'm going to go see Robin today; I'm going to see what she has to say.

"But, I have nothing more to tell you. I have to clear it with Sarah first ... Yes, I know the story's going to come out. I'll deal with it when it happens. I mean, how can you prepare yourself for something like this? I'm not some weak little thing. I know the story's going to get done, yes; so, good luck. Still, there's nothing more that I can tell you. All I can say is go for it."

J.P., perhaps speechless for the first time since he learned to speak fluent sentences in the cradle, glances sidelong at me for several kilometers, wheels spinning, questions forming, blessed silence reigning while we take turns steering A-M-T up one mountain and down another heading east on our search for a woman who claims she's Sarah McLachlan's birth mother.

Slowly, over jump-start juice at a Hymns just west of Truro, J.P. eventually arrives at the conclusion I'd reached after speaking with Judy during our *tête-à-tête-à-telephone* conversations.

"Fitz, every time we turn on the radio, they're playing *Building A Mystery*, right?"

"Yeah, right. So ...?"

"Well ... it's kinda weird ..."

"No kidding. Lines about 'rastawares,' 'a suicide poem,' 'a beautiful fucked-up man' and 'razor-wire shrines' and shit. *Man ...*"

"Hear the video's good, though."

"Wouldn't know."

"Don't own no boob-tube," he chimes.

"You got it, *Pontiac*."

"It *is* weird, Fitz. You just don't fit the picture of an unauthorized biographer, you know? Kitty-Kelly-esque, eh? Too bad McLachlan doesn't know you like us guys do."

"Well, she doesn't know you, either; not like I do, at least. You can't know everybody, you know?"

"You think you'd like to know her?"

"Who?"

"SARAH! Our Sarah!"

"Our Sarah doesn't seem at all keen on even speaking with me for a 20-minute 'phoner, let alone developing a friendship, eh?"

"Yeah, I see your point. So, how do you know this Judy's her mother for sure?"

"Well, let me put it this way. I did a little legwork, so to speak, thanks to *RPM Chart Weekly*, the 'Net, Ma Bell, regional libraries *et soforthia*. (Got that off Thomas Pynchon.) Also, *FRANK* mag. It provided me with a lot of information I couldn't possibly secure from any other source; and, with the info I received, I let my fingers do the walking and all kinds of sources started talking. Freely."

"Like who?"

"Like *whom*."

"Whatever."

"Well, I called a source on the West Coast concerning a related matter; and, in the course of our conversation, my source asked me if my questions concerned McLachlan's birth mother."

"No!"

"Seriously. I gave no indication I was looking for this information. I called my source simply to establish that what I'd heard concerning this particular aspect of the book was factually true (and it was).

"Out of the blue, my source starts talking about rubbing shoulders with McLachlan and crew on various occasions and hearing from several different individuals the same story concerning McLachlan's adoptive parents and biological mother."

"Like?"

"Well, the source asks me, quite bluntly, 'Does this have anything to do with Sarah's birth parents?' "

"What'd you say?"

"Might."

"What'd the source say?"

" '*Hmm-mm*.' And, when I ask how the source knows about the birth parents, I'm told, 'Well, she's adopted, so obviously . . . I don't know it any other way than just having heard it so many times. Can I prove it? No. But it's never been something I've ever been too concerned about. I just happen to know that the people who raised her were not her birth parents . . . That's not a secret, by the way. That has come up from so many people . . . So, I do know a fair bit about some of the circumstances under which she came to find her birth mother. . . .

" 'This is information that has been passed to me by third parties, okay? Obviously, I wasn't there. I've never been to Halifax; so, but, what certain parties have said to me is that there was a certain jewelry store in Halifax; and, it just so happens that this was a place that Sarah, I guess as a young teenager, I think that's the period, you know, really liked to frequent. She really liked the stuff that they sold there; and, it turns out — I'm not sure if she officially did a search to find her birth parents or vice versa; but, the story, as I've heard it, is this:

" 'It turns out that this woman — who was either the proprietor or the main salesperson of the store whom Sarah had gotten to know a little bit just because she liked going to the store — ended up being her birth mother.' "

"Hmm-mm."

"Hmm-mm? That's corroborating evidence from an ethical source, a person I believe would never fabricate nor prevaricate in any way, given the source's track record, professional relationships, and career-related accomplishments. Besides, Terry McBride considers said source 'the Antichrist incarnate', or so he says."

"Funny, Fitz. Are you 'the Antichristess incarnate,' then? Oops. 'Scuzee. Bad joke. . . . So, why are we going to Halifax? You've got proof and evidence up the ying-yang already . . ."

". . . Well, see. I do and I don't, at least, technically speaking. I absolutely believe Judy's telling the truth. I absolutely believe my main corroborating source (plus a lot of other sub-sources including high-school friends, ex-band members, *etc.*, *etc.*) are also telling the truth; but, I have to see her for myself, to prove this is not an elaborate hoax, for one thing.

"Secondly, I want to see how far away she lives from McLachlan's adopted parents. Thirdly, I need photographs of a number of locations where McLachlan hung out; and, you know, these are not the kinds of photographs I can ask someone else to take."

"Now what?"

"The line forms on the right, right? Now, we go to Halifax and snoop around the neighborhood, quietly, of course. We don't want to alert anyone to our being there on officially unofficial biz, if you get my drift."

"So, what's she like?"

"McLachlan or Judy?"

"Judy."

"She's wonderful, J.P., really kew-l-l-l, as I think your generation would say."

"Yeah?"

"Yeah, like when I started talking with her, you know what she said? She said she couldn't tell me anything about Sarah without Sarah's permission (and she didn't); but, she did tell me quite a lot about herself."

"Like?"

"Well, stuff. Stuff that gives you a pretty good idea about the kind of woman she is and all that. Personal — but not deep-secret private — kinds of stuff.

"For instance, I called her on the eve of Canada Day, right? You know what she says? 'I've been partying quite a bit — it's Canada Day — and we've had major celebrations. I just got in, and I've been drinking . . . Actually, we're doing the Canada-Day thingie tomorrow. We've had, like 35-degree weather which is, like, rare here. Thirty-five degrees. That's hot. Especially on the ocean, it's seriously warm; but, oh, well. It's all right with me, so long as I can get to some body of water, at least down here, there's lots of bodies of water I can jump into . . . Not like Ontario, like Southern Ontario. There's nowhere I can jump into a body of water there. Here, in Nova Scotia, there's tons of clean water. You can jump into any body of water and be where you want to be; but, in Ontario, you actually have to line up and pay to swim in those bodies of water. Actually, I went swimming at Niagara-On-The-Lake last summer and I expected to glow in the dark,' " I paraphrase fairly accurately.

"Then she goes, 'Uh-huh. It was hot, sticky and humid. So, I had to be in the water. I took my shorts off and went in in my underwear, in broad daylight. I said to hell with it. I wanted to get in there, it was so inviting; and, it was so hot; and, I wanted to get in some water. I said to hell with it!' The dame's got class."

"Weird, Fitz. She likes swimming and water. Sarah's always going on and on about swimming and water, isn't she? Like, in her videos, songs, interviews? She's wet, wet, wet. Like mother, like daughter, eh?"

"Well, I like the mother, that's a fact. And, you know what else? Judy says it freaked her out when she knew Sarah *was* her daughter. She says it was 'extraordinary' because both she and Sarah had the same kinds of mannerisms and movements and she could see so much of Sarah in her and vicey versy. I told her I understood exactly what she meant by that, having seen my own birth mother — after not seeing her for over a dozen or so years — and experiencing exactly the same kinds of feelings. You want weird, Japes? *That's* weird.

" 'So,' says Judy, 'Sarah's friends are always amazed at how much like me she is; and, I always find it really weird because I used to think your mannerisms were part of your upbringing; and now, maybe they're not, maybe they're genetic or a combination . . . ?' "

"No kidding. The book's still out on that one, Fitz."

"Well, did I tell you she loves cats, just loves them to bits?"

"Yup. Two cats. One husband. No kids. What's her hubby like?"

"Don't know much about him except his name and what he does for a living and the fact he's also from Newfoundland. Talked to him twice on the 'phone when I tried to contact Judy. Sounds like a decent guy. Called me 'Dear,' *e.g.*

"But, Judy? Judy sounds like the kind of birth mother I wish I'd had. Seriously. She genuinely cared about the well-being of her daughter and was intelligent enough to do what she thought was best for her daughter. My birth mother never gave a damn about her kids. She only cared about herself. I told Judy that, too.

"Judy clearly felt it was the only honorable and responsible thing she could do, given the time and place and circumstances surrounding the pregnancy. I can imagine it was a much more difficult decision for her to make than she lets on, too. But, I can also see how she'd realistically view it without artifice and pretense and, since she seems a very strong woman, I can also imagine she's more honest and candid with herself than a lot of people on this planet. I mean, I respect her very much because she respected the child she'd conceived, and she additionally recognized she could not practically give her child the kind of life she felt all children entitled to receive. Funny, eh? McLachlan's quote, unquote 'good' corporate sponsors are donating big cake to battered women's shelters, rape-crisis centers and Planned Parenthood...

"But, you know, that's quite a bundle to deal with when you're just a kid yourself, practically. I think she handled it extraordinarily well.

"I really liked this woman's forthrightliness the first time I spoke with her and, you know, in a different world, I'd like to bring her a bottle and share it with her."

"She likes to drink, eh?"

"Yeah, she likes lots of drinks. Too bad I quit drinking. I was a Scotch woman myself; but, I can't drink (and don't want to, either). Didn't drink for a dozen years, eh? Then, I fell off the wagon for a year after I got deathly ill in France and all that. You remember?

"Anyway, I forget what Judy said she likes to drink...Vodka, I think...But, that might be McLachlan. McLachlan's favorite drink's Russian Vodka and her favorite food's swordfish. Picture that, if you can."

"I'm trying, I'm trying. McLachlan a big drinker?"

"Gawd, how would I know? All I know is one of the songs on FUMBLING, *Good Enough*, opens with, 'Hey, your glass is empty' and I don't think she means milk . . .

"So, know what else? At one point in our chats, Judy really loosens up and it's just two dames talking. She says she'll be 50 in September, right? And, she adds, I'd never know it by looking at her. Says something like, 'You should see me' and I say, 'I have, in the picture of you I've got. You look great! I never would've pegged you at 50. No way.' Then, I tell her we've got the almost exact same shade of hair color."

"'Red? I dye mine,' she says, 'and, I tell people that this year I'm going to celebrate the 20th anniversary of my 30th birthday. I like to celebrate my birthday. For this one, I want all my friends to really celebrate, and give me a really big party, and celebrate forever. You know, I still feel like I'm 28. I wear miniskirts. I can still wear them, with bare legs. And, I bike everywhere I go. It's the only thing I drive. I live in a third-floor walk-up and I bike everywhere I go. That's the only thing I've ever driven — besides driving men crazy,' she says, 'I've never driven a car. But, let me tell you, living in a third-floor walk-up, that keeps the respiratory system healthy and, I don't smoke a lot; but, I do drink . . .

"'So, you're a Judith and I'm a Judith,' she also says to me. 'Do people call you Judith or Jude or Judy?' And, I say, 'Fitz,' of course, 'cause that's what people call me. Only my biological mother and my adopted family called me Judy. When someone accidentally calls me Judy, I correct them . . ."

"I'm sure you do, Fitz, I'm sure you do."

"Well, then, Judy says, 'I've been called Jude. All my friends in St. John's used to call me Jude. I've mostly been called Judy here in Halifax. I'm also called Carmen. Carmen? I've been called Carmen by a number of friends for a number of years because I'm a Gypsy and Bizet's Carmen is a Gypsy, right? It's a nickname that stuck; but, I've never been called Fitz,' she adds, laughing. Then, she tells me, 'Judith is Hebrew for "The Praised" ' " and wants to know if I knew *that*.

"I ask her how *she* knows that, right? She says, 'Because I've researched my name. It's a Hebrew name. And, I've been praised a lot all my life' . . .

"When I point out I've heard she's a fine artist, she concurs and explains she's 'done a lot of stuff; and, in the past few years, I've sort of drifted away from doing anything seriously artistic. I don't do jewelry anymore. I just paddle and dribble along . . . I still do research and I restore antiques. I do watercolors, cards and things, but nothing serious.' "

"She sounds really neat, Fitz. Do you think she's telling the truth?"

"Absolutely. I knew it the first time I saw the picture of her."

"Can I see it?"

"Yeah, if and when we hit Halifax. *And*, if *and* when we do, I'll show you a picture of McLachlan or two *and* you can compare their facial characteristics, their naturally curly hair, their body types, *etc.*, *etc.* for yourself *and* you can tell me what *you* think, okay?"

"Whaddya mean, 'if *and* when' we hit Halifax?"

"Well, at the speed you're driving, we'll be lucky to get out of New Brunswick in this century, I'd say. You know, El Japo, I just can't figure it. You talk a mile a minute and drive like an old fuddy-duddy."

"Do not."

"Do so. Look, you're doing 80 in a 100, fer chrissakes. My truck's not used to all this, uh, fastidiousness. Adam likes to go fast. He's used to it."

"You know what, Fitz?"

"What?"

"You bitch way too much, you know that? Bitch, bitch, bitch! You ever hear the expression about catching more flies with honey than vinegar?"

"Sure. And, when you're a fly, I'll remember it."

We stop at Hymns, change drivers and arrive in Halifax just after lunch. I make three calls — Greg Clark, the local reference library, and Judy — all of them necessary to the book's various stories.

J.P. and yours truly head in the direction of Judy's home (despite the fact her answering machine announces she is not available).

"Well, if she's not there," opines J.P., "I don't know why we'd want to visit her."

"No harm in looking," I explain, "besides, if there are neighbors about or whatever, now would be a good time to chat them up, wouldn't it?"

"Well . . . It would also be a good time to take a nice long nap, right? I mean, we left Windsor on Wednesday and it's only Saturday. Besides, since we picked up this bacterial infection in Moncton, I feel kinda shitty. You think the Holiday Inn would've posted a sign telling travelers not to drink the water, eh? Geez, now we're both sick with this stupid thing."

"Stupid is right. Eat yoghourt, okay? Lots of it. And, if the acetaminophen don't help, we'll get you something stronger. Either that, or we get you to a doctor like I first suggested."

"Naw, I don't need a doctor. But, some sleep *might* help . . . Uh . . . Oh . . . Oh, okay, Fitz, okay. Where's the picture?"

I hand him the photo of Judy along with a range and selection of McLachlan shots. I tell him to study the photos closely before he says another word. I map out our route to

Judy's place, the McLachlan residence, the Maritime Conservatory of Music, Queen Elizabeth High School, the Nova Scotia College of Art and Design, Dalhousie University, and the corner of Prince and Barrington in downtown Halifax where McLachlan used to hang out busking or goofing off with her friends in the latter half of her teens at a place called Backstreet Amusements.

"Fitz, you know what?"

"What?"

"In these early shots of Sarah, she's got, well, the kind of nose just like Judy's, right?"

"Right . . ."

"And, in these recent ones, her nose is, well, different, you know?"

"Yeah, I know. No big deal. A lot of stars — both female and male — opt for cosmetic 'enhancement,' so to speak. It's because we live in an electronic age, right? Image is everything. It works for some people and that's okay. It's a highly competitive business and every edge helps."

"Well, I see what you mean. Sarah is definitely Judy's daughter. Look at the big mouth, the smile, the jawline, the eyes, all of it."

"Yeah, now we need to prove this picture is the picture of the woman known as Judy. And, that's where you come in."

When we arrive at Judy's place, I verify that the name on her mailbox matches her last name; and, when I walk up the flights of stairs leading to her apartment, I ring the buzzer on the off chance she's returned home in the interim.

No answer. No surprise there. Probably, with this heat wave that has moved from west to east with us, Judy's swimming. On her street, however, a middle-aged couple is working on the garden of the house beside Judy's third-floor walk-up.

"Hi," I say, "do you live around here?"

"Yup," says he, "this is our house."

"Nice house," I say, "you live here long?"

"Eighteen years," he says proudly, "lot's changed since then, though."

"Oh, I bet. It's the way of the world, right?"

"I guess so. How come you're asking?"

I introduce myself and explain I'm visiting from Ontario and that I'm looking for a woman who lives on the third floor in the building next to his house and was wondering if he knew her or her husband.

"Yeah, I know them a bit. Why?"

"Yeah, why?" asks his wife, "Are they in trouble or something?"

"Gawd, no," I assure her, "no trouble at all. I'm looking for Judy for good reasons, not bad ones."

"Well, who are you?"

"Fitz."

"Hi, Fitz."

Judy's neighbors introduce themselves to both J.P. and me.

"So, why you looking for Judy?"

"Well," I begin, "she's an artist . . ."

"Oh, she is!" enthuses Mrs. Neighbor. "She's really artistic. She does all kinds of things — jewelry, painting, you know?"

"Yeah. She's really good, I hear."

"Really good," she concurs, "really creative . . ."

"Say," says Mr. Neighbor, "you wouldn't know Sarah McLachlan, would you?"

"Yeah," says the Mrs., "do you know her?"

"Sarah who?"

"Sarah McLachlan. She visits Judy sometimes. You know her?"

"Nope. I don't. Never met her. Have you?"

"No. But, we've seen her. At least a couple of times. She visits Judy, you know?"

"Yeah? When was the last time she visited?"

"Geez," says Mr. Neighbor, "I guess she was here last Christmas, eh?"

"Yeah, she visited around this past Christmas."

"Well, kewl. Who is she? Is she related to Judy?"

"No. She's just one of Judy's artistic friends, right?"

"Right. Judy knows lots of artistic people."

"Wait a minute!" says Mrs. Neighbor, "You look a little like Judy. You related to her or something?"

"You never know," I say, "but, I've come from Ontario to find out a lot of things like that."

"Well, your hair's almost the same color as hers. That's it. You're her daughter!"

"No, she ain't," says Mr. Neighbor, "no offense, Fitz, but you're too old to be Judy's daughter."

"No offense taken. No. I'm not her daughter. I'm looking for her to talk to her about her artwork. I understand she's some kind of artist and I have this picture and ..."

"So, you're from Ontario? Judy's dad lives in Ontario. So does her twin sister. She works for some film company or other. Makeup? Costumes? Something like that. Lemme think ... Remember *Kung Fu*? That David Carradine fellow? She worked on that show, I think. What's her sister's name, Dear?"

"Uh, wait a minute, it's on the tip of my tongue," says Mrs. Neighbor. The couple throws names back and forth between them and tell me her twin sister's name, occupation, and latest project. "So, you see, it's a very artistic family."

"I thought so," I say, "any idea where Judy went or when she'll be back?"

"Well, they left yesterday with a huge canoe in the back of a pickup, didn't they?"

"Yeah, her husband and a couple of other guys we didn't recognize. They've probably gone out to the camp for the weekend, I'd say. They do that a lot, eh? But, I'd guess they'll be back tomorrow night. He's got to get up early for work Monday morning, you know?"

"Yeah, he leaves for work pretty early. There's always different kinds of cars around their place. There's a Taurus. And, the pickup; but, you know, even if you were the police, I couldn't tell you what kind of pickup it was. Never noticed. You know, Judy just loves to swim, eh?"

"She does. She loves water. She's mentioned that to me, too. So, do you folks ever visit with each other, neighborly drinks, stuff like that?"

"Once in a while. We went to their wedding celebration, you know?"

"Really? When was that?"

"Oh, must of been about four-five years ago, eh?"

"Yeah, it was about four years ago, anyway. They moved in about eight years ago, right, Dear?"

"Yeah, must of been at least eight. 'Course, the street's changed since then, too. This siding wasn't installed then, eh?"

"No-o-o-o. The siding was done after they moved in."

Mrs. Neighbor describes various changes on the street, the kinds of vehicles connected with Judy's husband's business that regularly park in the vicinity, their current water-hose/sprinkler problem, what they're doing for the evening, *etc. etc.*

I thank them both for the time and friendliness, remarking they could give Westerners a lesson or two. Just before J.P. and I make tracks back to Adam, Mrs. Neighbor says to him, "You look like John Lennon. Do people tell you that?"

J.P. says, "Well . . . Not recently."

"Weird," I add, "now that you mention it, he does, doesn't he?"

"Who's he?" asks Mrs. Neighbor. "Your son?"

"Nope. Godsend," I slur-mumble, "he's never seen an ocean before so I brought him along for the heck of it."

"Oh, you'll like it here."

"Yeah," drolls J.P., "I already do. The ocean's more beautiful than I could've imagined *and* the air's a little salty *and* all the stuff going on in the harbor *and* the light's kind of different from . . ."

". . . *And*, we're just heading out for dinner, right, J.P.? We're celebrating, aren't we?"

"Yeah, but, it's also a very nice view, too," he tells Judy's neighbors, "and, you really think I look like John Lennon?"

I jingle-jangle the truck keys.

"Well, you kids enjoy your stay," says Mr. Neighbor.

"Yeah, nice to meet you," adds his wife. "Have fun!"

Of course, when we reach Adam (parked a few blocks away), J.P.'s still going on about how she thinks he looks like Lennon; and, of course, since we have verified all that needs verifying, our job is done in this neck of the world.

J.P. can't fathom why I'd come so far and not wait around to see Judy in the flesh.

"Well," I say, "I've satisfied the technical requirement that I definitively prove she is who she says she is and she lives where she says she lives; and, well, I don't want to intrude any further."

Sunday afternoon, as we prepare to leave Halifax after

shooting off four rolls of film, we stop for Java juice at Hymns and, as J.P.'s my witness, the moment we walk through the glass doors, the intro to *Building A Mystery* floods the place.

Then, because it *is* Sunday night, J.P. insists I watch this TV show he loves, this *Due South* thing; and, again, as J.P.'s my witness, the show concerns the sale of an infant to parents desperate to adopt a baby; and, as J.P.'s my witness, this particular episode, *A Cop, a Mountie, and a Baby*, features a Sarah McLachlan tune, *Fear*, from FUMBLING TOWARDS ECSTASY.

"Fitz," says J.P., "that's *really* weird. It's everywhere . . ."

"Nope, J.P.," says yours truly, "that's just something that happens naturally, especially when you hang out with me."

I fell in love with the music of Sarah McLachlan the first time I heard *The Path Of Thorns (Terms)* in the backseat of a Toronto taxi. When the song ended, I asked the driver to turn up the radio so I could hear the backsell on the creator of this gloriously raw and achingly crafted six-minute masterpiece.

"Oh," said the driver, "you don't know Sarah McLachlan?"

"No," I'd responded, "but, I'd like to know her music better, judging by that tune. Who is she?"

"A gal from the East Coast," she'd replied, "from my hometown, Halifax. They play her a lot these days."

"Well," I remember saying, "that song's the story of my life writ large. I've got to hear it again."

"Oh," gushed the driver, "don't you worry about that. You'll be hearing from this little girl for a long long time."

Of course, I immediately bought both McLachlan cassettes, played each straight through, marveled simply and sadly over the vocal maturity and lyrical catastrophes she articulated so plaintively in much of the material, especially the compositions on SOLACE. Inexpressibly blue. Inarticulately red. Tracks etched razor sharp by screeching steel wheels sparking fire on a grid of lines crisscrossing the heart.

McLachlan had described it otherwise, of course; but, I had only to listen to *The Path of Thorns (Terms)* to hear the story I'd learned by hurt.

I knew you wanted to tell me
In your voice there was something wrong
But if you would turn your face away from me
You cannot tell me you're so strong
Just let me ask of you one small thing
As we have shared so many tears
With fervor our dreams we planned a whole lifelong
Now are scattered on the wind . . .
In the terms of endearment
In the terms of the life that you love
In the terms of the years that pass you by
In the terms of the reasons why
Through the years I've grown to love you
Though your commitment to most would offend
But I stuck by you holding on with my foolish pride
Waiting for you to give in
You never really tried or so it seems
I've had much more than myself to blame
I've had enough of trying everything
And this time it is the end . . .
[Chorus]
There's no more coming back this way
The path is overgrown and strewn with thorns
They've torn the lifeblood from your naked eyes
Cast aside to be forlorn . . .
[Chorus]
Funny, how it seems that all I've tried to do
Seems to make no difference to you at all.

— from *The Path Of Thorns (Terms)*

What I had heard in that particular song stays with me even after writing my adopted parents a letter ending our 26-year relationship forever.

I met them when I was already a high-school student on the cusp of 17. Through the years I came to love and cherish their presence in my life. I had moved from foster home to foster home throughout the Muskoka lake district. Bob and June provided me with stability, love, and security. My mother taught me how to sew and supported me in a million ways I had never known a mother could; my father was simply an amazingly kindly man who, like my mother, accepted me as one of their own.

My two brothers, my parents' natural children, did not. The elder of the pair called me a gold-digger the last time I saw him (on Christmas Eve some years ago). He also told me our parents felt exactly the same way about me. Shattered, I confronted them immediately, asking them to explain how they could possibly believe such a monstrous thing of a woman as independent of them as I am, particularly since I had already made it clear among the members of my family I did not wish to be included in the Will, especially since my mother and father's support and love meant so much more than an inheritance to me.

When Marjorie, my natural mother, returned to my life a decade after she'd abandoned me (because an indiscreet administrator at York University had given her my home number), I immediately told my parents she had made contact with me. I also told them about the day I stood in her kitchen and began sobbing uncontrollably.

"You're not my mother!" I'd bellowed, "You're not my mother! My mother's up north! In Muskoka. You're not my mother. You let that monster hurt me. You let Jack do those terrible things to me. No mother of mine would do something as awful as that to me. You're no mother to me!"

My parents, heartbroken I had attempted to establish any kind of relationship with my biological mother (despite the fact I had no desire to maintain even a friendship with her), never really forgave me (or so it seems to me now, the past allowing reflective distance on that which we never truly resolve. Rather, we accommodate ourselves to the dislocation, the low-grade ache, the inexpressible sadness which occasionally rolls down our cheeks). It is then, strangely, that *The Path Of Thorns (Terms)* comforts me.

My mother succumbed to Alzheimer's Disease several years ago; she currently resides in a Seniors' Nursing Home (and does not remember me). My father lives alone in what was once our family's home. Both my brothers reside elsewhere, too busy to stay with our father until he leaves us forever (since he's endured several major surgeries and currently labors under an inoperable-aneurysm death warrant).

The last time I saw my Dad, I explained to him a father who believes his daughter to be a gold-digger does not deserve such a daughter; further, by definition, a father who loves his daughter could not possibly inflict such a condemnatory judgment on his daughter. Rather than again risking a rewrite of the abandonment script bequeathed me by my biological mother, I shook hands goodbye with my adopted father.

I have not seen Marjorie in almost two decades. I do not know of the whereabouts of her common-law husband, Jack, the monster who raped, beat, tortured, and psychologically damaged me until the police removed me from their home and placed me in the Children's Aid Society. I became a crown ward in the Province of Ontario on 25 April 1966.

It is in this context that Ms McLachlan's beautiful song spoke such strength, sadness, and solace to me.

(Left) Sarah McLachlan's birth mother, Judy (Kaines) James.

(Below) Judy's neighborhood, Halifax.

(Left) The home of Jack and Dorice McLachlan, Halifax.

(Below) Queen Elizabeth High School.

(Left) Maritime Conservatory of Music, Halifax.

(Below) Former home of Backstreet Amusements, Prince and Barrington Streets in Halifax.

two

MEDUSA'S CAREER

or Out Of The Shadows

Y ou know, it occurred to me as I sat down to tap out the story of Sarah McLachlan, it's a story and a half.

"Yeah, it is," avers David Kershaw, McLachlan's long-time keyboardist and certain special someone who, by all accounts, loved her very much.

"Truth is such an evasive thing; but, personally," he says, "I find the story so remarkable because everyone has their own take on it. I know there's such a camp that is against her in the law and, I guess, philosophically; but, you know, I was there from the beginning and we got so involved. We were such good friends . . ."

"You were her lover."

"Yes. She was such a close friend for such a long time; and, you know . . . Truth. Ethics. That kind of thing."

Kershaw, who left McLachlan's band to work in the film biz sometime between FUMBLING TOWARDS ECSTASY — the disc which includes the photographs of McLachlan snapped by him — and SURFACING, declines an invitation to provide readers with some sense of McLachlan's personality, primarily because he considers it off-limits to kiss and tell, preferring instead to honor the years the pair spent together. In fact, when I explain to him that I do happen to know quite a lot about their past association and had rung him up in order to ask more general questions — Is she a southpaw or rightie, for example? — Kershaw politely changes the subject by interviewing the interviewer.

"So, I wonder, what story do *you* know?"

"The story I know — the stories I've heard — about your relationship, you mean?"

"Yeah, that. What story is *that*?"

Well, I tell him, *that* doesn't interest me. What does interest me is this story, the one about the kid on the skid marks of a dream who, come hell or hurt city, would land on top of the world.

And, that was that. One can see why McLachlan would fall for such a circumspect and protective guy (or, given his musical ability and hunka-punkin' good looks, this one can).

What does interest me — what I find so utterly captivating — is McLachlan's story, the story of a woman blessed with one of the finest sets of pipes on the planet determined to share her sonorous gift with her obviously adoring audience for, when all is said and sung, McLachlan's indelible voice — her finest instrument and premier asset — takes center stage in this story, the story of McLachlan's non-stop to-the-top musical chops.

So, naturally, this is the story of a voice instantly recognizable and absolutely unforgettable, a voice built to endure and mature, a drop-dead stunner of a voice articulately distinguished in its most fitting and proper sonic milieu (despite the fact McLachlan began her career scoring a number of prestigious firsts singing opera in Kiwanis Music Festivals, most notably when the Grade-Six sensation entranced 2,500 sets of ears at the Rebecca Cohn in Halifax). McLachlan's music takes up residence in listeners' nervous systems, lodges permanently between divinity and desolation, makes itself right at home with a singular sound and sense not often identifiable on the popular-music samescape of clone-drone dynamics (currently kicking the shit out of originality).

Invariably, a gift of McLachlan's caliber comes with a price. She paid — and continues to pay — her dues with the material wrought predominantly from both the obvious and obscure details of her personal life.

Listeners, invited to participate in her musical melodrama, generally hear an earful of adequately penned, competently composed, beautifully arranged, and exquisitely produced tunes created on popular-music principles (despite the "alternative" designation often attached to her still-growing body of work). Not overly sophisticated in her poetic outpourings, the "goddess" of her generation rarely disguises the first-personal point of view of her songs, preferring instead to provide her audience with living proof those most visceral of emotions — love, loss, grief, despair — do, at least in McLachlan's view, still matter.

McLachlan the reassuring human being — in tune with McLachlan the sensitive songwriter — waxes ecstatic in several media about the way in which *this* tragedy affected her or *that* injustice infuriated — or horrified or immobilized — her, all the while reinforcing Abbie Hoffman's prescient 1970s' observation, cited in Hilary Mills's *Mailer: A Biography* (1982), that the original Stormin' Norman viewed "feminism as the decline of civilization. Technology is taking over and women are leaving kitchens to go to press buttons along with the men."

Self-scrutinizing, quasi-cryptic, and excruciatingly confessional, the lyrics of her songs unquestionably push all the right buttons with her target audience, Rainer Maria Rilke-skimming listeners given to pondering the imponderable in search of a musical soundtrack with which to fill the inexpressible gaps of their disaffected lives, an emotional sounding board allowing them to gauge their personal growth (or lack thereof) and, most importantly, a point of express entry for therapeutic sessions with their equally narcissistic psyches.

And, why not? Lopsided lyrics packaged with incongruent melodies undeniably appeal, in the current musical marketplace, to millions of listeners lost in the detritus of cultureless utilitarianism, the phenomenon leveling the building blocks of life-on-earth (upon which civilizations simultaneously sustain and renew themselves).

So, for the superstar-in-training, making music would nec-essarily create both cause for celebration and ready-made refuge from the ubiquitous external restraints and internal pressures afflicting the star and star struck alike. Peer into the depths in which individuals given to finding themselves wallow on the road to redemption. Then, try to tell me it ain't just as illusory as time, the human construct, the one we dreamed up to dis-tinguish night from day.

One day, she woke with a dream; a decade later, she realized it — all in the trademark name of Sarah McLachlan, the one-time Medusa hell-bent on parlaying her liquid assets, plat-stat signature, and a string of solid compositions into discs astutely promoted to the millions of precious outcasts convinced, as their goddess is, that paradise both hurts like hell and equally signifies "heaven to no one else but me" (*Elsewhere*).

When Dr. J. L. (Jack) McLachlan and Dorice McLachlan, M.A., brought baby Sarah Ann home to meet her broth-ers — four-year-old Stewart and six-year-old Ian — for the first time, the ecstatic couple had no way of knowing how short-lived her stay with the family would ultimately be; by contrast, the "pre-Raphaelite vision" most likely already intuitively knew what it was she must needs do. After all, throughout the preg-nancy, her biological mother, herself a reputedly fine artist and singer for the sheer joy of it, had sung her daughter into life.

Life. What does a biographer tell readers about McLachlan's life? The dilemma becomes one of privacy, the limits one must — and ought never — cross in a way that both protects the subject and enlightens the public (which comprises all of us bozos on this bus). The long and short of her personal upbring-ing, well-documented as it is, revolves around private family matters (and, as such, does not belong to the realm of the pub-lic since McLachlan herself had not yet abrogated, by the nature of her chosen field, her right to privacy).

By the time McLachlan turned four, she had fallen in love with sound and wanted only to make music; but, because she could not hold a full-sized guitar, she pretended she was Joan Baez and picked out all the right notes on the ukelele to accompany herself, an activity her parents encouraged throughout her adolescence. It was, after all, at their insistence she began to study classical piano and guitar with a view towards one or the other of the instruments coming in handy in the accompaniment department.

Her mother's afternoon-tea group, impressed by the precocious ukelele-strumming toddler, no doubt bestowed lavish praise upon the little girl with the big voice since, according to damned-near every music critic across the continent, young McLachlan's love for live performance blossomed during these formative forays when she first strutted her prodigious stuff.

According to Klaro M. Mizerit, Director of the Maritime Conservatory of Music during the years McLachlan undertook her intensive studies, "Sarah was a fine student, a bright student. She only decided later what she wanted to become. At the time, she hadn't shown what she would like to be, which direction she would be taking; but she was very dedicated, very determined and she progressed rapidly. She did perform at our school concerts, but she sang classical music."

In 1985, Mrs. Margie Farmer presented McLachlan with the "Dr. Vega Dawson Voice Award" and a tuition-scholarship check in the amount of $50. The following year, McLachlan shared the $200 "Teodor Britts Memorial Scholarship" for voice with Leslie Stuckless; plus, that year, she was also the recipient of an Alumni Prize "awarded to students that made the highest mark over 80 in each grade."

The year she completed her studies at MCM, McLachlan earned a First in Nova Scotia's 1987 Kiwanis Music Festival, a fact which no doubt delighted her teachers, Diane Oxner (voice), Barbara Glencross-Shortliffe (guitar), and Marilyn Vance (piano), who had worked intensively with the "quiet and studious young woman," to use Mizerit's words. "A revolutionary she was not," he adds reflectively. "She was definitely not the rebellious type. She was extremely dedicated to her music, especially her vocal work. I believe she saw the guitar more as an instrument to accompany her singing."

Ray Childerhose, who describes himself as "an old sailor," recalls "Sarah was a little lost, in a way. She was a good kid. I've known her since she was just a little thing, 12 or 13 or so.

That's when she first started chumming with my daughter, Buffy.

"She had goals; but those goals were sort of not directed yet. She had ideas; she was sort of running around in circles; but she sure straightened out. I went backstage to see her the last time she was here in Halifax performing," he says, "and, I've known all kinds of good singers in my life; but, Sarah's the first one I've known who's made it to the top. All the kids she chummed around with turned out really well, thank God. They've all left, now, of course. Sarah's on the West Coast and Buffy's in Montreal and they're both doing really well. Back then, though? Well, you know, parents always worry about the directions their kids are taking."

Sarah's father, Dr. Jack McLachlan, described as the disciplined and dedicated scholar in the family of five — and keenly concerned about the direction in which McLachlan was heading — rarely speaks to the media, preferring instead to keep a great deal of public distance between himself and his daughter (about whom McLachlan, understandably, rarely speaks). According to Dalhousie University's *Home Biology Page* on the 'Net, Dr. McLachlan, an Honorary Adjunct Professor at Wolfville's Acadia University as well as a Research Associate with Dalhousie's Biology Department, undertakes and oversees "culture and field studies of marine microalgae for taxonomic, ecological and physiological investigations with emphasis on benthic species; species producing diarrhetic shellfish poisoning (DSP), factors affecting production of these toxins and other secondary metabolites, biosynthesis of DSP toxins; winter species of microalgae in shallow-water embayments of the southern Gulf of St. Lawrence."

In his recent work, Dr. McLachlan has co-authored two articles based on the results of said studies and investigations:

McLachlan, J. L., Sequel, M. R. and L. Fritz. 1994. Tetreutreptia pomquentensis, gen. et sp. nov. (Euglenophyceae), a quadriflagellated, phototrophic marine euglenoid. *J. Phycol.* 30:538-544.

McLachlan, J. L., Marr, J. C., Conlon-Kelly, A. and

A. Adamson. 1994. Effects of nitrogen concentration and cold temperature on DSP-toxin concentration in the dinoflagellate Prorocentrum lima (Pronocentrales, Dinophyceae). *Natural Toxins* 2:263-270.

Additionally, while browsing through my well-thumbed copy of Trevor Platt's 1981 *Physiological Bases of Phytoplankton Ecology* published in the Canadian Bulletins of Fisheries and Aquatic Sciences Series ("designed to interpret current knowledge in scientific fields pertinent to Canadian fisheries and aquatic environments") by the Department of Fisheries and Oceans, I came across a footnote citing some of Dr. McLachlan's earlier analyses in a pair of issues of the *Canadian Journal of Microbiology*:

McLachlan, J. L. 1960. The culture of Dunaliella tertiolecta Butcher — a euryhaline organism. *Can. J. Microbiol.*6:367-379

McLachlan, J. L. 1961. The effect of salinity on growth and chlorophyll content in representative classes of unicellular marine biology. *Can. J. Microbiol.* 7:399-406.

I sent Dr. McLachlan an e-mail respectfully requesting information about his daughter's various academic pursuits. His wife, Ms Dorice McLachlan, later told me he'd received it (although he did not show it to her, nor did he reply to my request for information).

Dorice — despite her daughter's request I not speak with her before clearing it through McLachlan first — and yours truly chatted concerning a variety of subjects; and, in the course of our conversation, I listened carefully to her voice, her beautifully spoken sentences, her tentative almost self-deprecating wisdom, and her intuitive intelligence. Even in hostile mode, this Ms McLachlan charms utterly with her tact, grace, and obvious regard for the feelings of others.

Ms McLachlan? She tried very hard to break it to me gently (so as not to hurt my feelings). She knew she was not to speak with me. I know that for a fact. She started out by telling me she knew who I was, why I was calling, and explaining she couldn't talk with me.

"Well," I replied, "nobody else will and really, Ms McLachlan, I'm just trying to get a few fact straights, not pry into your closets or anything private. I'm trying to write a celebration of your daughter's contribution to Canadian music on the global soundscape."

"If it were a celebration, I would think it would be an authorized biography. I don't know; you sound sincere to me . . . I really think Terry McBride must have had some reason for [denying access] because he's a successful person. I mean, I don't know him well; but, of course, I've met him on a number of occasions and he seems to me to be a rather practical person."

"Practical or pragmatic?"

"I don't know; but, I think he must have some reason for it. To me, you sound sincere. I would say that right now. You do; but, still, I think Terry must have some reason for not wanting you to write about Sarah . . . Why did you call Judy, though?"

"I tried to contact Dr. McLachlan at the university . . ."

"Yes, he did notice that message . . ."

". . . and, I tried calling you too many times to count. No answer."

"We've been at the cabin. But, I still wonder why you'd call Judy? Sarah did say last night that she'd heard that you called Judy."

"I called Judy because I thought she might have info on Sarah's upbringing and I couldn't get in touch with anybody else."

"She's the last person who would know anything about Sarah's upbringing. Obviously, this is all interesting to you; but, the fact is, just the fact that you called Judy, would make me think I certainly shouldn't talk to you. The person to talk to is Sarah . . ."

"Believe you me, on this score, we both agree. I'd prefer that, too; however, before I'd even written a word, right after I spoke with Mr. McBride requesting an interview, he said he'd think about it and get back to me if I'd put in writing what I was doing. So, I did. Next thing I know, your daughter's manager's hired a Hollywood lawyer who starts heavying me by fax and stuff."

"I don't know why he would . . . I really can't talk to you because I have to clear it all with Sarah. I can appreciate your problem; but I don't want to say anything that might be detrimental to Sarah. I imagine you'd realize that and I understand Judy said the same thing?"

"Judy said she couldn't talk about Sarah without getting her permission first, yes."

"Well, I understood she said that. Sarah's adoption's never been a secret here; so, if you did print it, I would have to say that we have never made a secret of it. In fact, as soon as Sarah was able to understand anything, I told her quite clearly that she was adopted . . ."

"I understand you're the one who turned Sarah onto Margaret Atwood's novel *Surfacing*?"

"Yes, I had lent her that several years ago; she'd just forgotten about it. . . . You know, Sarah's a really good person. I mean, I don't know, you sound sincere; but, I am always suspicious of people who are writing unauthorized biographies. I would have to say that Sarah is a good person. She truly tries to do the best she can in every way. She's not the type of person who would hurt anyone."

"I'm not planning to write anything to the contrary about your daughter."

"I hope not. I certainly hope not; because Sarah doesn't deserve that. So many of these unauthorized biographies that come out are just ones that dig up all the dirt they can on people; and, of course, I don't know the truth of those. But, I do know Sarah does not deserve such a book."

"Ms McLachlan, my book will say nothing damaging to the reputation of you or your family. . . . And, I don't want to upset you, either."

"Good. I certainly hope not. You haven't upset me because I was talking with Sarah last night. We hadn't known you were writing the book until we read it in *Maclean's* . . . But, of course, I'm not always up on what's . . . I'm not always knowledgeable, you have to remember that."

"Well, I haven't heard that. Actually, I've heard quite the opposite."

"No, no. My husband's the smart one. My husband's the one with the Ph.D. You've got it wrong."

"I'm sorry to contradict you, Ms McLachlan; but, I understand you're a student of English literature with a couple of degrees of your own; and, since I have a couple of degrees in English myself, I know it takes some kind of smarts and discipline to do that; and, if you're into the field, you certainly know that."

"Yes, I got my Masters in 1994 from McGill."

"What a coincidence. My manuscripts and archives are on deposit at McGill!"

"Really? That is a coincidence."

"No kidding. What was your major?"

"Well, I wrote my thesis on Samuel Richardson's *Clarissa*."

"That's another coincidence! My honorary nephew, Adam? He's at Oxford as we speak and he's a huge Richardson fan! You'd like him. He loves Richardson. Have you read Pynchon's *Mason & Dixon* yet?"

"No . . ."

"Oh, I recommend it, Ms McLachlan. I sent a copy to Adam because, once I'd read it, I knew — knowing how much he loves Richardson — he'd love Pynchon's new one. Still, if you completed your degree in '94, I can imagine you must have felt pretty good about it? I mean, an accomplishment's an accomplishment."

"I did feel good about it, yes. It was an accomplishment, for me. It's not much in the eyes of the world; but, for me, it was an accomplishment. It was something I'd always wanted to do."

"Can I brag about you?"

"Oh, well. I wouldn't bother putting that in . . . No, I mean, it's not important. I just hope you are kind to Sarah; and, as I say again, she is a very good person and I do hope you'll take into consideration she always tries to do the best she can for everyone, I think."

"I think so, too, Ms McLachlan. You won't get an argument from me; but, if you don't mind, I'd like to point out to the public — particularly the media — you're not a lifelong student at all. You're a graduate. At least, I can correct that misinformation, if you'll allow me to do so."

"Well, I suppose you can say I do have the degree; but, when I say that, it almost sounds as if I want to see my name in print. And, I don't . . ."

"No, it doesn't. I'll take full responsibility for coaxing you to do so, which I have done so, clearly."

"Well, I suppose so . . ."

"Ms McLachlan, I don't know you and I've never met you; but, I can say, just from talking with you, Sarah's a lucky kid. You sound pretty wonderful, at least to me."

"Go on. If you flatter me like that, I *will* be suspicious of you."

"I appreciate you taking the time, Ms McLachlan. I won't flatter you; but I do thank you for what you have told me."

"Good enough."

Don't you know that why is simply not good enough
So just let me try
And I will be good to you
Just let me try
And I will be there for you
I'll show you why you're so much more than good enough

— from *Good Enough*

The portrait of Sarah McLachlan which slowly comes into focus highlights her years of disciplined training offset by the image of a quiet child and introspective young woman variously considered weird, committed, wild, and "a little lost" in her alternative passions, especially her fashion tastes and musical preferences. When McLachlan speaks of her childhood, she speaks of leading a sheltered life growing up in Halifax, a harbor city on Canada's East Coast, a coast renowned for its picture-postcard views of the Atlantic ocean, its rich and varied heritage and history, plus its near-reverential worship of traditional Canadian music and its indigenous makers, including OneOfs Dr. Stompin' Tom Connors, Stan

Rogers, Theresa Doyle, the Rankin Family, Anne Murray, Nathalie MacMaster, Ashley McIsaac, and suchlike, all deservedly enshrined in the country's collective musical consciousness.

McLachlan's naturally curly hair (inherited from her mother) provided her classmates with a physical basis for her adolescent Medusa monicker (which, coincidentally, according to literary lore, was also the nasty high-school nickname of *Surfacing* author Margaret Atwood whom, in 1989, McLachlan singled out as one of her favorite authors despite the fact, as she told *Vancouver* magazine, she'd "hated her in school"). In Greek myth, the Gorgonian Medusa has snakes for hair, and if a guy gets an eyeful of her, he gets turned to stone (which, not to put too fine a point on it, isn't such a bad gig to have among myths, given the way in which most guys still insist they don't behave).

Anyway, McLachlan was apparently ridiculed often by groups of careless kids who would engage in bathetic and boorish impromptu theatrics whenever they encountered the co-ed in the corridors, cafeteria, and such: writhing, grasping, and gasping for help, the Queen-Elizabethan offenders pretended they were being turned to stone simply by looking into McLachlan's eyes.

"Yeah, and Queen Elizabeth High is still filled with idiots," writes Haligonian Don Whiting in one of his early posts to the Fumbling-Towards-Ecstasy List, a free-for-all subscription-based cyber-forum (allegedly owned and monitored by Nettwerk Productions) where "The Fumblers" (a.k.a. Sarahmaniacs) endlessly debate, dissect, and discourse on everything from the meanings of McLachlan's songs to aspects of her personal appearance (only her hairdresser knows — and needs to know — for sure).

"The kids at her high school thought her to be very strange," continues Whiting, "and her alternative way of looking was ridiculed and she became a target for a lot of cruel jokes and name-calling like 'Medusa.' It had quite an effect on her . . . ."

Whiting cites McLachlan's jewelry, album artwork, posters and T-shirt designs (often created around Medusan motifs) as concrete evidence of the aforementioned effect the typically brutal nickname had upon McLachlan.

"Now," Whiting positively crows, "these same people come up to me as a Sarah McLachlan fan and say, 'Hey, I went to high school with her!' expecting me to think of them as special in some way. In a lot of cases the phrasing is more, 'Hey, I was friends with Sarah in high school' when the truth is that she had maybe four or five friends . . . I have only met one *honest* Queen Elizabeth High grad, who I was talking to as he taxied me out to K-Mart: 'Yeah, this is a cool song . . . I went to school with Sarah McLachlan . . . I, along with most of the school, thought she was fucking WEIRD, Man!' "

Whiting concludes his post by pointing out the effect of those years "still stings . . . There is an article on my wall where she says she would like to forget a lot of things that happened while she was growing up in Halifax. Halifax doesn't hold a lot of fond memories for her."

During an interview in August 1997 with Denise Keeley of London's *Scene*, McLachlan confided that "someone passed an e-mail on to me of a guy who read an article about how I felt I was picked on as a kid. The very ring-leader, in his e-mail, said, 'You know, I just wanted to tell you the reason we called you Medusa was not because you were ugly but because of your long curly hair. We teased this guy mercilessly because he had a crush on you.' This guy was an asshole to me. He just wanted to say, 'You may not believe this; but, we're proud of you.' It totally warmed my heart. It was really nice because he was aware that he was a real shit."

Still, despite the real shits we all necessarily encounter on the road to restitution (or retribution), Medusa took the shit, and, as a testament to both her unflinching honesty and market-savvy moxie, McLachlan made something like an art of it.

Let's face it. It's almost a truism to remind readers we all get beaten up, knocked down, and pushed around throughout our lives, one way or t'other. Likewise, as a corollary, it almost echoes without saying that not all societies or family units comprising said societies function perfectly all of the time. It's the nature of the beast, best summarized by the notion that nobody's perfect (or everybody is); and, by extension, the gift of life — the curse and blessing that ultimately marks us all as utterly human beings muddling through its miraculous vistas — necessarily involves the gift of death.

When an individual elects to pursue her dream, shape her life, or realize her true function and potential in the grip and glare of public adulation (which maintains, endorses, and usually enriches said individual), it generally goes without notice that all those who neither require nor achieve fame keep the precious driven few who do so in the limelight. What, after all, would McLachlan be without ever-escalating sales and the kinds of lavish media attention she obviously, almost obsessively, needs? (Probably, a woman on the brink of 30 from a family of five ready to make room for one of her own.)

By the time she completed her formal studies at the Maritime Conservatory of Music — then located in the Sacred Heart School on Spring Garden Road — and after several years of private lessons, McLachlan had transformed herself into both top-ranking student and top-flight pop singer who, given the depth, color, and technical proficiency of her first-class asset, desperately and profoundly knew what it was she was meant to do.

As she told *Flare*'s Constance Droganes, "I used to think most pop music was just a lot of crap. In fact, even though I know there are many fine musicians out there producing good work, on the whole most of what I hear even now is a lot of garbage." Two years earlier, two days prior to her twenty-first birthday, McLachlan confided to *The Calgary Herald*'s James Muretich that she had "wanted to become a musician, be like Kate Bush or Peter Gabriel, have a cult following and create the most amazing music."

There was a time, before 'cult followings' and 'the most amazing music,' when Sarah McLachlan signed her name simply for the beauty of it. Naturally, that was before the now-legendary night when a shrewd wannabe rec-exec turned her attention to far more impressive signatures, signings and related Sarahgraphs.

"Well," recalls Haligonian dance-club entrepreneur Greg Clark, "there was this one spot, right? Like, nobody but *nobody* puts graffiti on the front of *my* sign, right? Like, I used to have a major problem with graffiti, mostly in the washrooms; of course, that was sort of hard to defeat, you know? But, my sign? Nobody touches *my* sign. It's just that simple.

"I come in this one day? There's this really small, really *tiny*, really beautiful signature. I can remember looking at my sign and saying, 'Well, *who the hell* is Sarah McLachlan?' "

Clark laughs easily and openly. When I catch up with him, he's listening to the Jays clobbering the Yanks 3-1 and preparing to check out the Saturday-night action at the clubs he still runs in downtown Halifax, N.S., especially Birdland, his most ambitious project to date. But, back then, when McLachlan signed her first autograph, Clark oversaw the video arcade Backstreet Amusements and the Club Flamingo situated on Gottingen Street where McLachlan worked part-time, selling tickets and such.

"Might have been as early as '83 or so. It was a place where a lot of the people involved in the initial phase of the alternative scene in Halifax congregated. The kids hung out there."

Clark's venue subsequently featured the 17-year-old Haligonian high-school student fronting the band October Game, fresh from a pair of pick-up nights at the local YMCA before the band jelled and made its way over to Dalhousie University's Greywood, a popular student watering trough in the Student Union Building frequented by the staff of CKDU, most likely because many of the personnel who pushed the anything-but-mainstream hits at the on-campus station — King's College students — also wore alternative hats as members of October Game.

Allegedly, October Game was comprised of Jeff Semple on lead guitar, Patrick Roscoe on keyboards, Bug Walsh on rhythm guitar, Jim Parker on bass, McLachlan on vocals, and, apparently, either a drum machine or, alternatively, an ever-changing roster of drummers. All of the aforementioned alleged former members were *not* interested in identifying themselves in any way, shape, or world with Nettwerk and Sarah McLachlan: not only did they not wish to grant me an interview unless authorized by "Nettwerk and Sarah," they uniformly refused to even divulge who played what in McLachlan's first profession-al band (which, it would appear, recorded tunes by Roscoe and Semple).

According to one of October Game's originals, bass player Jim Parker mysteriously presented McLachlan to the band one night when it dawned on the guys they might actually benefit from acquiring an individual who might actually know a thing or three about the art of singing. Actually, she did. She sang the guys' songs — exclusively penned and composed by the ultra-shy guys — plus a handful of covers (including Lulu's *To Sir With Love*, Siouxie and The Banshees' *Cities In Dust*, Blondie's *Hangin' On The Telephone*, and, appropriately, *Every One's A Winner, Baby* by Hot Chocolate).

"Nobody really remembers where exactly she came from (and if *he* does, he never said so)," writes one of The Game's members on a webpage (hosted by Dr. Mike [Phloem] Sugimoto) in cyberspace coyly dubbed *Out Of The Shadows* (after the first cut on McLachlan's 1988 Nettwerk début, TOUCH, which echoes the title of the 1986 vinyl record album October Game made — with four tunes featuring McLachlan on vocals — OUT OF THE FOG).

"We recorded a song called *Grind*" — McLachlan's first commercial recording currently available on 1993's OUT OF THE FOG TOO, a reissued cassette/CD compilation from the indie label, Flamingo, along with a dozen-plus singles from a slew of alternative bands recording at that time — "that the guitar player [allegedly Semple] wrote and it got a lot of airplay on CKDU because, well, we all kinda had our own shows at the station and we all played the hell out of it! But, actually, that song started to become very popular at the station and soon lots of people were playing it. So, we started writing more stuff."

"October Game?" snorts Clark, one of McLachlan's most steadfast supporters still in close touch with the woman who then beautified his sign with her first autograph and now beau-tifies the covers of leading publications throughout large por-tions of the western world, that same distinctive autograph front and center on many of same. "October Game? Well, I think they knew that the voice was there; but their own egos were too big. I mean, she was obviously the only thing that people were interested in. The other members, the bass player [allegedly Parker], the keyboard player [allegedly Roscoe] — whoever [allegedly the drum machine, *etc.*] — would actually do the between-song patter. Talk to the audience. That kind of thing. Sarah would never really get to do that, even. I felt like throwing my beer at them; for God's sakes, shut up and let her talk! That's who the people wanted to hear from, not those guys.

"I mean, in the long run, it was a good thing for Sarah. If she had felt differently about that band, she might not have gone; or, at least, she certainly would've had a harder decision in going. She had been courted by Nettwerk. It was a process for her to decide to go. I mean, she did ask a lot of people what they thought she should do. She was a kid, remember? I don't want to overemphasize my role in it; but, I was certainly there and I did say something like . . . I told her to get the hell out of there, I mean, given the situation she was in at the time."

At the time, McLachlan was on the cusp of graduating — apparently with barely passing marks — Queen Elizabeth High School while holding down various part-time jobs, including one stint as a dishwasher/counter person and another busking for handouts on Barrington, Halifax's main drag.

Understandably, her parents nixed their youngest's request to relocate to Vancouver until she'd satisfactorily graduated Queen Liz and explored post-secondary options or, at the very least, reached the age of majority. Besides, it seems, McLachlan had very much wanted to attend the Nova Scotia College of Art and Design (NSCAD) in order to work in textiles and jewelry design as well as to perfect her favored medium, pen-and-ink drawing. At the same time, she worked for a children's camp affiliated with NSCAD and, from 1985 to 1987, attended the not-for-profit Maritime Conservatory of Music, perhaps one of the finest and most respected musical academies in the country, studying classical guitar, piano, and voice. Also, of course, this *was* right around the time McLachlan happened to meet her birth mother, Judy. Various circumstances on the adopted home front additionally presented their own sets of anxieties.

"Yeah, she had a lot to deal with; and, all of it hit at once," recalls Clark. "She was really young, after all; and, of course, her parents didn't want her to go. But, October Game? Those guys? They were pretty stupid, really, about the whole thing. They should've just realized what they had, right? I mean, you don't have to be a brain surgeon to figure stuff like that out. You hear that kind of voice? You see the kind of presence she had on stage? Right from the start, it was pretty damned impressive.

"And, here's October Game. Yeah, yeah. It was almost similar to a Motown sort of situation: Sarah's the talented vocalist; but, the talented vocalist has absolutely no input. Go figure. Of course, those guys changed their tune once they realized that she might be going away . . .

"You know, though? Nobody but nobody would've guessed that this would've happened, although . . ." — Clark suppresses something between a sigh and a guffaw — "Well, it was pretty obvious from the start she had the talent. I mean, the wild card that was unanswered when she left here was whether or not she could write songs. She'd never been given the opportunity to do it."

Opportunity came knocking the night techno-pop dance-band Moev's guitarist, Mark Jowett — then also working at Vancouver's Odyssey Import Records as well as University of British Columbia's alternative-music station CITR — discovered McLachlan singing at October Game's first official concert doing the warm-up honors for Moev. Jowett flipped over McLachlan and promptly offered to sign her and two of October Game's four members, apparently the guitarist and keyboardist, to his then-fledgling independent-record outfit, which he, Terry McBride, and Brad Saltzberg had started with a round of handshakes in Odyssey's back room in the early '80s.

The enchanted Jowett marveled at the young woman's acrobatic dexterity, charismatic intensity, and unearthly beauty. Himself a quiet, sensitive, and somewhat studious soul slightly older than the object of his undivided attention, Jowett listened with acuity tempered by awe when McLachlan delivered exquisite versions of tunes penned by her October Game band mates, a fact which troubled Jowett not.

Clearly, McLachlan possessed the soul and temperament of a poet; clearly, her back-uppers hadn't taken the time to know it; and, clearly, one doesn't require an Einstein injection to figure out the boys in the band were a few tracks short of a CD.

"In our brief two-and-a-half-year existence," continues the October Gamester's cyberspiel, "we recorded a handful of songs, including *Shadows, The Warning Light, The Bower* (personal fave of mine; but then, hey, I wrote it, so . . .), *Irvine* and a number of others that escape me at the moment. In addition, there were a number of songs we wrote that never got recorded, including a ballad which was just Sarah and piano that somehow never really acquired a title, and another song we kept calling 'Amaretto' 'cause we couldn't think of a name for *it* either. We all had strong influences, especially Peter Gabriel and Kate Bush, though our songs didn't particularly reflect these influences.

"Our very first concert was played at the Dalhousie Student Union Building. We set up a rather spectacular rear-projected lighting system behind each band member that looked really cool. Anyway, on that fateful night, our little diva was offered a record contract right after the show by Nettwerk Records, although I didn't actually know this at the time. I think I was drunk, actually. I was very impressed with our first little concert and was probably celebrating somewhere. Anyway, although it was our first show, it was also the beginning of the end, because we knew she was gonna go."

Jowett knew it, too. Simultaneously stunned and utterly smitten, the Moevitian fell in love with the vision before him that night: a goddess, a new-age angel, an artist in possession of perfect pitch, a two-plus-octave range, and vocal gorgeosities to the nth degree. Jowett additionally knew that, if McLachlan would consent to either joining Moev or signing on with Nettwerk, her autograph on the deal's bottom line would ensure "our little diva" big-time success.

Two tumultuous years later, 2 October 1987, McLachlan signed a solo contract on that dotted line after McBride, in Halifax with another act from Nettwerk's then-tiny stable, Skinny Puppy, talked McLachlan up and allowed her to get an eyeful of the Pups' $80,000 tour bus. A decade after the fact, one "former member" — who obviously prefers the mystery of anonymity — still hasn't cottoned on to the simple notion that a few titles enshrined in Cyberia will never hold a candle to McLachlan's complete set of works.

The works — TOUCH, SOLACE, FUMBLING TOWARDS ECSTA-SY, and SURFACING — tell the story of McLachlan's education in the trenches of popular music, warts, wounds and all. It's the story of that kid, that skinny kid with braces on her teeth who skidded into paradise in possession of a voice built to last a life-time, despite the fact she's currently oiling, as one of her pri-mary influences Joni Mitchell calls it on a "Free Man In Paris," "the star-maker machinery behind the popular song."

The smoke-saturated mezzo who considers Mozart her clas-sical icon cites the movie *Amadeus* as one of her all-time faves, apparently right up there on her list with *Barfly, Blue Velvet, Angel Heart,* and *Blade Runner.* "I was so happy when I saw *Amadeus,*" she told *The Vancouver Sun*'s John Mackie in September 1988. "[Mozart] was this supposedly repulsive little fellow who made this absolutely beautiful, incredible music. I thought, 'That's me'."

McLachlan, who had started lessons on classical 12-string guitar at seven and piano during her preteens, made no secret of the fact she favored the female voice in opera; additionally, she credits her opera training with teaching her about ways in which to control her throat muscles, vocal cords, and breath-ing. The little diva, however, abandoned classical singing because she felt constricted and confined by its rigidity and rote methodology, considering it a formalism too rigorous for her need to create a musical environment allowing for impro-visation.

"I also used to listen to a lot of Joan Baez, Cat Stevens and Simon and Garfunkel," she explained to *The Boston Globe* in August 1989. "They were my mother's influence. And, when I was 16, I started to listen to progressive music and new wave by the Cocteau Twins and Kate Bush. Then, I discovered Peter Gabriel, who is a god to me. He just opened up a whole new meaning of music. He's so articulate, he writes great lyrics and has explored so many different kinds of music. He makes me want to achieve more and more with my own music."

McLachlan apparently engaged in quite a lot of soul-searching before facing the fact she could not envision herself pursuing a career in classical music. But, when she accepted October Game's invitation (allegedly tendered by Jim Parker) to join the band, she kept up with her studies at MCM, most likely because, as she repeatedly puts it, her parents freaked out when she informed them of her decision to explore alternative musical options.

"When I was a kid," she told *Now*'s Kim Hughes, "you'd give these recitals where everybody's parents sit there and say, 'That's my kid that I've been paying all this money for. Well, you better do good or you're going to get whacked when you get home.' All the proud parents were there; and, of course, all the kids were just shitting their pants because their necks were on the line. . . .

"I didn't give a shit about high school; but, I'm glad [my parents] made me finish. And, then I went to art college. But, you know, there's so much emphasis put on education. There's people out there with Ph.D.s driving cabs. . . .

"I don't see myself ever going back to classical music. God, no! I don't have the discipline. And, I don't love it enough. I love this more. Always did. I did spend years and years studying classical music; but, I always resented it.

"And, I don't think there's anything wrong with making a living doing what you love to do. I'm very lucky to be able to do that."

That, as she has repeatedly said, numbered one among the first serious things she'd ever wanted to do; and, as such, her parents reluctantly — perhaps a little wistfully — respected their youngest's decision to move 5,493 kilometers in the opposite direction (against the weather), yielding to her desire and obvious determination to make the kinds of music she felt most comfortable making.

"I think," she confided to Canada's premier popologist, *The Globe and Mail*'s Chris Dafoe, "they resigned themselves to the fact that I'm not a little girl anymore (although my dad still calls me his little girl)." And as she also confided to Richard

Cromelin of the *Los Angeles Times* some years later, "By the time I was 19 I was hell-bent to get out of there. . . . I was bored, and my parents and I didn't get along at all the last couple of years I was there."

Daddy's girl, all growed-up and gorgeous, didn't fulfil the McLachlans' dire prediction she'd sign her life away and wind up either dead or strung out on cocaine in a business dominated by sex fiends and drug addicts if she relocated to Vancouver.

"This was my ticket out, as far as I was concerned," she told *The Winnipeg Free Press*'s Stephen Ostick. McLachlan also admitted to *The Record*'s Jeff Bateman that she was an "average teenage rebel with a skateboard and a bad attitude" who, like most kids, craved independence, even if it meant crossing the country to gain same.

"Now, they're quite proud of me. My mom was in a mall and heard my voice and saw these kids watching my video on a television. They were talking about how they remembered me from school and my mother was just beaming," McLachlan happily tells her earliest admirer and biggest booster, Tim Arsenault of *The Halifax Chronicle-Herald*, on the eve of Valentine's Day 1989, right around the time her début disc, TOUCH, floors the aforementioned critics and goes through the roof in sales.

She said, "I haven't written a song before. You sure you want to do this?"

They said, "We'll give you six months and see what you can come up with."

The rookie recording artist, freshly arrived on the Vancouver scene in October 1987, came up with an enduring attachment to the cosmopolitan city so unlike the hometown she'd once called parochial (qualified, naturally, by her delight both coastal centers afforded equally spectacular ocean views). Modern, diverse, and pulsing with life as the heart of culture and commerce in western Canada, Vancouver allowed McLachlan the freedom anonymity confers as well as providing her with a place where she might finally make up her mind about *who in the hell* Sarah McLachlan *was*.

Despite the fact she was just a kid, she became a member of Local 145 and rented an apartment in close proximity to Nettwerk Productions Ltd., now a company comprised of principals Mark Jowett, Terry McBride, and Ric Arboit. Legend has it that the original business was supposedly founded on a loan of four grand. McLachlan worked in a submarine joint by day and did her damnedest to concentrate on the business of writing songs for the first of five records under the terms of her contracts with both Nettwerk and Nettoverboard, a general partnership consisting of Jowett, Arboit, McBride, and Gillian Hunt.

"For the first little while," McLachlan admitted to Dafoe in the spring of '89, "I was really lazy. I was just getting to know the city. Then, when I tried to write, I kept writing songs with too many notes. I had so many ideas floating around, I guess I was trying to cram everything into one song — a bass duet and an orchestra and . . . It was just ridiculous. Finally, I realised that I had to simplify things. I looked to how someone like Peter Gabriel wrote and tried to keep things a little simpler. . . .

"Then, I realized that you've got to keep at it; this is my profession now. I don't always know how a song is going to sound when I'm finished — the process of writing is important; I can spend four months on a song, leaving it and going back to it. But I know now what I want and don't want in a song. I'm feeling a lot more comfortable."

Also feeling both a lot more comfortable and even more convinced McLachlan could and would write songs, Nettwerkers put their eggs in one basket and bet the farm on Jowett's initial assessment that the singer's potential would take them to the market with a product that could, by conservative estimates, go gold (50,000 units) in Canada.

A month after she signed on the dotted line reports *Vancouver*, McLachlan "had these little ditties; but, I had never structured anything into a whole song. It took a long process of trial and error, of forcing myself to sit down for hours at a time to just play."

In November 1987, Jowett contacted 54-40's then-drummer Darryl Neudorf in Toronto and invited him to relocate to

Vancouver (all expenses paid) in order "to collaborate on the composition of songs with McLachlan" according to *Statement of Claim* No. C950847, registered with the Supreme Court of British Columbia 16 February 1995 (when Neudorf claimed he co-wrote songs on TOUCH). In February 1988, McLachlan's then-manager, Dan McGee, contacted Jeffrey Sawatzky in Edmonton and invited him to relocate to Vancouver, "bringing with him his original lyrical works," in order to assist with McLachlan's career by co-writing musical compositions with her, and join her band for the purposes of recording and touring, according to *Statement of Claim* No. C951105, registered with the Supreme Court of British Columbia 28 February 1995 (when Sawatzky likewise claimed he co-wrote songs on TOUCH). Around the same time, Nettwerkers enlisted the services of various personnel from their own roster — most notably the Grapes of Wrath (a.k.a. Ginger), Moev, and After All keyboardist Darren Phillips — to perform a variety of production and performance services.

McLachlan described, to various media reps across the continent, the obstacles she encountered during her apprenticeship days, repeatedly marveling at how much work goes into the making of a popular song, a craft in which many labor but few succeed. Right off the bat, she discovered that writing angst-driven lines of the high-school confidential variety bore little resemblance to the rigorous discipline the highly specialized genre demands. It most likely dawned on her that Marshall McLuhan's declaration concerning media and messages applied to the art and craft of shaping a successful composition created to appeal to millions.

It is a fact universally known that few poets additionally possess the ability to write memorable and lasting songs; it is also a fact universally known that few — if any — songwriters could (or would want to) match the genius of T. S. Eliot's *The Waste Land* or Emily Dickinson's body of work, primarily because songwriting is a craft directed towards mass consumption while poetry is an art for its own sake. And, when it comes to popular music, since the medium *is* the message, the product is obviously its purpose.

McLachlan would later defend TOUCH by agreeing with James Muretich that "the lyrics aren't always great; but, they're the first I've ever written. "I focused on my own emotions but kept them vague so that it wouldn't seem like I was writing about my boyfriend. This album is my innocence. I was really into writing beautiful music, all very pretty sounding. That's why TOUCH is so soft. It's just that I enjoy being taken somewhere by music. I enjoy being able to put the headphones on, close my eyes and forget about my worries."

McLachlan did worry. She worried she'd never reach a level of success that would afford her a house with a backyard for her cats (and eventually, a dog). She worried she'd wind up slapping down subs instead of climbing up charts. And, like all artists of the perfectionist persuasion, she anguished over her work.

Would anybody like it? Would anybody hate it? Would anybody ever get to hear it, given the fact she'd never written a song in her life? On especially dark days before she found her groove, McLachlan still found herself wondering — privately and publicly — whether *she* was even sure she *could* write a song. "I'm wondering how people can have 400 songs in their repertoire," she marveled in *Vancouver*'s December 1989 issue: "I'm a slob and I'm lazy; but, I'm a perfectionist with my music."

Once McLachlan realized the now-or-neverdom of her situation, she turned her attention to the task at hand, the task of creating a repertoire of songs worthy of preservation on vinyl. "More than anything," she explained to Mackie in September 1988, "I just tried to find words that sounded nice together. If they meant something, well, great; but, the intent was to have it flowing."

TOUCH, despite its flaws — lyrical incoherence, compositional disintegration, and jejune preciosity foremost among them — most certainly flows, a veritable deluge of water imagery and bleeding heartiness, from the flooding memories dripping with "pain and anger" on the disc's lead-off cut, *Out Of The Shadows* —

Crouching down inside a deep ravine
Those angry cries pass quickly by, he can't be seen
So many ways spent hiding in so many undone plans
Forgetting what it's like to fight when no one understands
Close call there in the shadows
There's a fear in the dark
There's no one out there
All those memories, pain and anger, flood back one by one . . .
The hours pass so slowly
The life's slipping out of me
No way's the right way
Is there a way out for me?
Is there no way out for me?
There must be a way out for me . . .

— from *Out Of The Shadows*

— to the "brooding storm" of *Vox* —

In the desert of my dreams I saw you there
I'm walking towards the water steaming body cold and bare
But your words cut loose the fire and you left my soul to bleed
And the pain that's in your truth's deceiving me has got me scared
Oh why?
Through your eyes the strains of battle like a brooding storm
You're up and down these pristine velvet walls like focus never forms
My walls are getting wider and my eyes are drawn astray
I see you now a vague deception of a dying day
Oh why? . . .

— from *Vox*

—and the recurring references to oceans, tides, dew, rivers, tears, rain *et soforthia* throughout her first full-length recorded (and endlessly remixed, remastered, rearranged, and repackaged) performance.

"Water," McLachlan earnestly insisted to *The Toronto Star*'s turfaceous Peter Howell in the summer of '91, "plays a huge part in my life. I need to be near water. I love being in it. It's like being back in the womb."

One might wonder what's so great about being back in the womb; but one must also remember that McLachlan, despite her trademark vocal precision and clarity everywhere evidenced on her first foray into the art of recorded sound, was, for all intents and purposes, still wet behind the ears, a fact which entranced both media as well as like-minded masses of brooding mood mongers willing to overlook the mediocrity of McLachlan's first and worst effort.

On 15 April 1989, *Billboard* published the following assessment of the young chanteuse: "Canadian 21-year-old with astonishing vocal range recalls Kate Bush. McLachlan's voice has those same swirling ethereal qualities that cause both chills and delight. She also wrote or co-wrote every tune and plays keyboard and guitars. [TOUCH] is certain to be a critical rave and strong word of mouth should help move it along."

Citing early Black Sabbath, Peter Gabriel, Kate Bush, Brian Eno, Talk Talk, German and Italian opera, Mozart, Simon and Garfunkel, Billie Holiday, the Eurythmics, Ella Fitzgerald, Nat King Cole, Tom Waits and the Stranglers among her personal listening pleasures in 1989, McLachlan endeared herself to rock-oriented popographers who approved of her willingness to sample music across the spectrum; it also hurt her not at all that the majority of mainstream musical commentators were, by and large, guys not above being smitten by the contradictions embodied in McLachlan's public image — misty-eyed Celtic princess — and off-stage personality — best described as a playful blend of virgin and vamp.

Cute, coy, and raggedy-jaggedy (on both compositional and lyrical fronts), the motley mix of traditional folk, orch-pop, and art music on TOUCH suffers from an irritating lack of synthesis, yet the title-track, for example, eerily reminiscent of the music of the oft-dubbed "savior of polyphony," Giovanni Pierluigi da Palestrina (c.1525/6-1594), particularly the five-voice motet *Ascendo ad Patrem* from the *Motectorum liber secundus* for five, six, and eight voices, proved McLachlan could sing circles around most of her contemporaries (but precious little else).

By the time McLachlan and band sold out Toronto's Diamond Club, played Ottawa's National Arts Centre, and

Montreal's Spectrum, she felt confident enough to return to Halifax, this time headlining a three-night mini-series of 75-minute concerts presented at the renamed Flamingo Café and Lounge Greg Clark and two partners had subsequently opened, apparently now located on Salter Street (attended by Jack and Dorice McLachlan, vocal-coach Diane Oxner, various alleged components of October Game, and so many Haligonians she broke all house records all three nights).

Flags For Everything stoked the audience's fires before McLachlan took her front-and-center place in the limelight with Darren Phillips on keyboards, Sherri Leigh (wife of Dan McGee) on drums, Stephen Nikleva on lead, and Jeffery Krosse on bass as the crowd erupted with a sonic welcome so encouragingly proud and protectively adulatory that McLachlan often fought back tears of joyous gratitude when she humbly and proudly introduced either her own tunes or covers of Simon and Garfunkel's *Emily*, Led Zeppelin's *D'yer Make 'er*, and Peter Gabriel's *Solsbury Hill* just prior to delivering a pitch-perfect *a capella* version of Scottish trad-ballad, *My Laggan Love*.

Yes. McLachlan expertly handled the between-song patter, chatting up the intimately familiar audience in a way October Game would never live down.

Clark? The guy already in heaven because "our little diva" had strutted some pretty impressive big-time stuff, simply beamed and beamed. He had finally and deliciously discovered just who the hell McLachlan was: a young woman in possession of an extraordinary voice and a commanding stage presence, ready, willing, and raring to turn the global musical community on its ear. Shortly after her spectacular Haligonian return, McLachlan headed off for a two-week promotional tour in Scandinavia, France, and Holland.

So, what had McLachlan and company ultimately come up with? An eight-record deal with Arista/BMG inked 1 December 1989. The Americans repackaged TOUCH, requested the additional track *Trust*, and allowed McLachlan to contribute her own cover design, a gorgeous hand-tinted photograph of the comin' upper on the steps of one of Halifax's landmark churches (or graveyards of same).

Two weeks after TOUCH's American re-release, McLachlan

told Arsenault she felt "very lucky that something happened so quickly. I came along at the right time."

So, natch, back home in Vancouver, McLachlan said:
"Hot damn! I did pretty good, eh?"
And, natch, Nettwerkers responded:
"You will do better. We've got a few more options."

Medusa and Dracula

Beneath a gibbous moon, beside a boiling sea

Medusa and Dracula set out for a walk.
He averts his eyes;
She looks out for her neck.
"So much Sturm-und-drang," she scoffs,
"All this blood-renewal, eternal life,
That messy striving of the undead —
My lovers are luckier;
One brave glance gains them
The elegant serenity of stone.

But then —"
As snakes writhe in the pewter light —
"Women, labyrinthine, wrought in you,
Incarnate, their necessary image of love."

— by Mary Dalton

(Left) Medusa silkscreen poster designed by Sarah McLachlan.

(Below) Medusa image on cover of LIVE.

(Opposite top) TOUCH *Cover (Arista release).*

(Bottom) TOUCH *Cover (Nettwerk release).*

three

MIDAS' TOUCH

or Black

By 28 June 1991, TOUCH had gone gold in Canada and had sold in appreciably higher numbers of units State-side. McLachlan had distinguished herself as an up-and-comer worth watching on a number of fronts. The big deal with Arista/BMG acting as bankroller and licensee for discs with copyrights on the compositions held by the Music Corporation of America, Inc. (MCA Music Publishing) would go a long way towards guaranteeing McLachlan increased North American visibility. As well, similar licensing, distribution, and publishing agreements were secured internationally, most notably in the U.K., Japan, Sweden, Denmark, Finland, Iceland, Belgium, Luxembourg, Norway, France, and Germany. McLachlan's willingness to hit the road, tour extensively, and speak to media with perceptive alacrity certainly provided the 23-year-old with an advantage over more reclusive, protected, or wiser (a.k.a. jaded) colleagues.

Thirty-three months later, SOLACE arrived in retail outlets across the country and its lead-off video/single, *The Path Of*

Thorns (Terms), began to turn eyes and ears in McLachlan's direction, most likely because the videogenic nubbie friskie had risked it all on maximum exposure to gain same. Yes, she had shucked her clothes for the video because she had elected to do so. Yes, it was the market-savvy attention grabber that jump-started her musical career. Yes, her mother felt it was tastefully, beautifully, and artfully done. No, her father didn't.

"When I talked to my dad," she confided to one of the country's more sensitive musical commentators, *Now*'s Hughes, "I asked him if he liked the video. He said, 'No, little girl, I didn't. You didn't have to do that.' There's just some things dads shouldn't see. It's one thing to see your little girl naked, but not on television."

One wonders, idly, where the father of "daddy's girl" was when Joni Mitchell, John Lennon & Yoko Ono, or the cast of *Hair* doffed their duds in the '60s and '70s. One can only conclude the American academic, born in 1930, was too busy with his book-learnin' to take much notice of the dawning of the "Age of Aquarius."

Just before the release of SOLACE, McLachlan met *mano à mano* with *The Globe and Mail*'s Liam Lacey in a Chinese café across the street from Nettwerk's Vancouver HQ at 1250 West Sixth. In the story he filed on 15 June 1991, Lacey describes the atmosphere at the record outfit as "something like a bustling campus radio station. Posters for the company's acts — Grapes of Wrath, Skinny Puppy, Lava Hay — cover the walls. The staff, in shorts, sweatshirts and sneakers, work at Macintosh computers, with telephones chained to their ears."

Meanwhile, back at the café, McLachlan impressed Lacey with her cursatorial savvy — or what he called her "salty vocabulary" — in an effort to dispel any and all myths concerning her previous incarnation as a well-dressed ethereal (*or* new-age angelic *or* pre-Raphaelitic rustic *or* misty-eyed moor-walkin') Celtic fairy princess, an image she already believed she'd crushed with the video she'd conceived and created for *Steaming,* the one featuring a sexually fantastic tart delighting in her role as sleazy chanteuse, the one that had set her back $17,000.

"I didn't know what 'image' was," avers McLachlan, "but

people told me, 'This is what you are' so I figured I better play along. My manager at the time [Dan McGee?] thought that it was a good approach to be this ethereal, whimsical waif. It wasn't particularly easy to live up to. I think I disappointed a lot of people when they actually met me."

Ah, the image, the all-important image. Several sources with whom I spoke concur McLachlan did, in fact, learn a little lesson or two about "image" after she entered the business primarily because, as "Hot Stuff" puts it, "she'd been prepped and put through her paces over and over. Naturally, she fell in with the party line, most of the time. I mean, she'd rebel occasionally and say something she shouldn't — especially live, especially radio — because she was a bit of an agitator, in her own way.

"But, look at the reality. Here's McBride and crew with a five-record contract where it looks like she signed her life away; and, here's McLachlan who hated that 'image' because it wasn't her at all. But, if she got of out line, she'd be perceived as difficult to handle and nobody would touch her in the biz. By the time she'd had a little success, she'd figured out how the business worked. She figured out the rules pretty quickly.

"Of course, of course. She fretted about her image right from the beginning, not necessarily because *she* gave a damn; but because *they* did. She'd tell an interviewer one thing; and, the next thing you know, Nettwerk's breathing down the guy's neck for a rewrite because it didn't jive with the image of the socially conscious clean-cut straight babe they wanted her to project.

"So, what do you do when you sing like she sings? A born singer. You dummy up and dive in or get out of the business forever. Remember, there's no such thing as a naïve popular musician; it's an oxymoron. But she hated that image; she just hated it. She wasn't that kind of person at all. She couldn't even pretend to be like that. I mean, she's really open and forthright and she says what she thinks.

"McBride was always out running around trying to put out little brush fires she'd started, not because she was malicious; but because she'd get going with someone she liked and she'd just naturally slip into being who she was, or who she became, shortly after she'd tasted a little success.

"I don't mean she took on a persona — more like, she began to grow up and into who she was and had begun to sort all of that out; and, to her credit, she got tough pretty fast, I mean, tough enough to last.

"It took guts to continue; but, it took her a bit before she saw the whole picture. By the time she'd gotten around to SOLACE, though, she could see it all too clearly; and, she couldn't very well just flick that ol' remote and change the channel."

"In the past three years," McLachlan confessed to *The Canadian Press*'s Nelson Wyatt, "I have sort of grown up. It's not like I'm mature or anything — I'm still a kid. But I just started asking questions. This is the time when most people do it, I think, from age 19 to 23.

"Part of me is really romantic," she admitted, "but generally, I'm as crass as anyone else . . . [SOLACE] is a lot more me. I'm singing lower. I'm not being this little angel singing really high up in the clouds."

Hughes had queried the gifted singer-songwriter on her wispy-waspy romantic image for the aforementioned *Now* profile a month after SOLACE came down the chute: "I designed [TOUCH's] cover and there was that image," allowed McLachlan, "I can be like that; and, I'm very romantic at times. But, I'm also just a normal person. I'm a goof sometimes, crass sometimes. Sometimes I dress nice, and sometimes I dress like a pig. I think that comes out more on SOLACE."

Enter Pierre Marchand, the rookie producer (Kate & Anna McGarrigle) and protegé of ex-Manitoban Daniel Lanois (Emmylou Harris, Peter Gabriel, U2, Brian Eno, the Neville Brothers, *et.al.*) who'd caught her eye and ears when, as a short-listed candidate for the producer reins on her second effort, he'd sent along some of his own music with his specs (which included his keyboard work with Luba, a Montreal band he'd joined because he'd needed a creative musical outlet).

A born musician, Marchand, not unlike McLachlan (or his Svengali, Lanois), never settles for second-best on anything to which he contributes. He'd spend days hammering and shaping a six-line verse or bridge until it exactly duplicated the way he'd already heard it (or sensed it should or could) sound. Ruthless (as all artists must necessarily be), he'd spend 12 to 16 hours on a single riff, kicking it around, dragging it all the way up and all the way back downtown until, miraculously, he'd nailed that sucker to the wall.

Eureka! The McLachlan-Marchand combination, a musical match as inspired as Rosanne Cash & Rodney Crowell or Glen Ballard & Alanis Morissette or Shania Twain & Robert (Mutt) Lange, proved to be the secret weapon she'd needed in order to go toe-to-toe in the down-and-dirty trenches of what Van Morrison calls "the music-business scene," the combat zone where hits, charts, shots, and bullets either turn a good singer into a great musical competitor or a coulda-been-woulda-been-shoulda-been contender.

The pair clicked. Marchand, itching to up the ante after the raves he'd received for his impeccable studio work with the McGarrigles' HEARTBEATS ACCELERATING, signed on with McLachlan and band (for better or best).

When she spoke with *The Record*'s Jeff Batemen, the scribe explained that "after spending much of 1989 touring and promoting TOUCH, McLachlan plunged into a lengthy pre-production cycle with Marchand, first in Montreal, then at Le Studio in Morin Heights, QB and last fall, in Vancouver. The project shifted to New Orleans in December, both to combat mounting studio expenses and to find a hermetic atmosphere where everyday routine would focus entirely on recording. SOLACE openly takes the emotional baggage McLachlan had acquired in the transition from youth to adulthood. The overriding theme is one of lost innocence."

"I named it SOLACE," McLachlan told Batemen, "because that is basically what everyone wants out of life, some comfort, some shelter, from all the crap we go through or bring down on ourselves. . . . Basically, it's an album of experience, though, God knows, I'm not all that experienced.

"Pierre [Marchand] and I have built this cocoon around ourselves and the music, and the album is like our child almost."

A year later, McLachlan confided to *The Los Angeles Times*'s Pop-Music columnist Richard Cromelin concerning her song-writing process for SOLACE: "I have to bring myself to a point of hysteria sometimes before anything good comes out. . . . But, that's when the good stuff comes up, when you push yourself so hard and so long that you're on the brink of bursting into tears — that's usually what happens. I usually just lose it. I burst into tears and bawl and bawl and bawl and then five minutes later say, 'Oh, there's a chorus. That's what I've been looking for'."

"I knew I wanted a musician to work with," McLachlan told Liam Lacey, "not just some engineer who was turning the knobs in the studio." McLachlan got what she wanted with Marchand (and then some). If there is one individual who deserves credit for her success (besides McLachlan herself, of course), Marchand is that one individual, a fact consistently underplayed or overlooked by both media and star-maker machinists who generally consider techno-nuts-and-bolts analyses of artists' recorded (as opposed to live) performances beside the point or beyond the interest and/or comprehension of the average consumer of musical products.

The Vancouver Sun's John Mackie, the exception who makes the rule, laid it on the line when he led off his review of McLachlan's October 1991 concert at the Discovery Theatre thusly: "In the high-tech world of modern music, the ability to actually sing isn't always a prerequisite for stardom. Provided you've got the proper physical attributes, know a few dance steps, hire a hot producer and songwriter and cut a way-right video, you can get away with a minimum of warbling. And, hey! You can always get some snazzy gizmo to fix up your vocals so it sounds like you can sing."

McLachlan, naturally, could sing, a fact she'd taken great pains to prove with TOUCH, an album she later confessed was heavily influenced both by other singers — *cf.* Mary Margaret O'Hara, 10,000 Maniacs' Natalie Merchant, Jane Siberry, Kate Bush, Sinéad O'Connor, Clannad's Maire Bhraonain [Brennan], Joni Mitchell, Enya, Joan Baez, and Liz Frazier of the Cocteau Twins — and her innate need to show off her heavenly gift; but, without the expert production services rendered by Marchand on the follow-up, one can only speculate on the course McLachlan's career might have taken.

"Musically," writes Lacey, "the Marchand-McLachlan combination may have been a marriage made in heaven; but, from the record company's point of view, it was more like a disaster. Both musician and producer were painstaking perfectionists in a business where efficiency and crisp professionalism are treasured.... Arista expected a record that would take, perhaps, a month and half to record. After two months, they asked for some demonstration of what McLachlan was doing."

McLachlan was doing all she could to overcome the sophomore jinx. "The next album had to be really good," she had already decided, "it had to be really huge. I felt these expectations were on me, and it was what I wanted as well. I was determined that I would give everything I could to make this a good record."

McLachlan rattled "some bare skeletons of what we were creating. I knew they weren't ready. They needed work, nurturing, but I hoped they would see I was on the right track. The answer that came back from Arista was that they were 'very disappointed' with my progress. I knew what we were doing was good work; and, I was almost devastated that they couldn't see it."

To his credit, Marchand could both see and hear it. "He made me sing lower, so my voice was closer to my speaking voice, and showed more of my own personality. We concentrated on using the voice for the purposes of the songs ... [In other words, Marchand instinctively understood McLachlan's voice better suited a conversational as opposed to an oratorical delivery] ... On the first record, I did a lot of classical wanking, you know, look at what my voice can do. This time, I was really singing the songs."

This time, a year after Marchand signed on and the pair had made tracks from Montreal to New Orleans to Vancouver laying down tracks, radio was really playing them. "I could care less about radio," she told Lacey, "and while I've eventually come to understand that record companies are businesses whose job is to make money, I found them pretty short-sighted. I wasn't about to stick some hip-hop sounds on the record to make it sound like the radio. I figure if it's good, it has the best chance of becoming a single. And, if it doesn't become a single, at least I have the satisfaction of knowing it's good anyway.

"I got sick of the pressure," she elaborated further, "so, I said, 'Screw it,' and we went to New Orleans. . . . When Arista finally heard [SOLACE], they flipped."

So, too, did the record-buying public, yours truly included. I'm not sure whether the cabbie who cranked up the radio for me that day when *The Path Of Thorns (Terms)* poured out of the tinny twin speakers of the beat-up Plymouth Fury she expertly negotiated through downtown Toronto's rush-hour traffic had a Ph.D. or not; but I am sure she knew a thing or two about longevity and the little girl with the big voice about to make a huge continental splash with one of the greatest pieces of music ever recorded.

"Making this record was the best musical education I've had. And, right now, I'm as happy as I've ever been because of that, because making music is what I want to do. I don't need to sell a million records to feel satisfied," she told Lacey over fortune cookies and green tea. "I just need to make a living from creating music. And, you know what?

"I'm a long way from rich; but, right now, I've got a nice apartment, I've got a record I'm proud of, and I am making a living from music."

A month later, McLachlan told *Now*'s Hughes the same thing. "I'm far from rich," she reiterated, "in fact, I'm flat broke; but, I'm really happy. I have a record that I'm really proud of, that I love. I'm touring with a great band. I've got a really great life right now."

Writing in the throes of agony for SOLACE in her apartment a stone's throw from Nettwerk's offices, McLachlan looked long and hard at both her current position and future prospects in the business of making music for a living.

"I've been figuring out my own life," she told Mackie just prior to her appearance at Vancouver's Pacific National Exhibition (in a free-stage series sponsored by Coca Cola Ltd.). "I stepped out of my own pathetic existence for a while and looked at other people's lives. Generally, I write because I'm pissed off or messed up about something; but, I didn't have anything to write about [because] I was really happy in my own life. So, I looked out of myself and into the world, and that's really when I started discovering there were all these horrible things going on."

At the same time she was telling Mackie she'd discovered that "this whole world revolves around greed in a really big way," her TOUCH had sold 200,000 copies internationally and its finest composition, *Ben's Song*, had been put to work softpeddling automobiles in a major motor-vehicle corporation's commercial in Japan. (Ben Askavold, an 11-year old with whom McLachlan had worked during her NSCAD children's camp days in Halifax, had passed away as a result of a brain tumor. She dedicated TOUCH to both the boy and her parents.)

Although McLachlan retained creative and artistic control of her career (including writing and composing the bulk of her material as well as designing the inevitable merchandise — jewelry, postcards, T-shirts, pack sacks, hats, mugs, posters, *etc*.), she obviously had to answer to the companies holding the purse strings in order to achieve the kind of financial success that would allow her to vacate her current False Creek premises and buy a house with a garden and a backyard for her pair of cats (and that dog she could only dream of adopting).

"Somehow on the first record, I didn't know what I had. I just did it. This one I cared so much about, it was so personal, it ran so deep for me. When people came to me and said, 'We don't like this because it doesn't sound like a single,' I just wanted to kick them in the head," she candidly tells Mackie elsewhere in *The Vancouver Sun* front-page profile.

"That's another horrible realization, that this is a business, these things are units, a commodity and product to these people. Not Nettwerk, but the major label [Arista]. I just couldn't take it. It horrified me, the thought that these people wanted me to create music — which to me is a sacred beautiful thing — and put a hip-hop beat on it so it can get played on the radio. I just couldn't take that."

Naturally, after several SOLACE vid-singles — including *The*

Path Of Thorns (Terms), Into The Fire, and *Drawn To The Rhythm* — had gone into heavy rotation and received priority treatment at radio, McLachlan changed her tune slightly, most likely because her "anti-capitalist pig" stance, best represented by the *Black* track on SOLACE, was ringing a little hollow, at least from management's point of view. Chances are, since McLachlan was knee-deep in the business of recording products for mass consumption on the commodified samescape of contemporary popular music, it had finally dawned on the prepackaged kid that the rec-execs she had so vituperously and vehemently attacked in several publications weren't the only ones who had gotten "sucked into the machine."

> 'Cause I can't see no reason
> What is blind cannot see
> 'Cause I want what is pleasin'
> All I take should be free
> What I rob from the innocent ones
> What I'd steal from the womb
> If I cried me a river of confessions
> Would I drown in shallow regret
> As the walls are closing in
> And the colors fade to black
>
> — from *Black*

Curiously, it was shortly after this time that McLachlan began to sign autographs with the now-customary peace plus love equals ecstasy symbols which were to become an integral part of "the whole package" her old friend, Greg Clark, had predicted she'd become.

In another context a while back, I visited with MCA-Nashville's prescient president, Tony Brown, something of a mainstream maverick who produced and continues to produce mostly platinum-plus platters for Wynonna, Lyle Lovett, Reba McEntire, Joe Ely, Nanci Griffith, Steve Earle, and George Strait, among illustrious others.

During the course of our get-to-get in his swank Twang-town office, the hot-shot rec-exec, a prototypical nice guy oozing unaffected humility, spoke candidly about the business of doing business in the music industry.

"Let's face it," acknowledges the guy who pounded the ivories for Emmylou Harris's Hot Band prior to his gig backing Elvis on keyboards from 1975 till the King's untimely death in 1977, "pop music is basically fashion, you know. Pop music affects and shapes fashion and that's the reason pop music, for the most part, is a young world. . . .

"I love the music business. There are things I hate about the music business, the things you probably hate about the music business. Politics and stuff; however, all that same stuff exists at Exxon and in every other business that calls itself a business.

"It just so happens, we creative people are so idealistic about what the music business should be, we occasionally fail to see what it really is. My greatest forte is the creative thing, that's what drives me; but, of course, the business side of it cannot be ignored. I can deal with the politics of it because it's endlessly fascinating and intriguing; but, I think, you have to hold onto a little bit of that idealism if you plan to last in this business.

"When you hear a singer sing, you want to look 'em in the eye and look down their throat. From a producer's point of view, I would say you would have to be able to live down the artist's throat."

"When I came to work at MCA, [Jimmy] Bowen had introduced digital to Nashville and insisted — *mandated* — that every record we cut at MCA had to be cut digital. And this town sort of thought he was full of it because pop-music people still favored analog recording.

"So, for that reason, Nashville became an innovator in recording. For years, there were more [producers and engineers using digital] here than in New York or L.A., and mainly because of Bowen. Well, everyone said digital wasn't as warm as analog tape. Because Bowen was such a maverick, people would say, 'I can't believe you work for him; I can't believe you listen to him; I can't believe he makes you use digital tape'.

"And I was going, 'Hey man, I'm just glad I got the opportunity.' I just shut it out; I realized I had to work within the confines of what Bowen wanted.

"You know what I learned? He was right. I love digital tape. I only use analog as an artist or co-producer. Some insist on it. I say, 'I don't really care; whatever makes you happy; I can work on anything'.

"If I had my druthers, I'd prefer to work with digital; but I can work with analog. Anyway, I learned about digital and I learned how to make it warm the more I worked on it — meaning, I found engineers who *enjoyed* working on it.

"Digital has more headroom. You can put more stuff on the tape. Wynonna or Reba's voices? They're so dynamic, they could hit a note and where analog tape would compress it, digital would let it expand or stuff. People who love the compression of analog tape love it because they're used to it.

"I love the fact that Wynonna or Reba or whoever can blast out a real cool note and I'll have all of it, in clear form and then I can use it.

"I can use the dynamics of a singer's voice because of digital tape; and, with the separation of all the instruments? Yeah, I use all that to my advantage, too. Whereas analog has natural compression, this way, you can clearly place everything.

"Some people say, 'I don't like that; it's too clean for me'. Well, you know, I say, 'I like it clean; so, it's just a matter of taste'.

"Yes," concludes Uptown Brown, "I guess every producer goes through this. There are moments I sit down and have anxiety attacks over whether my record sounds as big as so-and-so's record or maybe my record sounds too sterile or, maybe, fear's a great motivator, Fitz."

(That was the day the Awesome Possum hisself, George Jones, gold-inked his autograph on my copy of *Walls Can Fall*: "To Fitz: Thanks — George Jones." But, that's another story.)

This story concerns the fact that Sarah McLachlan didn't find her musical groove until technology caught up with capturing the full beauty of her exquisite vocal acrobatics. Pierre Marchand lovingly constructed a soundscape built to showcase McLachlan's splendorous instrument, pushing it forward and slightly upwards in the mix; at the same time, the constant combination/separation or re-situation of the instrumental tracks provided a warm foundation which reinforced and beautifully complemented the front-and-forward vocal tracks (due, one suspects, to a tapered oscillatory EQ which allows for vocals so pushed to weave in and out of the mix while still retaining their overriding prominence).

In other words, Marchand's techno-wizardry in the studio allowed for the creation of an aural context from which McLachlan's voice could reach out and wrap listeners in a storm of gorgeous sound so warm, rich, and clear, they'd swear it was better than her live performances until, when they did finally see her live, they'd swear she'd proven them dead wrong.

With Marchand on her arm, Lady McLachlan, best foot forward, stepped into the spotlight and out of her life.

The name of Norman Stein is a Vancouver landmark. It is at the heart of the early days of the West Coast's alternative scene, perhaps in more ways than one. Terry McBride's name is also there, allied at one time with Stein and then Saltzberg. Two record stores — Stein's *Cinematica* and Herman Saltzberg's *Odyssey Imports* — loom large in the rear-view mirror as McBride drives the Nettwerk vehicle, Sarah McLachlan's recording company, into the hell of Music-Biz City. He's going places. Fast.

And, I'm going nowhere. Sitting at my kitchen table in the dead center of summer '97, *not* thinking about Sarah McLachlan or Nettwerk or books or the bright day outside my window. Nope. Drinking coffee. Thinking about Orpheus.

Thinking about heaven and hell, as a matter of fact. Thinking about living, dying, immortality — the works. And Martin Luther and his hell. That gets me thinking about the hell of the ancient Hebrews, a hell where all souls ended up some place where either rewards or punishments were doled out by a certain somebody or other.

That gets me thinking about Hades and Orpheus looking back and losing Eurydice.

Now, there's a character.

Not to mention one hell of a musician.

Charmed his fellow mortals with his music; charmed the

wild beasts; even charmed the rocks and trees.

But one day he gets stinko-blotto and a gang of bitchy virgins tears him to shreds and throws his head into the river. *Whoa . . .*

Then, there's that whole business with the Muses, picking up the pieces of what's left of the guy and conducting a proper burial.

That's what stumps me — the part about the nightingale singing over his grave, apparently more sweetly than anywhere else in Greece.

How the hell can one nightingale sing *more sweetly* than any other?

I keep hearing Norman Stein's name. It keeps cropping up. He was *there*. I cold-call him, over cold coffee, after dropping by Canada 411 on my back-busting powerbook.

His number's there and he's there and he's different from many of the others who've expressed little interest — or even immense reluctance — in speaking with the author of an unauthorized biography (even a polite and pleasant one. Some have been well-nigh rude. Shucks, I'm just a workin' stiff. They may figure that one out some day).

Stein was only faintly hesitant to reach back into the early 1980s when Terry McBride, Mark Jowett, and Brad Saltzberg founded Nettwerk (who in turn found Sarah). The man has some painful memories. Yet, it's quickly apparent he was entirely *there* with his business and the scene; and it's even more obvious he loved what he was doing.

Norman Stein's 65, now. He is, inescapably, brilliant and sober. An alumnus of the Universities of Manitoba and Chicago with a doctorate in Clinical Psychology, a degree in Hebrew letters, and a background in sociology, Stein has always taken his avocation — music — seriously. At one time, he was an artistic director for an ongoing series of classical concerts; at another, he produced award-winning musical performances (on records).

Stein's done a stint in the A & R department (Artists and Repertoire) of RCA Records — back in the days of the Monkees and Jefferson Airplane. He's also served as a vice-president with Polydor/Deutschegrammophon — now Polygram — where he took care of the campus-radio record departments for more than 60 North American universities.

But he got banged up pretty badly in a '60s' car-crash in Winnipeg's North End. Rear-ended at a red light, he was pushed into an intersection and broadsided.

Unaware he'd been seriously hurt, he walked away from it, subsequently went into convulsions, and ended up in a coma after being treated with the wrong drugs, Stein states matter-of-factorily. He's suffered memory loss as a result. I certainly couldn't tell: his memories of his early Vancouver days are remarkably vivid and spry.

Norman Stein went into business because it was something he loved. "I attempted to apply Talmudic principles of ethics to business. There are conflicts ...," he says, quietly, rather wistfully, with characteristic understatement.

"I'm not a typical businessman, and neither is Terry," he reflects with wry precision.

Stein, St. Boniface-born, started in business in his hometown with a retail outfit called *Cult Opus 69*. Later, he exited Winnipeg, entered Vancouver's music scene, borrowed 20 grand and set up shop with his private collection of sound recordings, memorabilia, *et soforthia*.

He got busy, soon discovering his rather exotic stock — including obscure Grateful Dead recordings cheek-by-jowl with rare European imports — excited the local trendsetting rock jocks. Many of these either worked at — or volunteered their services to — CITR, the University of British Columbia's alternative campus-radio station.

Stein rustled up some extra income from a sideline of his at the time — consultant for props for Vancouver-made films. He loved films: he dreamed about the day he'd finally open his own film bookstore (and related enterprises that normally wouldn't be able to justify themselves financially in solo configuration).

Sure, he wanted to make a buck; but he also wanted to make art out of life. Stein's a diehard cultural preservationist.

Spring 1981. New Wave arrives. The folks in the air chairs are all over him about these blistering hot imports they've read all about in *Melody Maker*. They want them.

His own import collection has served him well; however,

he clearly sees an accelerating push for more. He tells the DJs he'll give it a shot. He'd already learned his import chops by bringing over appreciable quantities of in-demand products throughout the 1970s. He wouldn't mind doing it again, but he needs help. New Wave is, after all, well, *new*.

It's new to the radio people, too; but they've heard a few of these hard-to-acquire tunes at Vancouver's Love Affair club; so, they call upon Stein to contribute more of the same.

Stein digs around; finds himself a New York source for imports; and business takes off.

Enter Terry McBride. Barely out of his teens. He walks into Cinematica one day and offers his services as a consultant, says Stein. He hires him — 500 bucks a month — and tells him to help himself up to a certain limit — with Stein's approval — to records. "I'm not an astute businessman," Stein readily acknowledges.

McBride, a Richmond, BC twentysomething with a lifeguard certificate, had apparently fallen in with a school of like-minded public protectors of Vancouver's surf and turfers.

"He was short compared to the other lifeguards," recalls Stein. "I thought they were gay in their behavior and their dress, parodying Errol Flynn . . . They'd come into the store with their pointy shoes and ask me how I thought they looked," he sighs. "They liked Depeche Mode. They were all poseurs."

McBride had dropped out of Engineering at UBC. He wasn't bright in an academic sense, as far as Stein recalls, "but he *was* charming; he did do his research; and he was a very hard-working person. . . . McBride was an excellent salesman who generally believed in what he was doing . . . possessed, almost."

As Stein tells it, after hiring the guy, he finds McBride to be "so overzealous" about selling records that, at one point, he admonishes him to "ease up" on the customers. McBride's flabbergasted by Stein's attitude (sincerely believing he deserves praise for convincing some of the store's regular customers to spend $200 or $250 when they'd only intended to spend $100), remembers Stein. "He was driven." Plus, McBride possessed a strange talent: He could "gnash his teeth at the same time as he smiled at you." The disciplined and driven guy followed a rigid schedule, thanks to "a tremendous amount of adrenaline," he says. With respect to his utilitarian philosophy? "Ayn Rand could have learned from *McBride*."

Not long after that, Stein enters the hospital with gastrointestinal bleeding, and when he's discharged, he returns to work to discover McBride's virtually "taken over" his business, he says. The business owner's seemingly generous *help-yourself-to-records-just-let-me-know-what-you've-taken* arrangement had backfired on him, claims Stein. Quite simply, McBride "never submitted any such list" to him, he says.

Stein had worked hard to establish *de facto* "exclusivity" in the record-import biz. It didn't come cheap. By the time he'd paid its air-freight, duties, and broker fees, each imported album would set him back $13 before it even made it to the rack. Stein put his faith in volume and charged $16 for each record imported, thereby earning a profit of $3 per.

Cinematica carried various other lines of stuff, including material for the heavy-metal crowd as well as film and music books for (more scholarly) *aficionados*: "It was," reminisces Stein, "quite the eclectic group" popping in and out of the store in those days. "Many of the kids were idealists," opines Stein; and, a core group of them were so devoted to their music they'd spend "all of their spare time hanging out" at the popular musical magnet. "It was," as far as Stein's concerned, "a healthy atmosphere."

He knocked himself out researching new music for buyers who wanted rare recordings. Relaxed and paradoxically charged with the intense energy and excitement of youth, Cinematica's easy-pleasy atmosphere became more of a home than home for a lot of the kids. "Everyone wanted to help," recalls Stein, and the line between customers and staff occasionally blurred.

McBride, apparently, had his own business (in name, if nothing else): Noetix. That was McBride's preferred orthography. (You know, it's one of *those* words. New-wave semioticians play with it these days. It's a chameleon; but its Greek etymology fixes it firmly in the realm of *rational* activities of the mind.)

So, McBride has his own business and that business soon included various ad hoc "partners." And, lookee here, now he's got his own band as well. One day, some customers walk through Cinematica's doors; and, within the hour, these self-same customers are members of a band McBride's all-of-a-sudden managing.

"Moev," marvels Stein.

Three fellows — Mark Jowett, Thomas Ferris, and Calvin Stephenson — had put their musical heads together in June 1981, it seems, and *voilà!* Exactly three years and a million miles of heartache later, Moev's first commercial release returned from the vinyl pressers.

Buoyed by doing the seemingly undo-able just prior to shipping the final tracks to the manufactory, Stephenson, Ferris, Jowett, and McBride make a pact to become partners. Inside that year, they firmly cement the deal by filing a declaration for partnership in Nettwerk Productions.

At the time, McBride needed any kind of "edifice" he could find to lend his operations credibility, says Stein. Stein strongly believes he "presented that opportunity to McBride."

McBride needed to give the "appearance" of being a distributor of records, explains Stein, so he could promote his own group by throwing a Moev recording into the mix every chance he got (when he rubbed shoulders with the various radio and dance-club DJs he'd scrupulously get to know on a first-name basis). He also, explains Stein, obviously needed money to push for more demos and to run Moev.

At any rate, business was, in Stein's own words, "very good," good enough that he was "expanding to the point of going into partnership with another business."

That business? Odyssey.

Enter Herman Saltzberg, father of Brad Saltzberg, who, years down the road, becomes the treasurer and a shareholder in Nettwerk Ltd. when it legally incorporates in July 1985 (or so one story goes; it's the same story that would conclude with Brad Saltzberg selling off his Nettwerk Ltd. shares in August 1987). In one way or another, however, it was a deal in which Saltzberg was intimately involved.

The younger Saltzberg, an amiable and straightforward fellow over the 'phone, reveals he's been out of touch with Nettwerkers some eight years, now. The 36-year-old's presently employed in the field of computeristics.

"Distribution, specifically."

"Kewl," I say.

"It's not that cool," he volleys back. "It would've been cooler to own one-third of Nettwerk." Saltzberg readily volunteers the information on his current financial status. He's not a rich man, he tells me. Brings the subject up hisself, does he.

Still, he's pretty certain McBride's pretty rich by now; or, "probably, getting there. Her too. Sarah's probably pretty rich herself now," muses Saltzberg.

"You think?" I ask. "What's your take on SURFACING? You think it's a lasting contribution to Canadian musical feats of accomplishment? You know, like Gould or Peterson or so?"

Well, it seems to him McLachlan peaked artistically with FUMBLING; although, he allows, it may be a little early in her career to make such an assessment.

When it comes to more pressing matters, Saltzberg's only slightly reluctant to go back in time to the music-business scene during the early 1980s in Lotusland.

"I had a part to play in the early days. That's true."

In fact, Saltzberg was there "from the very inception of the company. I was there when the Grapes of Wrath were sleeping on Terry's floor." The guy's memory needs nary a jog when it comes to the names of Moev and Skinny Puppy, which, by association, introduce the names of Nettwerk acts such as Single Gun Theory, Manufacture, After All, Grassy Knoll, and the Waterwalk into the conversational mix. He's certainly familiar with all of them; but, as he says, "I wasn't there, then."

"And, McLachlan?"

"It was Mark Jowett who found her in Halifax."

"Were they in love?" I ask him.

"Yeah. I guess . . . He liked her at that time." But Saltzberg's not all that certain *they* were in love.

"I see; but, *they* had a relationship?"

"Yeah."

Saltzberg's quick to point out that Jowett discovered McLachlan, but "Terry made it happen. I liked Mark. I always liked Mark; but Terry's always been the driving force" in that company.

McBride's devoted himself for many years to the music

business, relates Saltzberg. His story goes back before Nettwerk, back to the time when he tried to start up a previous label, a pre-Nettwerk label that didn't click, adds Saltzberg.

Back then, McBride did work at Saltzberg's Odyssey, a business Saltzberg would ultimately sell off, in the early 1990s, he says. Nettwerk, Cinematica, and Odyssey were involved in each other's affairs to some extent, he admits; but he declines to offer much more, except to say that Cinematica and Odyssey *were* involved with each other. "Norman [Stein] and myself — my father was also involved — were partners in the beginning."

Whatever else happened, Saltzberg definitely concurs he became "a partner in Nettwerk."

Now he's older, he regrets not retaining his role as so-called silent partner. But, at the time, his role, as he himself describes it, was "marginal."

Saltzberg sold off his shares in Nettwerk (which was not a big company on the cutting-edge of computer technology in the star-maker biz at that time). "You know, I still have trouble dealing with the fact I did that," he admits, "I know I lost a lot of money by jumping the gun too soon."

Before the growing concern effected a major-distribution agreement with Capitol/EMI, Saltzberg (a.k.a. the distribution department) undertook the expeditious proliferation of all of Nettwerk's product; but, back in those days, recalls the man, perhaps a tad sentimentally, "it was very simple."

He was there when Nettwerk negotiated the Capitol deal that allowed it to "maintain indie distribution" as well. "McBride was overseeing all of this, of course; the guy was driven; and, he made it happen," sighs one respectful Saltzberg. He openly marvels at the company's inroads on the information highway, especially its elaborate websites promoting tours, discs, services, and related items of merchandise via the 'Net.

"What do you remember of the Ferrises?" I ask him, "what were those guys' names . . .?"

"Tom? John? Tom . . ."

"And one of them was the leader of Moev, right?"

"Yes. I think that was Tom."

"They were still around, were they?"

Saltzberg replies he believes he was still involved with the label when the Ferris brothers had some involvement with the company. He expresses surprise piggy-backing on dismay that those guys — or, so he's heard — are doing some kind of litigation line-dance. . . .

But Saltzberg, it seems, wants to talk Pretty Green and the Grapes of Wrath. He was really impressed by some of the GoW's stuff he heard on demos: "It sounded great!" For some reason, perhaps production-involved, the band "lost something" in the transition from demo to finished product. Saltzberg's pet project? "Pretty Green; but McBride didn't put his weight behind it," he says. And, although he managed Pretty Green "to some degree," he ran into some kind of difference of opinion with its leader who, it seems, was not ambitious in the commercial sense. Yet, Saltzberg also admits to his own naïvete at the time: "I thought the music was everything, then," he almost spits out, now.

When did Saltzberg meet McBride? He knew him in the early new-wave days, back when the guy was still DJ-ing at the Love Affair and listening avidly to stuff like Joy Division; however, the meeting that produced the formation of Nettwerk took place "in the back of the store" at Odyssey, with each of them — McBride, Saltzberg, and Jowett — owning one-third of the company, he says.

"Yeah. It cost me $10,000. It was a joke. I sold it for $30,000."

Saltzberg's as sure about McBride as he is about his own error in biz judgment: whatever happens, "Terry's always going to come out on top. He will make a lot of money. He'll come out of it with money and power, in some form."

Saltzberg again reiterates he could have remained a silent partner in Nettwerk. He could have held onto his piece of the company for all time and never even seen McBride who, Saltzberg says, didn't care what he did or did not do insofar as he was involved with the company. "He didn't care. No. He was going to make money. He was going to find a way. He's McBride. He's the next Bruce Allen [legendary Vancouver-based manager of Bryan Adams and Anne Murray]."

"You think so?" I ask.

"Oh yeah, absolutely; but, you know," notes Saltzberg, "McBride had a lot of failures. A number of his bands struck out.

If it hadn't been for Sarah —" he muses rather mysteriously, a half-finished sentence trailing off into meaningful silence.

"Who would have thought this Nova Scotia girl was going to have the impact she's had? She *was* good," marvels Saltzberg; however, he hadn't recognized her potential.

"Mark picked a winner?"

"Yeah, he did. I always liked the guy," he concludes.

"Who else was there, then?"

The company was small — McBride, Jowett, himself (in the role of silent partner), and the bands (who would help out with shipping). John Rummen and George Maniatis are a couple of the names he distinctly remembers. They all worked at Odyssey, he tells me.

"What's McBride like?" I ask.

"Very clean-cut. Doesn't smoke. Doesn't drink. Very clean living."

"Drugs?"

"Terry?" laughs Saltzberg in a chuckle best described as sardiculous. "Naw. The guy's too cheap with his money."

According to Saltzberg, "Terry's not interested in publicity for himself. He never has been. . . . He's a very astute business-man and he's driven. Whatever it takes to get there, he's going to do it. . . . I'd say he's a damned good businessman. . . . He's an extremely driven person; he's tough; and, he doesn't care what people think. I know that he was a very determined guy; and, you know, he would stop at nothing to succeed. . . . That's what it takes on that level."

Then Saltzberg does confess to a kind of mixed-feeling thing about all of this. He agrees there's something admirable in that kind of attitude; but, at the same time, he recognizes its costs: "Battle scars. Burned bridges."

H-m-m. Did *I* mention Elvis? Nope. Don't believe I did.

"Believe you me, there aren't many days that go by that I don't think about it," says Saltzberg. "Elvis may be a 'bit' big-ger than McLachlan; but she's got a long career ahead of her. I know that Sam Phillips sold Elvis's contract for $30,000; that's what I sold Nettwerk for, $30,000."

Back to 1981. Saltzberg Sr. and Jr. begin to visit Cinematica, says Stein. He meets the elder Saltzberg at Saltzberg's home, for breakfast. Herman wants to go into business," says Stein. To Stein, Saltzberg seemed to be, straightforwardly, "an honorable Jewish businessman from Halifax."

Brad had no part in any of these discussions, says Stein. His father had come up with the idea: he was going to set up a business for his son, as Stein recalls; and it was only later that Herman began to show interest in the venture by getting personally involved.

"I had the brains. He had the money," emphasizes Stein. "Herman was going to be putting up all the money; and I was going to put up the stock and savvy. The deal was this: he would leave it up to me as to what stock I would contribute to Odyssey; and we'd work out some arrangement."

Stein would put up records from his own stock while retaining Cinematica's autonomy; he would concurrently assume the role of buyer for Odyssey.

Boxing Day 1981. Customers lining up and down the block. Stein works the floor talking to customers and Madeline Morris (Moev's lead singer) operates the cash register. McBride as well as an ex-partner of his (from Noetix) are both on the premises that day, recalls Stein. That day, Cinematica does $14,000 worth of business, reports Stein.

Early in 1982, Stein decides to undertake an inventory of his stock, a preliminary step necessary to the Cinematica-Odyssey venture, he recalls. "Terry immediately said that I shouldn't do it. He would do it himself because he knew the product." McBride was insistent. He said *he* would take care of it, recalls Stein. "In fact, I noticed that he seemed rather alarmed."

Here's Stein's story (which doesn't disclose the identities of individuals peripheral to its telling, from his point of view):

'Fred' goes to Stein claiming McBride had approached him with a complaint that Stein was planning to go into the video business and ruin all the good work McBride and others invested on the record side of the biz. 'Barney' compares notes with Fred. He's been riding shotgun with McBride selling quantities of albums to various other record stores knowing that Stein doesn't conduct business this way. Fred and Barney agree: Things have gotten out of control. How, asks Fred of Barney, are you going to prove any of this?

Barney responds with the revelation that there is a pile of invoices out in the warehouse Stein's put at Moev's disposal. Barney walks into that warehouse; and, lickety-split, walks back out with a stack of invoices he'd been writing up in various retail record outlets around town.

24 February 1982. It's time all involved had a meeting. Jack McBride, Terry's father, attends the meeting. So does Terry. So do several others connected to Cinematica (where the meeting's held). Those several others have already 'fessed up *vis-à-vis* their "involvement" in the Cinematica crisis, most obviously evidenced in the large stack of invoices retrieved from the warehouse and piled neatly on the table.

Stein asks Terry if he won't at least offer him an apology for what's he's done and acknowledge its damaging effects on Cinematica. Stein gets the impression his father's a nice guy determined to avoid a scandal: Jack McBride gives Stein a check in the amount of $17,500. "That's what we settled for." Stein figures he's out between $35,000 and $50,000 in immediate losses, not counting hundreds of records that seem to have simply disappeared from his stock, somehow.

Later, he hears of sightings of "thousands of albums," many of them limited and special editions readily identifiable as Cinematica stock. Soon, "devoted insiders, friends, and new wavers" begin to approach Stein to apologize personally to him for having been witting or unwitting participants in whatever it was that had happened. Dealers and retailers return quantities of records to Cinematica. Some of them don't even ask for compensation for what they've paid out. CITR's executive board meets to deal with the affair when its members discover its volunteer program leaders have accepted "gifts." They returned them upon realizing that they were not.

Meanwhile, things are not going well with Herman Saltzberg and, understandably, Stein feels even less charitable towards him when he finds out McBride has been hired by him. His own loyal customers express their shock that McBride's now working at Odyssey.

Stein confronts Saltzberg.

Saltzberg shrugs: "I'll watch him like a hawk."

Stein's pissed. Saltzberg has apparently asked McBride for

his assessment of the Cinematica stock at the heart of the putative partnership. Now Saltzberg's privy to every last one of Stein's carefully guarded importation sources. He starts telling Stein he no longer needs him; he starts insisting on a business divorce citing, as grounds, McBride's unfavorable assessment of $65,000 worth of stock Stein's agreed to ante up for the new business arrangement.

Stalemate.

After only one month in business together.

Stein's got two choices: Bail out. Go to court.

Right. Court. Litigation might tie up his stock for years. Stein settles and loses again.

Through his lawyer he gives up his rights to Odyssey in exchange for $17,000.

His customers remain loyal; but Stein can't pay the bills. He folds at the tail end of 1982. Loses everything. Tallies his losses: "Certainly over $100,000."

Stein's take on McBride, now, in hindsight? "The music-business equivalent of a charismatic TV evangelist. . . ." Stein thinks he'd make a great case study. "Very very charming . . . Insecure . . . He liked total control . . . Nobody was going to step in his way . . . Anybody who stood in his way — including his own partners — he destroyed . . . He had certain goals . . . He was Machiavellian . . . and very bright."

That's part of Nettwerk's story, as Stein and Saltzberg tell it. Part of the music biz. And that's part of Sarah's story, too.

According to "industry gossip," Shawna Richer wrote in the *London Free Press* following a performance by McLachlan in June 1995, "McLachlan and her label, Nettwerk Productions, are facing lawsuits over the ownership of songs from a former bass player and an engineer who worked on *Touch*, her first album. And if that weren't enough, partners at Nettwerk are waging a war over ownership of the label that threatens to tear the company apart. But no matter. McLachlan proved last night she is Canada's premiere songstress."

"It's a funny thing, this stuff about bein' and becoming 'famous,'" remarked Chet Atkins, Certified Guitar Player (CGP), during an interview he'd granted me concerning his contribution to popular music.

"Yeah, fame," observed the virtuoso, "fame's a fickle filly. Sometimes a guy is running a hot streak and he can sell anything he puts out. For a while. But, it only lasts for a while. . . .

"Every time you come out of the chute, you've got to have a new sound of some kind or be dead. If I were still making records, I'd still be trying to do it that way, too. It's not just the producers. It's the radio stations who play the records, the songwriters, the businessmen and the attorneys taking over the record labels. It's the fact that it's a product and a market.

"Everyone's guilty of moving the music around here and there. But it's got to happen in order for the public to buy the product. It's got to change all the time. That's economics. That's business. That's good-ol'-fashion common sense, Fitz."

The innovator responsible for contributing a new axe attack — right-hand thumb-and-forefinger harmonics fused with discrete tones picked by the ring-finger — also created such techno-musical advances as the fuzz-tone effect, reverb, tremolo, wah-wah, direct-to-board instrumentation, and the echo chamber. One of RCA's legendary Studio B designers, Chet Atkins also arranged and played on such Elvis Presley hits as *Hound Dog* and *Heartbreak Hotel* before producing (or discovering) a Who's Who of talent, including Roy Orbison, Waylon Jennings, the Everly Brothers, Dolly Parton, Jerry Reed, Charley Pride, Floyd Cramer, Willie Nelson, and Eddie Arnold, among the stellars in his roster.

So, I asked the incomparable CGP how he felt the music business had changed since the early '50s (and the advent of the recording studio).

"People say, why don't you make records like you used to do? Just a small group. Piano. Steel guitar. Fiddle. Yes, I tell them, I could do that; but the market wouldn't take it because you've got to make records that sell. In big volumes. And, you lose ground in some things. There used to be room for classical and jazz music; now, all the cherry pickers working for the record labels want is millions of sales.

"There's no heart nor compassion nor any feeling toward giving an artist a second chance. You have one chance and that's it."

To her credit, Sarah McLachlan jumped at the chance to prove to millions she possessed the kinds of pipes that would generate millions. And, with a little luck and a lot of machinery, she landed head and shoulders above the crowd, thanks to a voice that plans to stick around and prove itself good enough to guarantee McLachlan a permanent address on Hall-of-Fame Lane.

And, that was just for openers, done, one might say, with a lovely touch of class and a flair for the dramatic.

Spend all your time waiting
For that second chance
For a break that would make it okay
There's always some reason
To feel not good enough
And it's hard at the end of the day . . .
So tired of the straight line
And everywhere you turn
There's vultures and thieves at your back
The storm keeps on twisting
Keep on building the lies
That you make up for all that you lack

— from *Angel*

T-Shirts — Shortsleeves: $18.00 Longsleeve

3 Panel T-shirt
Yellow & blue on
White #37101-5
Black #37101-6 L or XL
(Longsleeve XL
#38105-5/6)

Smiling Sun World Tour
Gold & bronze design
Available in 3 Colours
Black, Burgundy and White
T-shirt L or XL
#37100-6/5/7

M
T-shirt i
#37102-
#37102-

Fumbling...T-shirt
Eco-fibre (a recycled
cotton). Full colour front
design on cream shirt.
L or XL #37105-7

Tree of Life
Green, Black or White
(Longsleeve XL #38107)
Black or White
Shortsleeve L or XL # 37107

Star
T-shirt in L or XL
#37108-5 White
#37108-6 Black

Baseball Hat with Tree Design
Black (gold stitching) or
Natural (black stitching).
Sarah's name on back.
#34104 (Nat), #34103 (Blk)
$25

Cotton/Hemp Knapsack
with tree silkscreened on front, Sarah's logo on back.
Size:13" X 16"
#39101
$30

Please remember catalogue number when ordering.

Accessories

Rarities, B-Sides, and Ot
This Rarities and B-Sides collection contains
material never before available on

DEAR GOD • I WILL REMEMBER YOU • FEAR (LunaSol Remix)
SONG FOR A WINTER'S NIGHT • BLUE • DRAWN TO
AS THE END DRAWS NEAR (Extended Remix) Performed L
VOX (Extended Remix) • INTO THE FIRE (Extended Rem

Sarah McLachl

FUMBLING TOWARDS ECSTASY
A full length album featuring
Possession, Good Enough & Hold (
W-30081 $16, $9 Cass

SOLACE
2nd full length album fe
Path of Thorne, Into
& Drawn to the Rh
W-30055 $16, $

Pages from the Sarah McLachlan Catalogue *of merchandise available to fan club members.*

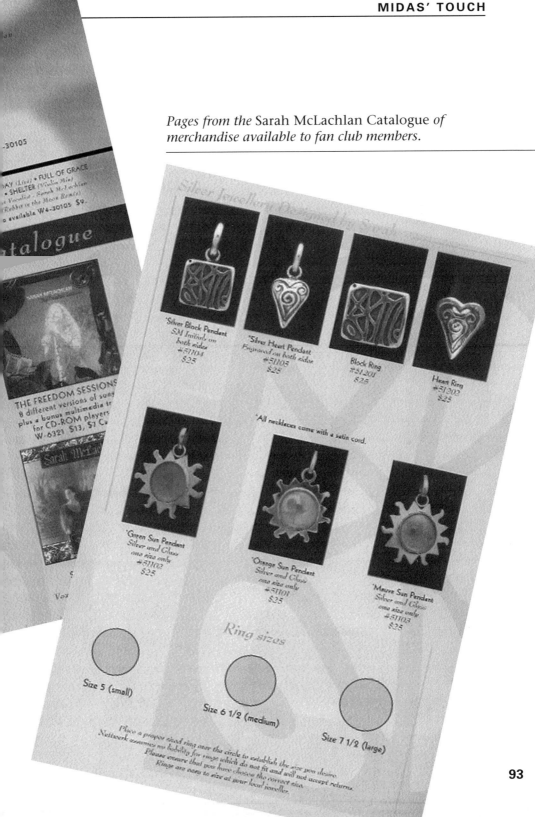

CANADA'S WEEKLY MUSIC BUSINESS NEWSPAPER

PUBLISHERS
David Farrell
Patricia Dunn-Farrell

SENIOR EDITOR
Jeff Bateman

NEWS EDITOR
Steve McLean

PRODUCTION MANAGER
George Finch

ACCOUNTS
Pat McSweeney

ADVERTISING/MARKETING
Pat McSweeney
Jason Taylor

CIRCULATION
Jason Taylor

WESTERN BUREAU CHIEF
Jeff Bateman
Phone/Fax: (604) 688-5635 / 5687
E-Mail: jbateman@mindlink.net

CONTRIBUTING WRITERS
Richard Flohil – E-Mail: rflohil@inforamp.net
Karen Bliss
Daniel Caudeiron

COUNTRY COLUMN
Martin Melhuish (905) 936-3989

RADIO COLUMN
Howard Christensen (416) 782-6482

RECORD REVIEW BOARD
Review Editor: Richard Flohil
Jeff Bateman, Daniel Caudeiron,
David Farrell, George Finch,
Steve McLean

PRINTING
Pro Art Graphics Ltd. (905) 475-7111

The Record is published 48 times a year by
David Farrell & Associates Inc.,
#502 - 124 Merton St.,
Toronto, Ontario M4S 2Z2
(416)322-5777, FAX (416) 322-7674.
E-Mail: record@ican.net
ALL RIGHTS RESERVED.
ISSN# 07128290   GST # R101285468

The Record was founded in 1981 by
David Farrell & Associates Inc.
Co-Founders - Richard Flohil, Larry LeBlanc.

Printed In Canada
SUBSCRIPTION RATES
CANADA (First Class)$250.00 + GST
ELSEWHERE $285.00 (US)
INQUIRIES (416) 322-5777

**CONTACT: THE ESSENTIAL
MUSIC INDUSTRY DIRECTORY.**
Published by David Farrell,
Patricia Dunn-Farrell, Martin Melhuish

ADVERTISING/MARKETING
Pat McSweeney/Jason Taylor
(416) 322-5777

Lilith Fair is launching pad

▶ *From page 3*

That said, she'll devote much of the next 14 months to touring if all goes according to plan and *Surfacing* begins to approach the five million sales figure that some have predicted.

Once Lilith wraps in Vancouver on Aug. 24, McLachlan will take a breather in September and shoot a video for the album's second single, *Sweet Surrender.* She'll headline her own North American tour in October and November.

Early '98 is set aside for international promotion, while it's hoped McLachlan's audience will have grown to the point where an arena tour is feasible in March/April. She's also committed to playing a central role in the second Lilith Fair, which will again roll in July and August next year.

Dan Fraser, McLachlan's former road chief and now her personal manager at Nettwerk, is handling the production logistics. The constantly changing Lilith talent bill was assembled by Little Big Man Talent, an S.L. Feldman & Associates division run in New York by agent Marty Diamond.

While Diamond was on the road with Lilith last week and unavailable for comment, Sam Feldman says that the opening show delivered on the caravan's theoretical promise.

"Everyone involved knew that it was going to be extremely challenging and somewhat risky going up against all the established and new festivals out there. It's really gratifying to see a great idea whose time has come executed so perfectly and without compromising in any way the incredible spirit of this event."

Surfacing into the limelight

Just as k.d. lang built an audience without benefit of much airplay, McLachlan has established herself fan by fan over nine years. Such has been her ability to plumb emotional depths and connect with listeners that she's built up a tribe of camp followers who call themselves "Fumblers."

"Radio hasn't traditionally been a big supporter of Sarah," says Nettwerk marketing VP George Maniatis. "They will play Sarah, but that's not how Sarah broke. She broke on touring. And because she makes timeless albums that will be around in 10 or 20 years."

Airplay has picked up substantially in the last nine months. *Full of Grace,* the de facto single off the *Rarities, B-Sides & Other Stuff* compilation, reached number 18 at pop adult

radio in Canada last Christmas. And a full-on effort by Arista in the U.S. succeeded in breathing second life into the vintage single *Possession* earlier this year.

"If you add up the 100,000-plus (U.S.) spins on *Possession* over the 12 months that we worked it — five months at the start (in 1993/94) and seven months at the end — we would have a top 10 hit," explains McBride. "We used *Possession* this year to show radio how big her fan base was, how well she researched, and how great she sounded on the airwaves."

The Nettwerk crew of David Hawkes, Shauna Gold, Sondra MacLeod, Terry McBride, Cathy Barrett, George Maniatis, Kim Hardy, John Rummen and Pierre Tremblay shows off its two latest projects. While the two acts might not sell the same numbers, it's obvious that this crowd is in a state of Delerium over Sarah's summer prospects.

The payoff is showing in the early returns for *Surfacing*'s lead single, *Building A Mystery.* American modern rock and adult numbers are strong. And in Canada "she's being treated as she should be — a major artist who has put out a monster single," says Nettwerk radio promoter David Hawkes. While the song is already top 20 at CHR without the benefit of video airplay (a Matt Mahurin video goes into heavy rotation at Much this week), rock radio is lagging behind other formats.

Notes McBride: "There's still that girly syndrome at male-dominated rock radio, which can be as bad for Sarah as Cancon ghettoization ... (*Building A Mystery*) has to go top five at rock radio for me to believe we've finally got a genuine hit record on our hands."

Two dozen stations in 10 Canadian markets participated last weekend in

various McLachlan and Lilith giveaways. Also on tap is MuchMusic's July 21 broadcast of an expanded *Intimate & Interactive* special that originally aired in late June.

The domestic launch includes television buys on Much, the Woman's Television Network and MusiquePlus. A Starbucks promotion is putting Surfacing tent cards into the chain's outlets nationwide.

"This isn't a circus, and we're not going out there with balloons," says Maniatis. "As much as Sarah is now becoming an international superstar, we are still developing her as an artist. Imaging is very important in terms of what goes out and what surrounds her. You don't want to piss off her fans."

As with all Nettwerk projects, the company has strict control over A&R, marketing and promotion. Distributor EMI Music Canada "is helping us with radio promotion this time," says Maniatis, "and I'm not one to say no to some help from people as knowledgeable and supportive as Peter Diemer."

Arista is running its own campaign in the U.S., though McBride stays in regular contact with everyone from senior executives Clive Davis and Roy Lott down to regional street reps.

"Terry understands better than most how you work an American record company," says Maniatis. "He knows that Arista is a great record company when they're focused on something, and they're definitely focused on Sarah."

From The Record, *21 July 1997.*

four

PANDORA'S BOX

or Plenty

After working on SOLACE for 6 months in New Orleans with Pierre Marchand, Sarah McLachlan returned to Canada to find herself surprised, as Stephen Ostick notes in a 15 November 1991 interview in *The Winnipeg Free Press*: 'This is great. I'm single, I'm feeling so confident. I love it,' and BOOM! You meet somebody, and it's like, 'Oh, man, I don't want this . . .' "

This?

David Kershaw, natch. McLachlan and Marchand, the musical marriage made in heaven, had returned to planet earth and simultaneously discovered, despite their amicable parting, they really liked working with one another as double perfectionists.

Like, right. Biz is biz. That's the kind of producer you want to worship for a long, long time.

Still, Kershaw — the weird, wacky, and wonderful keyboardist in her touring and studio band — turned the kid's world upside downside right all over again. And, apparently, that pretty much sums up their relationship; and, *fyi*, that's just about how much I'd tell any friend of mine about any other friend of mine. McLachlan's no friend of mine, of course; but we women gotta stick together, don't ya think?

McLachlan falls in love with a vengeance — or, so I've heard — a woman committed to her man. Lucky woman. Lucky man.

She even told one interviewer she thought ice cream a lovely way to love. Good for her. (I mean, if it works, why fight it?) As she told *The Vancouver Sun's* John Mackie when he playfully quizzed her on the sensuality of the song *Ice Cream*, "Well, when you bring food and love into the same sentence, sex is definitely going to come into play.... When you think of love and chocolate, personally I think of ... Well, I don't want to get into it! Lots of things come to mind. Ice cream, same thing. Licking ice cream out of someone's naval is wonderful. Especially if you're in love with them. Whipped cream and mangoes actually is the best...."

> *Your love is better than ice cream*
> *Better than anything else that I've tried*
> *Your love is better than chocolate*
> *Better than anything else that I've tried ...*
> *And, it's a long way down ...*
>
> — from *Ice Cream*

(Interesting. Nettwerk had released its Donovan-tribute, ISLANDS OF CIRCLES, which included a remake of *Wear Your Love Like Heaven* and featured McLachlan supplying BGVs for the "Chocolate Factory's" contribution, *Barabajagal*. Comprised of then lover-keyboardist Kershaw and now husband-drummer Ashwin Sood, one can speculate, idly, if one finds oneself so inclined, as to who was the "chocolate" and who was the "factory" in that particular pick-up duo.)

But, other than that?

The only other dirt I really want to dish (or diss) is about this pissing business.

I mean it. She does *CBC's Vicki Gabareau*? McLachlan tells

Vicki she's gotta pee. She does a 'phoner with Arsenault? She tells *him* she's gotta pee. She participates in a cyber-chatski? She works a piss into one of her answers. She drinks a little peppermint tea before she performs. She drinks wee little siplets. Just tiny wee tasticals.

Why?

Otherwise, half way through the show, the girl's gotta pee.

Now, this may be an unauthorized bio and all, but I got two words to communicate to somebody:

Kegel's Exercises.

And she thinks sex is great *now*?

On 6 February 1992, Elysa Gardner's "New Faces" features "Sarah McLachlan: Happy To Be Unhappy" on page 32 of *Rolling Stone*. Gardner leads off with message-track stuff, explaining to American readers that McLachlan's considered Canada's answer to Kate Bush and similar party-line palaver that's made the media rounds several times: "But McLachlan explains that she's not quite the mystical waif that her 1988 début, TOUCH, may have suggested. 'The album cover is a bit mysterious, and the songs are sung really high, so people thought I had an angelic voice. And then when people met me, they would go, "Oh, you're not at all like I thought you were.' "

Next, Gardner quotes McLachlan's assessment of SOLACE: " 'There's a lot more of myself in my writing — more the way I think, more the way I talk. . . . And there's not all this vocal aerobatics stuff.' "

Then her own critical assessment: "Indeed, her generally subdued singing on SOLACE only hints at the astonishing strength and clarity McLachlan is likely to demonstrate in live performance. Her voice may drift at any given time from a sirenlike middle range to a ghostly soprano. But McLachlan's upper register can soar, too, with the power and technical prowess of a classically trained musician."

Back to the message track. Studied classical guitar. *Tick.* Loves Joan Baez, Cat Stevens, and Simon and Garfunkel as "influences I've had throughout my whole life." *Tick.* Peter

Gabriel and Brian Eno. *Tick.* "In fact, Pierre Marchand — a protégé of Daniel Lanois's, Eno's sometime associate — produced SOLACE." Then the part about how McLachlan can only write when she's seriously bummed (although, for the record, Gardner doesn't quote — as too many others did — the way McLachlan bawls and bawls and pulls her hair out and climbs the walls and walks the floor and goes around the bend and how, suddenly, boom! Out comes the sun; and, *oh-oh*, lookee here! Here comes a chorus or a verse of a song or whatever). No, Gardner winds up her piece quoting McLachlan: "Depression does tend to get your juices flowing. . . . But I would like to be able to write about happy things, positive things. I guess I haven't tried as hard as I should. I'll keep trying."

All of a sudden, everybody who's anybody starts citing McLachlan's rave in *RS*. As the entire planet knows, *RS* represents the be-all and then some on acceptable "alternative" taste.

Four months later, in Halifax to receive her Best Female Vocalist pewter statuette at the Rebecca Cohn — she loses in six other categories — from the East Coast Music Awards, McLachlan performs *The Path Of Thorns (Terms)* complete with visuals: "More than a few heads were turned at the sight of her video," reports *The Canadian Press*, "in which the sultry songstress bares most of her upper body, her arms folded over her breasts. . . . Since leaving Halifax five years ago for Vancouver, McLachlan's career has steadily picked up steam. She's received two Juno nominations this year and has been written up in *Rolling Stone* magazine."

A month after McLachlan collected her ECMA honor, Arsenault provides Haligonians with an update on her up-steaming career, noting that "she had just flown in from California where she had performed at a big-deal conference for radio program directors, the people who decide whether their particular station will play her records. . . . Now an established Canadian star and nominated for two Juno Awards (Best Female Vocalist and Best Video for *Into The Fire*), McLachlan is also starting to make inroads in the gigantic U.S. pop-music market. The ebullient McLachlan could be spotted as a New Face in a recent issue of *Rolling Stone* magazine and New-York based *Interview* magazine also featured the singer.

" 'So far, it's been amazing," McLachlan said of her new-found appeal in the U.S., "[SOLACE] just got released on the 28th of January. I didn't think anybody knew who I was but there was a lot of people who wanted to do interviews and stuff.' "

When McLachlan arrived in Toronto for the 1992 Juno Awards presentation, management had booked her into the Winter Garden Theatre for three sold-out nights, 26-28 March. *The Globe and Mail*'s Alan Niester, a seasoned vet of the pop-music set who reviewed the first of McLachlan's three shows, remarked to readers that "Thursday's appearance showed McLachlan to be a total package. Her most obvious asset is her voice. . . . As a songwriter (she writes all her own songs), she is also unique. Thursday night, for example, she and her band worked through a fairly lively version of *I Will Not Forget You* from SOLACE. On the surface, the song would seem to be a lament for a lost lover, a life chapter to be savored but ultimately left behind. But, when McLachlan adds the line, 'nor will I ever let you go,' the song acquires a darker meaning, becoming a sort of *Fatal Attraction* scenario in the making, more like something Sinéad O'Connor would sing on a bad day."

And I will oh I will not forget you
Nor will I ever let you go
I will oh I will not forget you
I remember how you left in the morning at daybreak
So silent you stole from my bed
To go back to the one who possesses your soul
And I back to the life that I dread
So I ran like the wind to the water
Please don't leave me again I cried
And I threw bitter tears at the ocean
But all that came back was the tide

— from *I Will Not Forget You*

Perhaps, like Jeff Bateman's of *The Record*, the advance copy (less liner notes and credits) of SOLACE routinely sent to critics before shipping units to retail outlets, had originally listed the song's title as *I Will Not Possess You*. (Hold that thought.)

Niester continues. "McLachlan was backed by a surprisingly strong and sympathetic five-piece band. On faster numbers such as *Drawn To The Rhythm* and *Into The Fire*, the rhythm section of Ashwin Sood and Brian Minato offered the kick necessary to compensate for McLachlan's high-end vocals (her voice is really better suited to ballads or folk-singer material). And on numbers that tended towards a new-age jazz direction, multi-instrumentalist Kim Linekin's violin soared and swooped in the best Ben Mink-styled directions." (By the way, Linekin, who also supplied BGVs on McLachlan's 1992 tour, apparently kept a diary or journal she dubbed her "Black Book Of Secrets," a title, perhaps, subtly related to the "corporation pig" first-persona McLachlan adopted for her rendition of *Black* on SOLACE.)

"Nominated for two Junos, McLachlan recently appeared on *The David Letterman Show* and had a sold-out concert series in Tokyo," Paula Citron reports two days later in *The Toronto Star* (she had been sent to review the third and final of McLachlan's three Toronto shows), the night before the Junos — held further south on Yonge Street at the then-O'Keefe Centre and broadcast live on CBC-TV from Sunshine Corners to Big Ray Bay — would feature those duelling guitarroes, heart-bustin' Big Bad Bryan Adams *vs* Tom "Life Is A Highway" Cochrane — and McLachlan would snag her first pan-Can trophy.

"How to explain the phenomenon known as Sarah McLachlan," Citron muses thoughtfully in the lead of her review. "McLachlan's mass appeal would appear to rest squarely on the fact that her music is an antidote to bleak times. Her sound, both in voice and instrumentation, is dreamy, moody and wistful and washes over listeners like a blanket to cuddle up in. Ever her more spirited music is reflective rather than joyous. To hear the McLachlan voice once is to recognize it forever, although to categorize it is another matter. Think of Buffy Ste. Marie mixed with Joan Baez with a soupçon of soft rock and country-and-western for seasoning."

Over at *The Globe*, Niester had also offered his description of the McLachlan voice in his previously cited 'view: "Her most obvious asset is her voice which is capable of soaring to heights only dogs can hear, of suddenly lurching in a different direction like a carnival ride, of swooping like a hungry hawk, and ultimately making the little hairs on the back of your neck sit up and take notice."

March 29th, the biggest night of the year in Canadian music, McLachlan's voice had been heard by the dogs, obviously, in the vicinity of the O'Keefe. I attended the Juno ceremonies that year; it surprised me not that the McLachlan phenomenon had failed to vocally, if not visually, register with the country's musical movers: Best Female Vocalist — Céline Dion. Best Video — Phil Kates, *Into The Fire* (Sarah McLachlan).

It was right around the time SOLACE hit 200,000 in units sold another curious McLachlan phenomenon occurred: most media photographs of the young star issued from Nettwerk's HQ (while a flinty handful of plus-one photo passes were stingily bestowed upon professional snapshooters). More and more of Nettwerk's photographs bore the name of Kharen Hill, the woman at whose house McLachlan, Marchand, and crew had made their musical magic in New Orleans. Naturally, it's a very close family, this Nettwerk clan. Maybe a little obsessive about protecting its star. Yeah. It makes sound sense, right? A million-dollar vocalist with that kind of potential needs a little protection.

Still, it strikes me as odd, when Nettwerk grants an interview to the fifth largest newspaper in North America, *The Toronto Star* — an interview to its leading pop critic and ardent McLachlan supporter — in exchange for the entire front of its splashy "What's On" section (plus a lengthy three-quarter turnover), Howell feels pissed off enough about the treatment he (and his editor) had received from Nettwerk over an artfully done show-nuthin'-special full-page spread of McLachlan in the shadows, he makes a point of telling readers Nettwerk had meddled in his job and he doesn't like its attitude one goddamned bit. No, of course, that's not how Howell puts it; he couches his barb in an aside about how Nettwerkers were chewing their fingernails — a bad habit McLachlan couldn't shake for years — to the quick worrying about a tasteful shadowy techno-distorted outline of their naked star when, as Howell so prettily puts it, "she can be seen in her birthday suit on millions of TV sets across the land . . . ."

Then, 13 June 1992, *Melody Maker* takes McLachlan to task in a way that grates on several parties' ears. Writer David Jennings gives an approving nod to McLachlan's "nimble soprano voice, which often bears an eerie resemblance to Joni Mitchell. . . . There's lots of vague imagery drawn from nature; references to fire, the night, the Earth, the sun, the river. Hello trees, hello sky. You could see all this as new-age consciousness; but, really it's just old-school singer-songwriter preciousness. . . .

"But, too often, bad poetry ruins it all. On the Sinéad-like *Into The Fire*, for instance, it's a real pleasure listening to her performing graceful vocal aerobatics — as long as you don't listen to the words. I mean, 'Open the doors that lead on into Eden / You I see as my security'. It's like P.J. Harvey never happened. The concluding cover of Donovan's carefree *Wear Your Love Like Heaven* is good breezy fun; and, perhaps she should drape that voice in more borrowed material. Here, her own work is generally too precious to be valuable."

During the following months, McLachlan, doing her utmost in the promotion department, toured North America and the UK, introduced audiences to her "graceful vocal acrobatics" and precious lyrics, gave interviews by the dozen, a fact which Howell duly noted in his now-famous nail-biter profile in *The Toronto Star*. McLachlan, Howell pointed out, "will do a lot of things to promote her music. . . . She's happy to yak with the press or do whatever else it takes to sell records or advance her shows, even if that means waking up from a deep sleep, stopping her tour bus in Bruce Mines, Ontario — 'I have no idea where I am,' she says — and sitting at a pay telephone in a roadside restaurant. . . . She's also willing to appear absolutely buck naked — and this was totally her idea — in her arresting new video for *The Path Of Thorns (Terms)*."

But as McLachlan had told Constance Droganes a year earlier in *Flare*, her love of touring and promoting had a downside. "While touring is the part of her career that McLachlan loves most," reports Droganes, "she occasionally feels overwhelmed by the droves of fans on and off the road. 'It really bothers me at times. I just don't know how to deal with the attention. I appreciate it; but, I often feel like yelling, "Stop it already. I'm not on display.' "

McLachlan expressed a similar ambivalence towards some members of her male audience in an interview with Richard Cromelin of the *Los Angeles Times*. In L.A. on a make-up date reskedded and relocated from the Variety to the Troubadour because of The Riots, her début in the city of angles meant a great deal to both McLachlan and Nettwerk. McLachlan performed professionally and expertly 11 August 1992. Apparently, she really wowed the crowds, did the born singer doing what she loves since, for those in the know, McLachlan's best, Vocal Division, places her among the top-ten popular-music performers on the planet.

"For McLachlan," Cromelin explains to American readers, "performing for an audience is the ultimate experience. 'I want to take people to another place in the shows. That's when music really works for me. And that's what I want to do, bring people to a different place. When I'm really connecting, I almost feel a continual state of arousal. There's a heightened awareness.' "

Cromelin's August piece also includes quite a lengthy section given over to McLachlan's thoughts on her fan base. "She has also drawn a growing cult of fans attracted to her densely textured and abstract but intensely confessional lyrics. Not all the attention sits well with the 23-year-old singer: 'I get a lot of young lost males,' McLachlan says, 'they seem like early to late twenties, and they don't seem to know what they want to do with their life. I seem to fill some sort of void for them. I get a lot of letters saying that I'm singing to them, which kind of freaks me out, because I'm not . . . I don't know them; but, they know me. They know a lot of me because I'm really revealing myself — in my lyrics — to them. But I'm not gonna compromise that because of some psycho fans or anything.' "

As far as both Blake Bell (creator and maintenance-maestro of *The Quiet Touch of Solace* on the Web) and I can tell, McLachlan did not perform another concert in 1992 after her Troubadour date. She returned to Vancouver with firm plans to enter the studio just after the 1992 festive season to begin work on her third disc, but instead packed her bags for Cambodia and Thailand in the name of World Vision "to assist in the making of a documentary-style film," as McLachlan writes in *Network*'s February 1993 "On My Mind" forum.

"Our main focus was women and children and the plight they are facing with prostitution, AIDS and poverty. . . . Huge numbers of foreign men come to Thailand to have a woman for $10 a day. They justify their behavior by saying they are giving these women a living. I was so pissed off at all the fat ugly foreigners while filming in Pat Pong, a red-light district of Bangkok, that I was ready to kick the next guy in the nuts who made any advances towards me. . . . Nothing could have prepared me for the things I saw on this trip. We take too much for granted. It's time to give a little back."

The following month, McLachlan headed for Morin Heights in the Laurentians near Ste. Jerôme, a boulder's pitch from Montreal, QC, one of Canada's oldest and most beautiful cities, where her high-school friend, Buffy Childerhose, now the Arts Editor for Montreal's weekly *Hour* magazine, was within driving distance should McLachlan require an ear and shoulder (or any such refuge from the deluge of attention she'd begun to receive).

On 7 September 1993, McLachlan came down from the Heights to put in an appearance on *The Tonight Show*. When next she descended on 22 October, it was to embark on the most grueling tour of her life, in support of FUMBLING TOWARDS ECSTASY, the disc which proved to be, in both the eyes of the global community and McLachlan herself, the magical passport to the next level, where — like it or not — McLachlan would find herself the center of attention when millions of heads turned in her direction and millions of dollars passed from hand to hand to hand. McLachlan, if nothing else, was most certainly on display.

Perhaps, in the same way she hadn't finished reading either Atwood's *Surfacing* or Rilke's *Letters to a Young Poet*, Sarah McLachlan had likewise given up on the *Mentor Dictionary of Mythology & The Bible* half-way through the *M*s or so. Oh, "Lilith" probably thrilled the girl; but "Medusa" must've chilled the girl so, natch, she could not be expected to explore as far as *P*, where the entry describing "Pandora" might have finally set her free:

PANDORA. The first woman, she was fashioned from earth by Hephaestus at the request of Zeus in order to mitigate somewhat the gift of fire Prometheus had given to man. The gods contributed attributes (cunning, beauty, voice, *etc.*) and Zeus gave Pandora a container filled with misery and evil and warned her never to open it. She was sent to Epimetheus, who ignored his brother Prometheus's warning never to accept a gift from Zeus and took her as his wife. Pandora opened the box, releasing all the evil in the world. She closed the container before hope escaped.

Two days after the Canadian release of FUMBLING TOWARDS ECSTASY, Sarah McLachlan screwed up her courage and returned to the fray, this time with her long-awaited breakthrough disc doing one slow-and-steady burn up continental charts.

"That's it. You can see glimpses of it. You can get there for a second but it's always going to go away," she told James Muretich of *The Calgary Herald*. "FUMBLING TOWARDS ECSTASY is the perfect metaphor for life, as far as I'm concerned, because we're continually making mistakes but we're also always striving for that ecstasy."

Echoing Heinrich's "No more," Muretich doesn't miss a beat the Sunday *The Calgary Herald* features Hill's beautiful photograph of McLachlan's revamped image on its "Entertainment" front. He expertly commences his rapturous assessment of FUMBLING with a nod to SOLACE, a disc he considers as occurring "somewhere along the path from innocence to experience; it challenged but without completely letting go. *Rolling Stone* magazine described her in glowing terms. More albums sold. That is the past. This is now. And the time has come to sing of many things . . . for at the ripe old age of 25 McLachlan has just released her third album, FUMBLING TOWARDS ECSTASY. It is her most accomplished disc to date; songs will stroke the senses alive but do so with more of an edge. Her lyrics are romantic without being naïve, evoking the heart's passions with an earthy urgency, finding McLachlan more willing to bare her heart while accepting the fact she is fumbling towards ecstasy. . . .

"What makes this album more focused, more impassioned than her previous efforts is its lyrical grounding in reality and the fact the music is stark yet strong, buoyed by arrangements that subtly support McLachlan's expressive vocal range."

McLachlan tells Muretich she devoted too much attention to craftsmanship on SOLACE, and, this time out of the gate, she'd elected to "truly let go and only by doing so" could she be "truly honest": "Musically and lyrically, just digging way down deeper into myself than I've ever done before. That quest for self-identity has driven me quite strongly in the past year and a half, especially after being on the road for so long and feeling like I was skimming the surface because I had so much outside input 24 hours a day. I was never alone. Life can get diluted so easily through too many outside influences.

"Your brain starts to eat itself. . . . It's like the balance between mind and body. In some ways, I think there's a huge separation which explains why we're so fucked up. People are so completely out of touch with their bodies which is like the center of the earth. . . . I'd rather not be quite so radical but these people [out of touch with their bodies in their '50s and '60s getting facelifts and such] are ruining their countries because they have no concept of themselves so how can they have a concept of the land, the world around them?"

On 28 October 1993, McLachlan hit the road for her first worldwide tour. She told *The Vancouver Sun*'s John Mackie she thought she'd learned how to say things more directly prior to her two-night installation at Vancouver's Vogue (with Nettwerk's Ginger opening): "I'm allowing myself to go deeper into myself to pull out more honest stuff. And, I think I'm also more confident to allow stuff to come out that before I would edit."

McLachlan offers Mackie an example or two of how she's "learning to approach songwriting as a craft," and to step outside herself and play a character: "For *Possession*, I put myself into the rapist/murderer's point of view. I wrote it from his perspective. . . . I had to deal with that, 'cause it really was starting to freak me out. Some [fan] letters were getting really intense. There were a couple of people in particular. . . . It just got way too intense, way too close for comfort. . . . I'm writing these songs and leaving myself incredibly open, so that people are going to take them that way. I'm going to get people [with] a greater or lesser degree of obsessions. But, at the same time I can't not do it, because that's where I get the highest, when I get that deep inside me and that stuff comes out. The best stuff, that's so honest."

Listen as the wind blows from across the great divide
Voices trapped in yearning, memories trapped in time
The night is my companion and solitude my guide
Would I spend forever here and not be satisfied?
And I would be the one
To hold you down
Kiss you so hard
I'll take your breath away
And after, I'd wipe away the tears
Just close your eyes dear . . .

— from *Possession*

McLachlan also provided more details on her trip to the Pacific Rim, explaining what "really horrified me was all the foreigners, all the people from western civilizations going over there and picking up these 13 and 14-year-old Thai prostitutes. It's just really intense. All these guys would go, 'Yeah, I fucked her ten times and she's got a smile on her face the whole time. Five bucks. It's great.' I was thinking, 'Oh, man, if your mother could see this!' There are, like, 19-year-olds on a spring break, going for a fucking season, a fucking vacation."

The experience profoundly affected her and inspired *Ice*. "I've always tried to portray a sense of hope in the songs before; but that one doesn't really have much."

Mackie (rightly) singles out producer Pierre Marchand's lion's-share contribution to FUMBLING's title-track and McLachlan explains, "He was trying to figure out what it is that frightens people away . . . Where does that come from; from what mistake in the past, what problem? That song came from him having this huge fear of commitment, of letting himself go to truly be in love. And to be loved. The idea of loving yourself, and getting back that sort of childhood innocence of unconditional love."

All the fear has left me now
I'm not frightened anymore
It's my heart that pounds beneath my flesh
It's my mouth that pushes out this breath
And if I shed a tear I won't cage it
I won't fear love
And if I feel a rage I won't deny it
I won't fear love . . .

— from *Fumbling Towards Ecstasy*

(Oh, so that's what happened between the inseparable pair who had parted loving company but stood firm for their love of music. Mackie tells readers McLachlan wrote *Fear* at the start of a new relationship.)

McLachlan had hit her stride. Muretich and Mackie had flagged FUMBLING right out of the box. A month after its release, Nettwerk granted Arsenault in Halifax and Howell in Toronto an interview apiece.

The head on Howell's profile, "McLachlan Busy Fending off Fanatics," naturally caught the attention of each and every last subscriber who read *The Toronto Star* 25 November 1993. The same day in Halifax, Arsenault's editors had gone with "McLachlan Lightens Up" — an in-joke reference to the fact she'd dropped a few kilos and was back down to her acceptable weight of 56-59K? — and a sidebar file dubbed "Sarah Smile."

"Sarah McLachlan is in the Top Ten with her new album and a new attitude. As she heads to Nova Scotia for shows next week, the singer-songwriter is busier and happier than ever."

McLachlan cheerfully tells Arsenault she felt as though she had written FUMBLING from a spiritually higher place: "The only times I could write was when I was sad or depressed or angry about something and this time that wasn't the case. . . .

The way I look at it now is that you can still go through those things; but, you can go through it with a different sort of energy. . . . Before, I'd almost wallow in it and these days I have so little time for that. . . . I just came upon a place that was good and I've been trying to maintain that kind of equilibrium since."

Arsenault reports McLachlan's "amazed by the instant commercial success" of FUMBLING before turning down his rave a notch in order to digress on the subject of *Possession*, the breakout single all concerned agree fuelled McLachlan's incendiary rise to the top of the musical world. McLachlan responds to Arsenault's query concerning "disturbing fan letters" and the "obsessive notes" which had provided the inspiration for her biggest hit: "[Fans] do know a lot about me; but, I don't know anything about them and it's a bit of an unfair advantage and it's a strange one for me. I don't want to hurt people's feelings; but, at the same time, it's disturbing. . . . Most of the letters that I get are of that nature but to a lesser degree. 'I went through this really hard thing and your music made it okay and made me able to get through it and I thank you for that'. End of letter. Not like, 'We have to meet on a desolate shore and we have to be married and you were betrothed to me before birth'."

Back in Toronto, Howell gets right to the point. "Sarah McLachlan learned about the power of her music from fighting off the love-struck lunatics it attracts. Her songs attract a lot of perfectly balanced people, too, but it's the way the Vancouver singer-songwriter bares her soul, and the emotive reach of her singing, that seems to encourage dangerous devotion in some of her fans."

"A couple of them," confides McLachlan, "got a wee bit too intense and it started to affect my life. . . . Things like running into them a couple of blocks from my house, and saying they'd been there for a couple of days. It was pretty scary. . . . I stopped answering my mail a long time ago. I had my best friend answering it for a while and then she had nightmares so she's not doing it any more, either."

"The experience of being stalked by fans," writes Howell, "led to the writing of *Possession*. . . . For the striking *Possession* video, she is depicted both as a strong woman and as a victim, the former as a lover in a warm consoling embrace and the latter as a bound-up victim, swinging from a pendulum."

McLachlan relayed her intentions with the video to Howell: "It was trying to break down the image-making machine, where people look at a picture and create a fantasy world of who you are because of one image.... Which ties into *Possession* being the song about the fan who assumes he knows you and he knows all about you, because of a few things he's heard or read or seen."

McLachlan had spoken to both Arsenault and Howell from Elsewhere, somewhere on the road that had taken her from Vancouver on 28 October 1993 to Edmonton, Saskatoon, Calgary, Winnipeg, Thunder Bay, Sudbury, North Bay, Windsor, Hamilton, London, St. Catherines, Montreal, Kitchener, Toronto, Glace Bay, Halifax, Moncton, Quebec City and, on 8 December 1993, Ottawa before she'd head for the States on the second leg of her worldwide tour that would ultimately stop in Paris a year later before winding up in Bellingham on 5 April 1995 and winding down on 5 August in High River, AB.

McLachlan spent Christmas in Halifax before returning to Toronto in March to attend the Junos. She played in the snow a little, got reacquainted with her family and friends quite a lot, dropped by Judy's, chummed around with a few ol' buds (apparently, on one occasion, trying to buy underwear in a mall), and left Halifax one snow-woman richer, thanks to the artistry of McLachlan and Co. (despite her well-known disgust for the commercialism of Christmas).

The girl kicked back, took time to reconnect with the R.W., apparently really enjoying the spirit of the season for the first time in her life, probably because she'd either come to the realization such rituals bind human beings together or, like most of us bozos on this bus, she recollected said commercialism had served her well in the past when one thing we know she wanted was a guitar — or, what it became, a ukelele — around the greedy age of four. It's the nature of childhood. It's also the nature of the beast.

On Tuesday 15 February 1994, *The Globe and Mail* reports, on the front of its "Arts+" section, "Ron Hynes Wins Three East-Coast Awards." In the text of the *Canadian-Press*

wire-service story, readers additionally learn "Sarah McLachlan was named best female artist and best pop-rock artist, beating out such rivals as Roch Voisine and Figgy Duff. McLachlan, who was raised in Halifax and lives in Vancouver, wasn't present to collect her awards."

Naturally, McLachlan and crew had better things to do. After all, FUMBLING TOWARDS ECSTASY, just released in the U.S., had débuted on *Billboard*'s "Heat-Seekers Chart" at No. 1, an extraordinarily rare accomplishment in any format, let alone an "alternative" one. Shortly after its auspicious *Billboard*ing, Kim Germovsek (Knight-Ridder/Tribute News Service) interviewed McLachlan concerning the making of the disc for a print-journalism feature which several major U.S. dailies carried 17 March 1994.

"Basically, I hadn't had any privacy for 13 months. I was on a bus with 13 people; and, the only private place was the bathroom. And, even then, there was usually a line." McLachlan further tells Germovsek the only other way she could relieve the pressures of her extended roadwork was to hole up in the high hills of the Laurentian mountains to work on FUMBLING: "That's from a desire to figure things out for myself, a desire to be honest to myself. . . . Writing is just for me and is, really, a form of therapy, a catharsis. I respect honesty in songwriting; and, I tried to be as honest as I could."

"This self-enforced isolation," concludes Germovsek, "helped bring a new maturity to McLachlan's music, both in her voice and her lyrics. Another big part of her growing up was a documentary she shot on the sex trade in Thailand and Cambodia for World Vision. . . . McLachlan was the 'celebrity spokesperson' for the documentary."

McLachlan avers the nine-day whirlwind junket "totally changed" her life: "I mean, I've seen stuff like this on TV; but, I couldn't stand to watch it and always changed the channel. Ugly poverty. And, I was forced to deal with it daily, right in the middle of it. The kids all looked so old, just these souls trapped. I mean, I saw a baby die . . . People have always said that my first albums were kind of depressing and dark; but, I always thought they had this kind of naïve optimism. For the first time, I realized that for some people there is no hope."

That same month, in an interview/mini-set she granted to the World Café folks, McLachlan sets up *Wait*, FUMBLING's second cut, as being "sort of about loss of innocence and the feeling that, for every generation, there is a group of individuals who will go outside of the norm and outside of society. We'll be the outcasts; and, we'll try to make a difference. But, it seems, eventually, they all get sucked back in, or they lose their minds completely, so it was kind of a sad thing for me; but, I still have that idealism."

When all we wanted was the dream
To have and to hold that precious little thing
Like every generation yields
The new born hope unjaded by their years . . .

— from *Waiting*

Following her acoustic version of the tune, the interviewer gushes, "It's hard to believe that when you were signed, your record company knew you could sing and you could play but had no idea you could write."

"Blind faith," replies McLachlan, "I'm amazed. The longer I'm in the industry, and the more horror stories I hear about how artists sort of get eaten up, whether they know what they're doing or not, I mean, I was so lucky for Nettwerk to find me and give me that opportunity."

Next, on the front-sell for *Good Enough*, McLachlan waxes vertiginous on mother-daughterdom: "I don't know what grasp I had on it, except that it affected me tremendously, of the relationship that [Jane Siberry] had with her mother and the women of my mother's generation who were so completely out of touch with their bodies and who did not really have any friends to talk to about anything. I have amazing female friends and this is another thing about where the song came from. I can say anything to them and I trust them to be able to say these thing to and to talk about it and work things out. My mother's generation is of, 'Oh, let's just not talk about it'. So, I wrote that song for her, on the perspective of, 'I'm not just the daughter anymore. I want to be your friend, now.' "

I never would have opened up
But you seemed so real to me
After all the bullshit I've heard
It's refreshing not to see
I don't have to pretend
She doesn't expect it from me . . .

— from *Good Enough*

McLachlan concludes her set with smoldering and spare versions of *Ice* and the title-track of her heat-seekin' third disc, FUMBLING TOWARDS ECSTASY, a title she chose because, as she puts it, she'd been "trying to use those words. They came to me at first in a different configuration, from a Wilfred S. Owens [sic] poem called 'Dulce Et Decorum Est'. He was a war poet; and, he was describing the soldiers in the field who were getting gassed. For some reason, I just fell in love with his poems, I guess, because they were so beautiful but they were talking about something so horrible. The way he melded the two things together, two complete opposites, and made it so beautiful.

"I was a total romantic to this guy. He was talking about the ecstasy in fumbling. They were in ecstasy of fumbling as they tried to fit on the masks so they wouldn't die. He was watching people not make it and fall and that little phrase stayed with me all these years.

"I think I first heard it in the ninth grade. I've always wanted to use it; but, in 'ecstasy of fumbling' or 'fumbling towards ecstasy', how to fit that into a song. I thought, 'Wow! What a simple beautiful metaphor for my life, for what I'm trying to do'. I mean, you can put in place of 'ecstasy' any adjective, whether it's inner peace or nirvana or whatever. I'm definitely trying to reach that and being human and making mistakes, which I think is one of the greatest learning things I have."

Where, said the poet and ex-professor of English and Creative Writing, do I begin? All right, enough already. I won't remind readers ecstasy is a noun, not an adjective. (That would be cheesy, right? I mean, this is the new-age siren of poetry speaking of the all-seeing me.) I won't bore readers with the details of Owen's final tragic days in the trenches during the closing days of WWI or the way in which his poetry necessarily comes to us in this most important context, particularly Owen's ironic appropriation of lines from Horace's *Odes*, "*Dulce et decorum est pro patria mori*" (ii.13), which, in translation, reads: "Lovely and honorable it is to die for one's country." And, I will refrain from pointing out Owen (1893 – 1918), along with T.S. Eliot, James Joyce, W.H. Auden, David Jones, Ezra Pound, and an entire host of brilliant high modernists, also wrote horrifically beautiful work at the same time, work, apparently, beyond the comprehension of individuals considering the "romantic" elements of some of the most gruesome war poetry ever written in response to economically driven confrontations that claimed millions of lives.

However, it is incumbent upon me to apprise readers of the fact that another alternative outfit — then fronted by Natalie Merchant — 10,000 Maniacs, at the start of its recording career, had already released HOPE CHEST (which included a pair of Owen's poems set to music, *Anthem for Doomed Youth* and the above-mentioned *Dulce Et Decorum Est*) some time prior to McLachlan's FUMBLING TOWARDS ECSTASY.

In "Joni's Heir" (21 March 1994), *Time*'s David Thigpen commences his review of FUMBLING thusly: "Beneath the placid surfaces of Sarah McLachlan's songs runs an emotional torrent. As her piano and lonesome guitar sketch folk-rock tunes of elegant simplicity, McLachlan sings vivid tales of love gone wrong, of troubled souls grappling with infatuation, rejection and other extreme conditions of the heart. . . .

"In *Possession*, she sings of a love that has crossed into obsession: 'My body aches to breathe your breath / Your words keep me alive / And I would be the one to hold you down / Kiss you so hard, I'll take your breath away'. Far from indulging in simple emotional bloodletting, McLachlan creates exquisitely poised songs that resist anger or pathos. . . .

"Now 25, McLachlan cuts a refreshingly lyrical path against the rage pervading society by suggesting that the answers to life's emotional earthquakes can come through perseverance and compassion. . . . At such moments, McLachlan holds out hope for the desperately troubled. . . . 'To work through this stuff and come out on the other side,' she says. 'That's the ecstasy.' "

Perhaps a little less rapturously smitten than Thigpen, *Spin*'s Joy Press considered McLachlan's lyrics "mature with a capital M, to the point of sophomoric pseudo-profundity" and concluded that McLachlan "obviously places herself in the category of the self-defined strong female songwriter," thereby making of FUMBLING something of "an easy-listening portrait of a woman — a perfectly graceful, confident and smart woman — but, it's not the portrait of an artist."

At the same time, the perfectly graceful, confident and smart woman confessed to *The Baltimore Sun*'s J. D. Considine that she felt making music was a place where she could be "ego-less" just prior to explaining that she "used to listen to Peter Gabriel. I don't listen to anybody now. I just don't hear anything I like. Haven't for years. Or else it's a I-like-it-now-I'm-over-it kind of thing. So, I have my five or ten CDs that I've had for five or ten years — the music that I've liked. I've got THURSDAY AFTERNOON by Brian Eno. I've got CLOSING TIME by Tom Waits, SPIRIT OF EDEN by Talk Talk, and those are the only CDs I've listened to for years. I keep going back to them because they fulfil me."

Obviously, touring extensively also fulfils McLachlan who, along with her six-piece band, takes to the road for a dizzying array of engagements, interviews, and guest appearances which includes a spot on *The Today Show* (25 March), *Late Night With David Letterman* (5 May), and *Late Night With Conan O'Brien* (13 July).

Memorable stops on the Spring/Summer '94 tour include a 10 April performance at Montreal's Olympia (where a delirious audience showers her with bouquets and gorgeous floral arrangements, while she blesses her adorants in a frenzy of fandemonium with an unprecedented number of encores, simply because the crowd, on its collective dancing feet, has so lovingly embraced the diva Ms M. who, according to one individual in attendance that memorable evening, could barely finish a sentence she was so utterly overwhelmed), four sold-out shows at the University of Toronto's Convocation Hall (13-17 April), followed by several U.S. dates in Rochester, Buffalo,

Cleveland, Detroit, Columbus, Grand Rapids, Chicago, and Minneapolis.

It was during this time she gave an interview to *Mindlink*'s Kagin Lee, an interview in which she uncharacteristically lays it on the bottom line: "[Nettwerk's] been amazing too 'cause they've given me 100% control and complete freedom even when I had no idea what I was doing. . . . Musical freedom and artistic freedom. I've designed all the album covers. I do all the merchandising stuff. I do the videos. Unfortunately, you know, the Sarah McLachlan conglomeration of stuff now is becoming so big that I physically can't do everything anymore otherwise I'll end up doing a bunch of things half-assed."

When Lee asks McLachlan what she thinks about the glamor of pop-stardom, she responds that she "couldn't give a shit about the glamorous side. . . . I hate it. I don't want to be put up on a pedestal. I never asked for that, that's just part of the gig."

"What did you ask for? Just to be a musician?"

"*Mm-hmm*. I mean, I didn't ask for anything when I was getting into it. I didn't know what it all involved. You know, I don't necessarily enjoy celebrity status, that kind of thing, because as far as I'm concerned I'm as worthy as you, too, or anybody else on the street. I believe people are really equal; and, for me to be put up on a pedestal because I'm in the newspaper or in magazines or on television and people treat you differently, and I think it's just weird. It's not something I've totally gotten a grip on. I've seen so many people on the media, especially celebrities, who'll say something; then, if they change their minds, the media will just slag them because they expect them to be more than human. They expect them to be godlike and not make mistakes and that's bullshit. . . . Why? Why do people put musicians on pedestals or actors or actresses? Why do they get put up there? That's my frustration with society; but, that runs very deep."

So, suggests Lee, McLachlan must have found it "bizarre to be treated absolutely differently than before?"

"People I care about," she replies, "people really close to me, don't treat me any differently. If anything else, they give me more trouble than, you know, if they even see a glimpse of my head getting big they'll whap me and say, 'Hey, hey! Don't forget who you are'." To her credit, McLachlan never does.

Riding high on the ongoing success of FUMBLING TOWARDS ECSTASY in the sales department and on a promotion/performance tour to beat the band, she'd already stunned the crowds in St. Louis, Seattle, San Francisco, Sacramento and L.A. in May before drawing raves from NYC's tough critics when she puts in a highly publicized and much-debated "unplugged" appearance at that city's annual homage to gaiety in a soft-combo config at The Big Apple's Beacon Theatre 24 June as part of the LifeBeat benefit in support of its Gay Games and Pride Week.

Some months later during a radio show phone-in, the airchairist inquired about the meaning of *Good Enough*, one of fumbling's finest compositions, explaining he saw a little bit of a "gay subtext in its lyrics." Apparently, McLachlan had told a Houston daily that if she happened to fall in love with a woman, "then, so be it." As well, throughout that year, Nettwerk had placed several large adverts in *The Advocate*, a well-known print activist in behalf of gay rights. McLachlan, without missing a beat, replied that she'd written *Good Enough* for her mother; but she'd also had other motivations for keeping its meaning vague and ambiguous: she felt each listener had the right to bring his or her own meaning to the tune; and, yes, she agreed, that "gay subtext" was undeniably there.

In her own backyard, on 1 July, *Maclean's* chunks up its Canada-Day volume with a "special-issue" spread featuring a bevy of celebrities pondering their identity in their native land, including novelist Mordecai Richler's take on the separatist issue juxtaposed with McLachlan's opinion on important issues of the day: "Well, I have a beef," she says, "Brooks & Dunn, who are an American country act, are playing Canada Day in Newfoundland. We were supposed to play there; but, the promoters bumped us out. Can you believe that? I cannot play on Canada Day in my own country. Now, what does that tell you about nationalism in Canada?" That's all *she* wrote on that particular score. What does that tell *you*? (Need *me*, *myself* and *I* say more?) Later in the year *The Washington Post*'s Mike Joyce explains that McLachlan's "amazed" at FUMBLING's success and "thrilled that in America, unlike Canada, she's receiving plenty of airplay. 'I really think radio is opening up in America. . . .

Canada has the problem; it's entirely narrow-minded except for the *CBC*, which is great. We even have something called "Canadian Content," which means that every radio station has to play 30-percent Canadian music. I think that's great; but, I'm a Canadian and I don't get played."

For the record, on 2 July, McLachlan's handlers did manage to find a suitable St. John's, NF venue for Ms Patriotic, the Mount Pearl Glacier Theatre, where, it seems, every second person in attendance wanted the girl to autograph their 16 June copy of *Rolling Stone*, the one in which Elysa Gardner pulls out all the stops. "McLachlan's most compelling musical attribute continues to be her voice, a breathy soprano wail that transcends the waiflike languor characterizing some of today's more lyrical female singers by virtue of its technical strength and emotional vitality. Her producer, Pierre Marchand, is a protegé of Daniel Lanois's; like his mentor, Marchand knows how to craft atmospheric backdrops that support, rather than overshadow, emotive vocals. . . . The first track, *Possession*, opens as an airy ballad with only organ chords embellishing McLachlan's plaintive singing; then, chiming guitars and a lithe hip-hop beat kick in as she exhorts and tempts a lover." (Ah, the "hip-hop" thingie. Readers no doubt recall McLachlan's strident and vehement protestations concerning same? Sure. She wasn't about to put a hip-hop beat on her records just because her American label wanted one, was she? Nope. She wasn't about to pander to radio formats in order to satisfy the singles-oriented pop-music biz, was she? Nope. Not McLachlan. No "corporation pigs" were going to tell her what to do, eh?)

Over at *Vogue*, Jennifer Pierce elects to ignore the hip-hop-pity about-flop, preferring instead to focus on "percussion experiments on the album [which] sometimes render her music less certain than her words. *Possession*, the strongest song — which takes the point of view of an all-too-adoring fan — is proof that McLachlan's talent runs deep," a sentiment Michael Tearson echoes in his June *Audio* 'view of the chart-climbing CD: "[FUMBLING] is a collaboration with Pierre Marchand, a producer/musician with ties to Daniel Lanois. Marchand's greatest contribution is the Lanois-like mysterioso atmosphere that envelops McLachlan's songs and deepens them. Guitarist

Bill Dillon is also an essential component. . . . Among her strongest songs is *Possession*, which bookends the album — fully produced in the beginning and reprised much later as a hidden track (you won't find it mentioned anywhere) as a piano and vocal interpretation seconds after the album's final and eponymous track." (Apparently, for those in the know, this much-discussed hidden track is called, simply, *Possessed*.)

Enter Gregg Wagener, an electronics engineer with the U.S. Navy at California's Port Hueneme and one of the two-and-a-half members on the F-T-E List who responds to my call for contributions of anecdotes, *etc.* He e-mails me four stunning paintings (the guy's really got a way of expressing himself when it comes to the creation of beauty) and the following (which he graciously grants permission to reprint): "I painted a portrait of Sarah (oil on gessoed watercolor paper). I tossed it out on the stage when she played the Ventura Concert Theater (in '93 I think). [It was the Ventura Concert Theater on either 30 or 31 July 1994.] She picked it up, looked at it and she looked pleased to me. She put the painting up where the audience could see it. One of the bouncers was impressed, handed me a flower and said I could give it to her. (You don't argue with guys like that.) I managed to get her attention and she came over and got the flower. She squeezed my hand when she took the flower. I was QUITE distracted by this unexpected gesture; but, I managed to get out, 'The painting was from me!" She gave me a beautiful smile and said, "Thank you very much, it's beautiful.'

"I sent a photo of the painting to Nettwerk with a note requesting an autograph along with a self-addressed envelope and an international postal coupon. The picture came back autographed, "Gregg — Peace! S McLachlan" and "Peace + Love = Happiness" in symbols. She also sent me a postcard with a picture of one of her paintings on it, a nude woman with blue wings; it was autographed, "S McLachlan" and "Peace + Love = Happiness" in symbols. Until then, I didn't know Sarah was a painter. It is a little embarrassing to give Sarah a painting when she is a better painter than I am. What the heck? She didn't seem to mind."

At any rate, by the time McLachlan and crew blew into The

Big Smoke right after a pair of California dates for a back-to-back 19-20 August at Ontario Place, the summer's set-list had been polished and the loyal backline had been firmly established in a series of concerts she'd given in Philadelphia, Nashville, K.C., Elora, Las Vegas, Salt Lake City, Houston, Austin, Knoxville, Memphis, Chicago and Detroit. With David Kershaw on keyboards and vocals, Brian Minato on bass, and percussionist Ashwin Sood also supplying BGVs, lead guitarists/vocalists David Sinclair (also on dobro) and Luke Ducet (also on lap steel) nicely complemented McLachlan and Camille Henderson, the "ego-less" harmonist the star had brought on board sometime earlier to replace the more ego-solidified Kim Linekin.

Following warm-upper Stephen Fearing, McLachlan, clad in satin silver gown, opened with *Plenty*, FUMBLING's third cut, and immediately displayed the gorgeous warmth and fullness of her faultless voice before delivering pitch-perfect versions of *Ice, Elsewhere, Into The Fire, Drawn To The Rhythm, Ben's Song* and such with impeccable nuances of timing and phrasing. Neither the arrest of one woman caught pissing in the bushes nor the annoying and irritating lone voice repeatedly and passionately bellowing "I love you, Sarah" every chance he got diminished the first-rate performance the goddess of gloom-and-doomery gave the night some I know attended (and reviewed the show).

On the first eve of an eight-day break, a badly needed eight-day break, McLachlan perhaps forced herself not to think of the exhausting sked looming ahead, the one taking her to Oshawa's Durham College 9 September, London's Western Fairground Grandstand 10 September, and Montreal's St. Denis 11 September before first heading south (12 September) for shows in Boston, Philadelphia, Atlanta, Tampa, Denver, San Francisco, New Orleans (opening for Jackson Browne), and, on 27 October, points overseas, most notably Manchester, UK's Hop & Grape, the first stop on the European jag of a promotional tour (opening for Crash Test Dummies) that would build momentum in Glasgow, London, Dublin, and Copenhagen (6 November) before plateauing through Germany on a spate of dates and climaxing at the Vatican's annual Christmas concert where, on 14 December, McLachlan sang a hymn for His

Holiness. Along the way she scooped up a pair of Canadian Music Video Awards for female vocalist and her directorial work on *Possession* and gave a whimsical interview to *Rolling Stone* for its October 1994 "Raves," a piece in which she cites Peter Gabriel's *Passion* as "great music to make love to" as well as wantonly lusting after *Blade Runner's* Harrison Ford, the actor for whom McLachlan "just had a total chubby."

For those who need to know such things, the October 1994 issue of *Seventeen* features a quickie take on McLachlan listing her favorite artists, writers, films, *etc.* To my knowledge, McLachlan's favorite artists are Klimt and pharmaceutical jewelrist Colleen Wolstenholme; her favorite writers are Rilke, Owen, Atwood and the X-Gen dude; and a list of her favorite films cited earlier requires an important update, *Pulp Fiction.* By the way, her favorite colors are dead-rose red and green-gray-blue and her favorite McLachlan disc is FUMBLING, which had just hit retail racks on the other side of the pond, where *Q* magazine's David Roberts gave McLachlan's third effort two (out of a possible five) stars. "She has," opines Roberts, "a tender agile voice and there are times when her ability to spin a haunting intimate tune suffused with a slightly chilling, subtle passion makes sublime sense of such ambitions. Over the course of almost an hour there are also too many times when the almost endless succession of scrupulously neat, over-elaborate, relentlessly mid-tempo tunes and overly literate, self-analytical lyrics just drag."

Perhaps Sarah McLachlan had other things on her mind during that fall of 1994; namely, the fact some "psycho" fan had posted a bunch of crazy ravings on the Internet about her, attacking her personally and artistically for breach of moral rights and copyright infringement, using his letters for the lyrics of *Possession.* Former members of her band, collaborators on the recording of TOUCH and SOLACE, Darryl Neudorf and Jeff Sawatzky, were also preparing their claims to be filed in British Columbia's Supreme Court against McLachlan. (According to Jonathan Simkin, the preliminary hearing had convinced the judge the plaintiffs had a case. The trial, scheduled for 28 September 1997, has now been postponed because a judge could not be found to sit the case. Simkin confirms his clients will be in attendance at the trial now slated for the summer of 1998.)

In the other case, Paul Cantin broke the story in *The Ottawa Sun* on 16 September, and by the time she arrived in Atlanta 20-21 September, McLachlan was ready to talk about the lawsuit. Atlanta's *99X* threw open the 'phone lines for callers. She told the DJ she knew "whatever-in-the-hell-his-name-was" had posted to the Internet; and, in her own words, she "was very hurt by the whole lawsuit" and "pissed off" as well.

A week before McLachlan played Paris and Rome in December, the FREEDOM SESSIONS CD came down the chute in her native land; and, naturally, by then, it was time for one well-traveled songstress to take a much-needed breather. Christmas. Family. A port in the storm, especially since plenty had happened in her personal life of late, particularly the song in the key of ache:

I used to think my life was often empty
A lonely space to fill
You hurt me more than I ever would have imagined
You made my world stand still

— from *Plenty*

(Opposite) MURMURS *CD Volume 2, available to members of Sarah McLachlan's fan club "murmurs."*

(Following page) Cover of single, Possession.

five

SIREN'S SONG

or Possession

I t is quite true I wasn't doing anything that morning in the Metro Toronto Reference Library except tracking down newspaper and magazine articles to add to my collection of resource materials on Sarah McLachlan. It is also quite true I didn't expect to find anything but the usual media bumpf squirrelled away in the MetRef's holdings. So, there's no reason on this planet why I should have been on the lookout for either the unusual or the untoward that unseasonably chillish yet blindingly bright late-spring day in the dreaded Big Smoke.

In line to photocopy the recto-verso spread on pages 12-13 of October 1994's *Words & Music*, I scanned a glance at the ubiquitous snake of traffic inching north and south on Yonge Street and idly followed a pair of lovebirds, visibly thrilled with the acquisition of what looked to be a scaled replica of a delicately wrought gold-filigree bird cage suspended between them on a scarlet ribbon securely attached to a slim stick of dowelling.

Like a bird on a wire . . . Words & Music. Nice cover, nice guts.

I flip through the rag in order to flag the article and expedite the boring duplication process. When I can't locate the item, I automatically assume its numeric tags have been left off so prospective readers are unwittingly forced to gander at surrounding pages — a common advertorial gambit — usually stuffed with consumer pitches. So, I squint at the teensie 10 printed in the bottom left-hand corner, squint again at its mismatching 15 opposite, air and flap the periodical to ensure its missing pages have not been inadvertently inserted in the wrong sequence and apologetically make way for the guy behind me in the lineup stoically balancing a mini-tower of dust-brindled tomes bearing titles along the lines of *Victorian Valances* stacked on top of *Curtains of Fog, Masks of Iron, A Touch of Class, Edwardian Decor,* and such.

The thief who'd scoffed the obviously offensive story, I'd noticed, had also neatly razored the "Table of Contents" clean from the gutter of *Words & Music.*

"This *is* most unusual," allows the guy at the info desk, blushing a very-berry purple, "we don't normally see that kind of thing around here. Most users of our facilities are scrupulous and conscientious; most simply don't stoop to this kind of thing."

Over the clerk's left shoulder I spot a youthful queer by the Up and Down buttons pinning and adjusting a hot-pink triangle on the lapel of his perennially stylish Harris-tweed jacket, using a very pretty eyeshadow case with mirror to ensure its balance.

"Well, you're right about one thing," I reply, "whoever slashed those particular pages did so *most* scrupulously and conscientiously. If I hadn't been looking for the article, I never would have noticed it wasn't there. A real professional cut job. Look how close they got to the spine — neither a nick, etch nor ragged edge on the rest of the pages. Must've been a brand-new blade...."

"Anyway, I thought you'd want to replace your damaged *Words & Music*; plus, you wouldn't happen to have *FRANK* on file, would you?"

"Who?"

"It's not a *who*; it's a *what*; it's *FRANK*, the scandal-mongering, mud-slinging, shit-disturbing dirt digger."

"Excuse me? Frank?"

"Yeah, *FRANK*, the famous *FRANK* mag."

The blank look in the guy's eyes tells me all I need to know. In the elevator, Mr. Pink warmly remarks on the beauty of the day, a highly unusual occurrence in this neck of the world.

"Yeah," I chit-chat, "a real beaut. Tad cold for my liking, though. That's why I'm wearing my favorite NHL longjohns. See? I've got the Flames on one knee and Wings on the other."

"I didn't know girls wore longjohns," chirps my Down companion.

"Really?" I deadpan, "You don't know what you're missing."

"Ain't that the truth," the guy replies wistfully, "ain't that the truth?"

On the 300-kilometer trip north to Nowhere, my 23 acres of swamp plus shack mostly owned by the Royal Bank, I randomly poke around in a few dark recesses of my web-strewn memory vault trying to dig up the details of the *FRANK* piece on the McLachlan kafuffle since, as an ardent *FRANK*onian, I figured I must've at least hawked a boo at the thing when that particular ish first hit the stands.

Words and music, eh? Which words and music? And, songright suits to boot. What had some *Words & Musician* written that had so ticked off some razor-wielding wacko that they'd gone to the trouble of meticulously disappearing the offensive material from the public record?

A tiny bell — a belletino, if you will — distinctly tinka-tinkled in the remoter regions of the good ol' gray matter. By the time I'd left Jerks' Falls in the rear-view mirror and headed into the home stretch, that tiny jinga-jingling had swelled in amplitude to a five-alarm gong.

Naturally, I e-mailed frankmag@achilles.net and politely requested a copy of the story from 24 May 1995 on p. 6 cited in Worldview's CPI database at the MetRef. Frankmag@achilles.net obligingly re-mails the story; and, in the reply, gets off a smart-aleck remark about how everybody in the whole wide world but yours truly had a certain ancient yet beloved Canadian back-bencher in their Dead-Pool rosters.

That stung; nevertheless, I gritted an e-smile and thanked the barb-a-jabberist in the most drivelish way I could muster, primarily because I knew better than to bite the hand that had just electronically fed me the eye popper in question:

Sarah McLachlan Sued Over Song Rights

The legal woes continue for Sarah McLachlan, the hugely successful Canadian chanteuse and Grammy-Award Nominee.

McLachlan's last album, FUMBLING TOWARDS ECSTASY, which sold over a million copies, triggered a lawsuit from a deranged fan who claimed that his obsessive love letters were the inspiration behind McLachan's song, *Possession*. The $250,000 legal challenge came to an abrupt end last November when the man's body was found decaying in his truck near Manotick, ON — an apparent suicide.

Now McLachlan and her record label, Nettwerk Productions, are facing two new lawsuits over authorship of songs on her first album, TOUCH. Jeff Sawatzky, a former bass player in McLachlan's band, claims Nettwerk stiffed him for royalties on two songs he wrote for McLachlan. And Darryl Neudorf, a producer/engineer who worked on TOUCH, says he wrote four songs for the same album, without proper compensation or credit.

Neudorf says Nettwerk asked him to collaborate with McLachlan on songs for the 1988 release, TOUCH, and help out with the recording.

He says that he co-wrote the tracks *Strange World, Vox, Sad Clown* and *Steaming*. According to Neudorf's claim, Nettwerk told him it wanted to present McLachlan as the primary songwriter of the tracks on TOUCH, and proposed that he assign his ownership of the songs' copyright to Nettwerk, in exchange for royalties.

Nettwerk denies that Neudorf co-wrote any portion of McLachlan's songs. Neudorf says that since 1988, he has made numerous inquiries about payment of his royalties and fees for production services on Touch, but payments have been irregular and far less than the percentages he was promised. Nettwerk says it continues to pay Neudorf an agreed 1% of royalties on TOUCH, as compensation for his work on the album.

Vancouver musician Jeff Sawatzky has a similar complaint. He says that in 1988, the label invited him to Vancouver to work on McLachan's first record. On the night he met McLachlan, she was recording the single,

Ben's Song, but was having trouble completing the lyrics. Sawatzky says he suggested appropriate lyrics for *Ben's Song*, and his words eventually wound up on the final recorded version, making him co-author of the song.

Later that year, Nettwerk signed a deal with Arista Records to release TOUCH in the U.S. Sawatzky says he contributed music and lyrics to *Trust*, an additional track on the Arista release, as well as playing bass and singing background.

Nettwerk denies that Sawatzky co-wrote *Ben's Song*, but admits that he composed 5% of the song *Trust*. It says he has been paid a proportionate royalty for the song. After the release of TOUCH, Sawatzky went on tour with McLachlan's band, earning a per diem of $25. He says McLachlan's agent, Dan McGee, pressured him not to ask for songwriting credits or compensation.

McGee, he claims, told him he was "lucky" to be in the band and that he shouldn't press the matter if he wanted to continue to work with McLachlan and Nettwerk.

Sawatzky claims he was given the impression that if he didn't sign over his publishing rights to Nettwerk's publishing division, he would be bounced out of the band.

In December 1989, Sawatzky was dropped from the band because — according to Nettwerk — his previous conviction on drug charges meant he couldn't tour in the U.S. Both Sawatzky and Neudorf are seeking damages of unspecified amounts. They name as defendants McLachlan, Nettwerk Productions and Nettwerk execs Terry McBride, Mark Jowett and Ric Arboit.

The case is expected to come to trial later this year.

Maestro GM, my most trustable bud on the music beat, fills in the details on the song suits over duck soup at the Byline Bar and Grill by further explaining another musician/producer who'd also worked on McLachlan's début had similarly launched an action against Nettwerk, *et al.* for lack of payment on both songwriting and co-production work he'd contributed to the album (for which he had, after all, received full credit in the album's liner notes). As far as MGM recalled, Darren Phillips had accepted the out-of-court settlement. As for the general lack of public information in widespread circulation concerning the action, MGM cynically cited the M.Y.O.B. rule that most papers make a habit of following when it comes to their advertisers' internecine squabbles.

So, over dessert and café au lait, I quiz the guy about the so-called deranged fan mentioned in the *FRANK* exposé I'd brought along for the occasion. What, exactly, if anything, had he heard through the grapevine?

"Next to nothing," says he, dabbing sherbet from the corners of his mouth, "probably just about the same amount you heard and/or read at the time."

"Yeah, that's the thing; I wasn't around at the time. I was on the Riviera, remember? I left in September and didn't return till the end of November '94. But, it must've been big news in our neighborhood of the little village, eh?"

"Maybe in your neighborhood, Fitz; but, it barely made the gossip sheets, let alone the mainstream media, in my neighborhood."

"Whaddya mean? A deranged fan, surely, merits big coverage, even in little ol' Canada? Look at Lady Anne's deranged fan, for example, the Saskatchewan farmer who got kilometers of ink in the mainstream press, back when he couldn't get enough of our Annie, despite the cops' intervention, *etc., etc., etc.*"

"Yeah, didn't they issue a restraining order on that muzhik?"

"Yeah! As an ardent fan of Ms Murray, didn't the amorous clodhopper also do time in the slammer, if memory serves me correctly?"

"Search me."

"Okay, I will. What's the word on *this* deranged bird?"

"Lemme see. Yeah, guess it was right around the time you were in France, sucking up the sun. *Moi?* I was stuck in the newsroom sucking up to the bosses; but, I seem to recall, we started getting letters from the guy, letters about how he'd been morally maligned or some such. That was a while back now; but, as far as I can remember, it had something to do with his contention McLachlan had ripped off some of the lyrics to *Possession* from a letter and/or poem he'd written in one of his voluminous *billets-doux*. Also, he felt very strongly she'd ruined his reputation by going public with stuff in his letters he felt should have remained confidential, the most important point, in my opinion (unless, of course, McLachlan had other obsessive love-letterists on the go)."

"Not likely, if you ask me. Geez, what's happening to this country? Like, the fan shouldn't be fanned, kind of? He'll go away?"

"You kidding? The guy sent all sorts of media copies of his poems and letters and even went so far as to send along the Statement of Claim outlining his charges against McLachlan who was, by this time, sounding very much like she could just possibly be repeating his private communications to anybody in the media who would listen. He had a list of writers who'd quoted McLachlan in their stories who'd quoted him verbatim from his letters and it freaked him right out. He was most freaked out about an interview she gave to somebody at CBC."

"It'd freak anybody out. You think McLachlan's people would know better."

"Anyway, the guy who felt he'd been wronged was also a cybergeek, I think, a real devoted Netizen. He posted the details of his trials and tribulations on the Internet."

"Yeah? You remember the guy's name?"

"Uwe. Uwe Vandrei. He seemed normal enough, at least to me."

"Really, wonder who else might have chatted with Vandrei?"

"That's your department."

"You talked with him? When?"

"Two or three times back in the spring or summer of 1994. I only talked with him on the 'phone. He seemed upset, emotional; but, under control. He seemed eminently sane."

"So, did he inspire the song?'

"His suspicions his letters might have inspired the song are probably well-founded. It didn't strike me as being so completely out in left-field that I wasn't going to listen to him," says *The Ottawa Sun*'s Entertainment Editor, Brian Gorman. "He did sound rational."

"Did you know he was a musician?"

"No; but I did know he was a computer guy of some sort. He did tell me that. He didn't say much about his personal background at all. He was just a reader who'd called up, I guess, in his own words, 'Trying to get a fair hearing'."

"You gave him space?"

"We did. Paul Cantin did one piece. We were, however, understandably cautious. Someone can sound rational on the telephone, send you a rational letter; and turn out to be Rupert Pupkin [*The King of Comedy*]. There was always that concern, that we would be encouraging the stalker, contributing to his celebrity fixation.

"I'm not called upon to be a judge; but I am called upon to be cautious and to err on the side of caution where legalities are concerned. And there was also the question, at least in my mind (as well as the Editor-in-Chief's), about just how newsworthy it was. Plus, where do you cross the line into voyeurism and end up victimizing someone with a delusion? We were very concerned about that, more for Vandrei's sake than McLachlan's.

"In the fact that he was, at the time, contemplating bringing a lawsuit against her for appropriation of his ideas and private words, that is newsworthy; but you go beyond that, I think, at your own risk. We were very conscious of that fact."

"Would you say you felt any sense this man was self-destructive, capable of killing himself; or, on the verge of doing something like that?"

"No. I guess I couldn't say that. I didn't have any kind of gut feeling he even might."

On 16 September 1994, Paul Cantin provided the nation's capital with a brief yet balanced assessment of the action Uwe Vandrei had commenced against McLachlan. In it, he summarizes the details of the lawsuit and explains to readers that "the song, 'Possession,' has become a hit both in Canada and the U.S.," then reports that "Vandrei says McLachlan 'took unfair advantage of the confidential letters which had been received in confidence and profited from the wrong use of the ideas, emotions and character described in the letters.' ...

"In an interview with the *Sun* last October, McLachlan acknowledged the song was written about a number of fans whose admiration had grown 'too intense', and she described those people as 'really lost souls. They don't seem to have anyone else in their lives and they see me as their savior.'

"A spokesman for her record label said McLachlan denies the allegations and has specifically stated the song was not written about Vandrei. 'It isn't about one person. It never has been. It's definitely not about him,' said Nettwerk Records spokesman Catherine McLaren."

Naturally, Cantin makes a point of telling readers he had tried to contact Vandrei on 15 September 1994, most likely to see if he, too, had elected to go the "no comment" route: "Vandrei could not be reached yesterday and his lawyer refused to comment. However, earlier this year, McLachlan's lawyer, Andrew Atkins, sent a letter to Vandrei saying his 'repeated attempts at communication with Ms McLachlan are considered by her as an act of harassment.'

"Atkins refused to comment on the case yesterday."

That's all he, and most every other journalist in North America, wrote. Virtually every reference to Vandrei — with the noteworthy exception of "Object of Obsession," an article written by Jane Tattersall and James Hrynyshyn 18 January 1995 for the small alternative weekly, *Ottawa Xpress*. "Few people noticed Uwe Vandrei's disappearance last fall. His neighbors on Vanier's Barrette Street most often described him as a loner. Only the chance discovery in November of his truck parked in the Manotick woods, his decomposing body inside, brought to light the end of his tragic life.

"And yet, Vandrei was not an entirely unknown quantity. Those that did know him at all could point to the source of his pain. But, who could have predicted his love for Vancouver singer Sarah McLachlan would drive him to suicide?"

The intrepid journalistic duo next provides readers with a list of similar high-profile cases of obsessed fans and stalkers, most notably in connection with the names of Jodie Foster and David Letterman.

"Carey Stevens, an Ottawa psychologist who deals with obsessive-compulsive behavior, says fixations of any kind usually arise to fill a gap in someone's life. If the problem is smoking or nail-biting, it can be treated through behavioral modification, says Stevens. As long as there's a good reason to quit, the patient can. Fixating on a media star, however, is more difficult to treat because there's no obvious incentive to give it up. Its origins are also more mysterious.

'I don't know of a client who's been able to say, "This is why I do it." It's something that gradually forms,' says Stevens. 'I don't think they understand and I really believe they're telling the truth.' "

Hrynyshyn and Tattersall next explain to readers that many "gruesome or outrageous tactics" of obsessed fans have ended up as fodder for the voracious popular press. "But, Vandrei's story does not include dead animals nor body parts mailed to the star. There are no threats, no signs of violence nor otherwise dangerous behavior. Just letters. Lots of letters. And a bizarre lawsuit . . .

"As do many obsessed fans, Vandrei kept to himself. 'We never saw him with anybody or saw anybody at his house. He spoke with my roommate once about the court case; but, that was pretty much it,' says next-door neighbor James Buchanan. He also says Vandrei's home was well-stocked with computer equipment . . . In his basement he kept stacks of books and journals with titles like 'Poems' and 'Songs'.

"But, he didn't appear to have a social life . . . Details of his life — his age, birthplace, family — are hard to come by . . . Buchanan says he and his roommate only noticed Vandrei's absence when junk mail started piling up outside his door. 'We were cleaning it up for him. Then his bike got knocked over in the driveway and he didn't pick it up. It just sat on its side for days. That made us start to wonder'. . . .

"Rodney Murphy, a Carleton University student who met Vandrei at a McLachlan concert in December 1993 [8 December], spent several hours talking with him. 'He kept talking about how little faith he had in humanity,' recalls Murphy.

"McLachlan has always portrayed herself in her songs and videos as a mythic remote figure. . . . [On a national television network], she described herself as a 'sucker for tragic romance.' The image she has constructed has attracted more than one obsessive fan. In March of 1994 a restraining order was issued against a fan who moved to Vancouver to be near the singer."

On 23 January 1995, *The Indianapolis Star*'s "Entertainment" section published a feature on stalkers and stars, devoting the bulk of the article to Bloomington's Lisa Germano; however, Vandrei's name appeared in the context of Germano's story as a morbid side note on "the most bizarre stalking incident" which concluded when Vandrei was found dead, "an apparent suicide."

Date: Mon, 12 Sep 1994 09:40:55-0400
From: ae064@freenet.carleton.ca (Uwe Vandrei)
Subject: Possession lawsuit

I am the person who is the subject of the song ''Possession''. I am not a stalker, nor have I ever committed rape or murder. I do not have a criminal record.

Ms. McLachlan has just been served a Statement of Claim (City of Ottawa Court House file # 85502/94) in which she is named as the defendant and I am the plaintiff.

Based on my research of her press statements, there seems to be no doubt that she has undergone a series of negative experiences related to obsessive fans. These experiences seem to range from receiving disturbing mail, to someone stalking her to her residence. However, I contest her statements that these frightful experiences are reflected in the lyrical content of the song.

My claim that Ms. McLachlan has breached the confidentiality of my letters is sincere and has a factual basis. I have suffered profound emotional hardships because of the song ''Possession'' and the subsequent controversy associated with it. However, I have strong suspicions that the difficulty I am experiencing in resolving this matter with Ms. McLachlan is not caused by her, but by the actions of her management.

I perceive Ms. McLachlan to be a socially conscientious person and that if she had full knowledge of the nature of my complaint she would make visible efforts to resolve the matter. My suspicions are that her management has wilfully withheld information from her or has perhaps even deliberately misinformed her as to my personality and the nature of my claim against her. I have speculated as to the possible motivations for such alleged actions by her management, but such speculations are not suitable for public dissemination. The primary reason for my lawsuit is to establish a legal, public venue where these matters can finally be objectively, candidly examined.

Furthermore, I still contend that this matter can be resolved in a far more congenial, private, and economical manner if I were simply granted one conversation with Ms. McLachlan.

The only response to my Letter of Demand was a single telephone call from Mr. Atkins (her lawyer) to my lawyer on the 31'st of May, 1994. The highlights of that conversation are as follows:

- this telephone call would be his only response;
- that I was not ``normal'';
- the themes of the song ``Possession'' did not originate from my letters;
- he attempted to persuade my lawyer to convince me to drop the lawsuit;
- Ms. McLachlan wanted me to drop the matter;
- Ms. McLachlan has been made aware of all correspondence I have sent to her and she has no desire to communicate with me under any circumstances. Mr. Atkins declined an offer from my lawyer for a settlement meeting to be chaperoned by our respective legal representatives;
- Ms. McLachlan will not offer me any personal

confirmation of her wishes on the basis that no matter what she might tell me I would still not desist from trying to communicate with her.

Since her management indicated no inclination for discussion or negotiation I had no choice but to proceed with the lawsuit.

Documentation is available to all interested parties.

Uwe Vandrei Ottawa, Ont.

A brief history . . .

To give you a little background, I will confess to being quite 'taken' by Ms. McLachlan. Her artistic expressions and congenial personality have uniquely contributed to my personal growth. As a consequence, as early as October of 1991 I have been in the habit of expressing my appreciation for the richness she has contributed to my life. These expressions started in the form of offering notes of appreciation accompanied by rather elegant flower arrangements offered at various concerts that I was privileged to attend. I must confess that these expressions escalated to the form of rather confessional letters and perhaps inappropriately intimate expressions of affection.

I met her once, late April '92 and she identified me as the fan that had sent the flowers and thanked me. We had a polite discussion and I gave her a little hug before I left.

Since Ms. McLachlan never responded to any of my correspondence, I have no way of knowing what their ultimate effect was. I did not become aware of the controversy concerning ''Possession'' until the 27 October article in *The Ottawa Sun*. However, I had no problem identifying myself as the subject of the song when it was debuted on Ralph Benmergui in late March of 1993. Over the summer I sent four letters expressing my pain that she had taken my personal confidences and without asking me or at least warning me, displaying them in public. I received no response. It was only much later that I was to learn of the mail screen that was in effect, and I now presume that my letters were intercepted by someone of a malicious, or at least totally unfeeling nature.

After reading the October 27 article I was horrified. To learn of her opinion of the supposed subject was devastating to my personal life and demanded that I investigate this matter and arrive at some form of mutually acceptable resolution. On 1 November I called Nettwerk Productions. I initially spoke with Catherine McLaren (Sarah's PR rep.) and clearly identified myself (name, address . . .) and as being the author of the letters that seemed to have caused Ms. McLachlan such distress. I was then passed to Terry McBride (Sarah's manager), who assured me that I was 'not the guy' and informed me about the mail screen, which according to him had been in effect for about one year. I emphatically stated that whatever his current information may be, I was the true subject of the song and I had copies of the letters to prove it. I offered these letters to be subjected to an independent content analysis, but Mr. McBride declined. He also refused me a phone conversation with Ms. McLachlan. I countered that if Ms. McLachlan was accepting fans at the December 8th concert in Ottawa, I would take up the matter with her personally.

The following day I sent an apology to Ms. McLachlan to try and allay some of her apprehension, and presumably win enough of her confidence to merit an explanation. There was no response.

On the day of the concert I happened to be working from home and noticed two rather large men in a car, observing my residence. I took no notice because there were drug dealers living next door and I presumed the surveillance was intended for them. At the concert I noticed what seemed to be unusually heavy security, and after making inquiries learned that Ms. McLachlan had been personally threatened. It was not until much later that I connected these two circumstances and began to suspect that the supposed originator of those threats was me!

At this point I became suspicious that Ms. McLachlan's management's efforts to protect her went beyond her self-interest. I must confess that I was rather disappointed with her performance at the December 8th concert. She seemed quite troubled to me, small wonder in light of such rumors of threats. Based on her previous negative experiences with fans there clearly is a need to protect her, but I consider my efforts to communicate with her justified. At a minimum, Terry McBride is obliged to give my claim an objective consideration, rather than waving me off without even examining the evidence. I am determined to investigate this issue until I get confirmation or denial from Ms. McLachlan herself.

I formulated a strategy to generate a mail audit trail. My goal was to determine if Ms. McLachlan had been made aware of my efforts to communicate with her, or if my correspondence was being intercepted. The results were quite disappointing. Neither of the self-addressed stamped envelopes were returned to me, but I did receive a perfectly blunt letter from her lawyer stating that Ms. McLachlan had no desire to communicate with me, and the letter even went so far as to threaten a restraining order. Realize that this is the first official correspondence I have received from anyone associated with Ms. McLachlan. Note that the letter is carbon-copied to Ms. McLachlan, but I still have no confirmation that she has actually been informed of this ongoing confrontation.

(Service of the lawsuit has ensured that she now knows SOMETHING is going on. Stayed [sic] tuned for future episodes . . .)

When I arrived back at Nowhere, MGM had already taken the initiative and e-mailed the above-cited document along with the Internet address where he'd located it plus the name of the individual who hosted the website featuring Vandrei's extensive missive as its centerpiece attraction (John Shepard).

So, I sent an e-mail to Shepard asking him what he could tell me, if anything, about Uwe Vandrei. I also queried him about his reasons for maintaining the dead man's presence on the Web, something that struck me as a prurient and excessively gruesome pitch for attention on the poster's part. Shepard replied by explaining he considered Vandrei's document an important one to keep alive insofar as he believed it sent a strong message to other fans who might find themselves similarly obsessed with idols beyond their reach. Copyright regulations prohibit me from repeating Shepard's personal feelings on either the subject of Vandrei's apparent suicide or the victim's state of mind.

In a subsequent e-mail, I did ask Shepard's permission to quote from our correspondence as well as thanking him for his cooperation and information on where I might locate Vandrei's original Internet posting. I never heard from the guy again.

By the way, Shepard (a.k.a. Squid) wrote the original Frequently Asked Questions (FAQ) on McLachlan available at various Internet addresses on the Web. Shepard, it seems, occasionally updates the official-list FAQ for the Fumblers, a subscription-based forum technically known as the F-T-E List for hardcore Sarahmaniacs.

In his April 1995 version of the FAQ, Squid includes the following:

Who was Uwe Vandrei?

Where to begin? Uwe Vandrei was (and is) the textbook obsessed fan. From 1992 to 1994, he sent Sarah hundreds of flowers and letters containing remarkable poetry professing his love for her. He was a loner, who ''had little faith in humanity.'' (What does that make Sarah? A Vorlon?)

Well, Uwe's infamy began in the fall of 1994. He posted a message to this list, claiming that he was the one and only inspiration for the song ''Possession,'' which Sarah has repeatedly said is about an obsessed fan. In this message, Uwe gave very detailed and paranoid-sounding evidence that the song was about him. He stated that he was going to file a lawsuit against Sarah, for breach of confidence in writing a song about him. He did state, however, that the lawsuit need not go to court, that it could be settled in a one to one conversation with Sarah personally. Uwe Vandrei was found dead in late December of 1994, in his truck parked in the woods not far from his house: a suicide. He never posted again to the list, the lawsuit never went to court. To date, there has been no official statement from Nettwerk or Sarah concerning Uwe's suicide. Rumour has it the case is still pending. The ambiguity of Sarah's music, that unique quality that allows each of us to find our own meanings (or our own life stories) in her songs, unfortunately makes her a rather ripe target for obsessive fans. I speak from experience here; I was once a bit on the obsessed side myself. We find so much of ourselves in her music we think she must be more like us than she is; we fall in love with what we think is her, and pursue her, thinking that this construct in our minds would 'have' to love us in return. I eventually figured out otherwise, but unfortunately Uwe Vandrei never did.

In Shepard's March 1996 FAQ, he includes a second version of the Vandrei Q&A:

Who is Uwe Vandrei?
Between 1992 and 1994, Uwe sent literally hundreds of flowers and romantic letters to Sarah, making himself into a nearly textbook study of an obsessed fan. He was by no means the only fan doing such things, but you'd never convince him of this. When ''Possession'' was released, a song Sarah wrote from the perspective of obsessed fans, Uwe was convinced the song was written about himself, and filed a lawsuit accusing Sarah of breach of confidence for writing that song about him, based, he claimed, on letters he sent her. Uwe announced his intention to sue right here on FTE. Stop by http://www.iupui.edu/~jrshepar/ uwe.html to see what he had to say. The case never got to trial; in late December of 1994, Uwe was found dead in the woods near his home, apparently a suicide. As a morbid side note, Uwe's Internet account at the Freenet is still active. Rumour has it the case is _still_ pending; Nettwerk is extremely reluctant to discuss the incident (and I don't blame them). Sarah has had little to say publicly about the incident, except that it will not change how she writes her songs.

And, just prior to completing the manuscript for this book, Shepard provided newbies (a.k.a. Internet rookies) with yet another version of the now-legendary cybersaga:

Who's this Uwe Vandrei person?
Uwe was perhaps the consummate extreme example of the obsessed fan. From 1991 to 1993, he wrote literally hundreds of letters and poems which he sent to Sarah, some of which were cool, some of which were scary. As far as Sarah was concerned, he was just another of those damned obsessed fans

writing wacky letters - and in fact, she wrote
''Possession'' from the perspective of an
obsessed fan, to see if she could figure out why
they thought the way they did.

Apparently she hit the nail on the head — Uwe
Vandrei, after writing so many poems in a style
similar to Sarah's, heard *Possession* for the first
time and thought she'd swiped parts of it from his
poems. Heaven forbid any OTHER lunatic would send
her similar poems — obsessed minds think alike.
Anyway, he sued for $250,000 in damages for
''breach of confidence'' —whatever that means — and
the general consensus among Sarah and her lawyers
was that he didn't want the money, he wanted to
get the case in court, fire his lawyer, put Sarah
on the witness stand, and verbally have his way
with her.

Uwe posted a message to this list in September
1994, detailing his intentions to sue Sarah,
listing off all the probably-unrelated [sic]
events leading up to it, and generally proving
to the world that he was a nutcase. He posted the
note and disappeared. The case never made it to
court; Uwe committed suicide in December 1994.

The case is still pending and Nettwerk cannot
talk about it. Sarah has made no official
statement except to say it won't change how
she writes songs.

As a morbid side note, Uwe's account at the
Carleton Freenet is still active.

In order to verify the contents of Shepard's morbid side note, I
send an e-mail to Vandrei's Carleton Freenet address. When it
bounces back immediately, I discover the address, although
indeed active, rejects all e-messages because its mailbox is full.

Letters sent to Sarah McLachlan by Uwe Vandrei [from
Vandrei's media package]:

23 February 1992—there's someone out there like me
. . .
5 March 1992—I just had to write again
???-Tape: my favorite things
25 March 1992—Exhausted waiting for your response
27 March 1992—at the falls
???-Montreal Spectrum meeting: Sarah on drugs?
31 August 1992-post Harbourfront: tape A Love
Story
7 September 1992—no self control . . .
11 September 1992—apology for ''no self control''
???-CMVA card ''I voted for you 100 times!''
???-card: forever in celebration of you
December 1992-gift: swan album, assorted muds
29 March 1993—post Ralph Benmergui
31 March 1993—apology for post Benmergui
27 June 1993—fell in love all over again after
extended absence
3 July 1993—personal info & photos
2 November 1993—apology for ''disturbing''
letters, sent to Terry to be forwarded
31 November 1993—post ''Fumbling'', sent to
Catherine to be forwarded

March 1992

Dearest Sarah,
It feels like -30C outside and I am in the habit
of walking to work. I cursed creation all the
way. I met a woman on the elevator who has a
daughter in Vancouver. She says the daffodils
have been in bloom for three weeks. Tonight I got
claustrophobic and had to go for a run. I put on
the required ''protection'' and made a solitary
trip up the Rideau River to the falls (it's
4:00AM). It's curious how one learns to adapt. I
don't like winter, but it doesn't hold me back. I
have mastered its domain.

The falls are really something to see just
now. It's a glacier in miniature. Due to a
previous thaw the ice melted and ran over the
falls, piling right to the top. It's desolate.
In the sunlight the chunks have the clearest
blue, but all I can see now is grey. Somewhere
underneath I know there is life, but I have to
take it on faith, for this frigid scene does not
offer the slightest indication. I stood in the
condensation and it cut off my view. The crystals
tinged my skin and I thought of standing there,
letting it encapsulate me. I thought of how
similar this is to life, except that spring is
certain to come, and my winter is eternal. I
thought what malicious deity would condemn a
person to such a reality? And yet He is the
author of life. If He should choose that I learn
to master such a winter, who am I to decide
differently?

Uwe

January 1994

Dearest Sarah,
I must warn you that there is something evil
afoot! Are you aware that Nettwerk screens your
fan mail? These past two years I have poured out
my affections and have received no response. Now
I have no way of knowing if you have even seen my
d'expressions d'amour! Imagine, a perfect
stranger pawing these profound letters of love.
One must ask what the standard for censorship is
- does bad poetry meet the same fate as rotten
eggs (though I can't imagine anyone sending you
hate mail)!
    Due to this new development, I ask only one
thing — that you confirm receipt of this letter to
assure me that your holy eyes have graced my

persistent petitions for your affection. I am including an inventory of all correspondence previously sent in order to determine their ultimate destination or demise. Please check off the ones you have received and return the form in the SASE.

Please Sarah, if you find me an annoying low-life, indulge me this one thing and I will stop bothering you, but I must at least know that you have seen my letters. If not, I must continue this crusade against the evil Nettwerk Kingdom and free you from its tangled web.

Uwe Vandrei

Andrew S. Atkins
Barrister & Solicitor
1142 Keith Road
West Vancouver, B.C.
V7T 1M8

January 18, 1994
Delivered by Registered Mail

Uwe Vandrei
26 Barrette Street
Vanier, Ontario
K1L 8A5

Mr. Vandrei:
Re: Sarah McLachlan

I am the lawyer acting on behalf of Sarah McLachlan. I have been forwarded copies of various correspondence you have sent to Ms. McLachlan including the list of correspondence you provided on January 11, 1994.

Please be advised that your repeated attempts at communication with Ms. McLachlan are considered by her as an act of harassment. It is her express wish that you end all manner of correspondence and communication with her, her record label or any other person or party connected with Ms. McLachlan in any way.

Specifically, Ms. McLachlan does not wish to enter into any form of communication with you at this time or in the future.

I draw your attention to Section 264 of the Criminal Code of Canada and to the express prohibition contained therein with respect to repeated communications with a person where you are aware that the recipient may be harassed by such communication. Please be advised that any further correspondence received from you with will [sic] be considered by Ms. McLachlan as an intentional act of continued harassment and will be forwarded directly to the law enforcement authority responsible for dealing with such matters who will conduct themselves accordingly.

Please govern yourself accordingly.

Yours truly,
Andrew S. Atkins
Barrister and Solicitor
Encl.
cc: Sarah McLachlan

Lette McTaggart Blais Martin & Stein
Barristers and Solicitors
Patents, Licensing, Trademarks
100 SPARKS STREET, SUITE 1000
OTTAWA, CANADA K1P 5B7

April 25, 1994

Andrew S. Atkins
Barrister & Solicitor

1142 Keith Road
West Vancouver, B.C. V7T 1M8

Dear Mr. Atkins
Re: Sarah McLachlan

Mr. Vandrei has forwarded to me your letter to him of January 18, 1994. Might I point out that Section 264 of the Criminal Code is no longer in effect?

In response to your suggestion that Mr. Vandrei has harassed Ms. McLachlan, Mr. Vandrei denies any and all suggestions or implications that he has harassed Ms. McLachlan in any way.

Mr. Vandrei does claim that Ms. McLachlan has misused the letters he has sent to her and she has breached the confidentiality of these letters. Furthermore Mr. Vandrei claims that Ms. McLachlan has violated his moral rights in these letters. In breaching the confidentiality of his letters to her and in violating his moral rights in these letters, Ms. McLachlan has misused the letters to make considerable profits from them through her song writing.

Accordingly Mr. Vandrei demands an immediate acknowledgement from Ms. McLachlan of his contributions to her song writing and an accounting of all profits made by her through the misuse of his letters. If Mr. Vandrei has not received the acknowledgement and accounting within twenty days from the date of this letter, Mr. Vandrei will have no choice but to avail himself of any and all legal recourses against Ms. McLachlan.

Yours truly
Kenneth J. Bickley

File NO. 85502/94

ONTARIO COURT
(GENERAL DIVISION)
STATEMENT OF CLAIM
BETWEEN: UWE VANDREI
    Plaintiff
    and
    SARAH MCLACHLAN
    Defendant

TO THE DEFENDANT:

A LEGAL PROCEEDING HAS BEEN COMMENCED AGAINST YOU
by the plaintiff. The claim made against you is
set out in the following pages.

IF YOU WISH TO DEFEND THIS PROCEEDING, you or an
Ontario lawyer acting for you must prepare a
statement of defence in Form 18A prescribed by
the Rules of Civil Procedure, serve it on the
plaintiff's lawyer or, where the plaintiff does
not have a lawyer, serve it on the plaintiff, and
file it, with proof of service, in this court
office WITHIN TWENTY DAYS after this statement of
claim is served on you, if you are served in
Ontario.

If you are served in another province or
territory of Canada or in the United States of
America, the period for serving and filing your
statement of defence is forty days. If you are
served outside Canada and the United States of
America, the period is sixty days.

Instead of serving and filing a statement of
defence, you may serve and file a notice of intent
to defend in Form 18B prescribed by the Rules of
Civil Procedure. This will entitle you to ten
more days within which to serve and file your
statement of defence.

IF YOU FAIL TO DEFEND THIS PROCEEDING, JUDGMENT MAY BE GIVEN AGAINST YOU IN YOUR ABSENCE AND WITHOUT FURTHER NOTICE TO YOU. If you wish to defend this proceeding but are unable to pay legal fees, legal aid may be available to you by contacting a local Legal Aid office.

IF YOU PAY THE PLAINTIFF'S CLAIM, and $2,000 for costs, within the time for serving and filing your statement of defence you may move to have this proceeding dismissed by the court. If you believe the amount claimed for costs is excessive, you may pay the plaintiff's claim and $100.00 for costs and have the costs assessed by the court.

Date: September 2, 1994

Issued by . . . Tracey Powers <signed>

Address of court office:
161 Elgin Street
Ottawa, Ontario
K2P 2Kl

To: Sarah McLachlan
 Vancouver, British Columbia

1. The Plaintiff claims:
 a) damages for breach of confidence and breach of moral rights in the amount of $250,000;
 b) an accounting of profits from sale of the CD ''Fumbling towards Ecstasy'' and of the song ''Possession'';
 c) an order from the court requiring the Defendant to publicly associate the Plaintiff with the CD ''Fumbling towards Ecstasy'' and in particular with the song, ''Possession'' and to credit the Plaintiff with help in the

creation of the song.

d) pre-judgment and post-judgment interest in accordance with the Courts of Justice Act,

e) its costs of this action on a solicitor and client scale, and

f) such further and other relief as this Honourable Court may deem just.

2) The Plaintiff is a computer programmer and a resident of the City of Ottawa, Ontario.

3) The Defendant is a singer and songwriter and a resident of Vancouver, British Columbia whose residential address is unknown.

4) The Plaintiff is a fervent and admiring fan of the Defendant.

5) At various times during the years 1992 and 1993 the Plaintiff wrote many confidential letters to the Defendant and sent them directly to the Defendant personally.

6) During the years 1992 and 1993 the Plaintiff sent the Defendant flowers and other items designed to show his admiration, love and adoration of her.

7) The letters written by the Plaintiff describe a relationship between an avid fan with a strong and obsessive love between him and a pop singer.

8) The letters written by the Plaintiff to the Defendant were not designed to be used for any commercial purpose and were designed solely for the personal, confidential use of the Defendant.

9) To the best of the Plaintiff's knowledge and belief, the Defendant received and read these letters.

10) The Defendant issued a collection of songs in CD form entitled ''Fumbling towards Ecstasy''. One of these songs was the song ''Possession''.

11) On the CD, ''Fumbling towards Ecstasy'', and in the accompanying literature, with the exception of the song called ''Fumbling towards Ecstasy'', the Defendant claims authorship and copyright of all the songs in the CD including the song ''Possession''.

12) The song ''Possession'' reveals the experience and perspective of a fan obsessed with a pop singer. Its theme consists of an examination of a fan's worship of a pop singer and the transformation of this worship into a menacingly obsessive and overwhelming need to control the pop singer who is known to the fan only through the music of the pop singer.

13) The Defendant used the letters of the Plaintiff as the basis in whole or in part for the creation of the theme of the song ''Possession'', the song and the CD ''Fumbling towards Ecstasy'' and commercialized this theme.

14) In basing the song, ''Possession'', and the CD ''Fumbling towards Ecstasy'' on the letters of the Plaintiff, the Defendant took unfair advantage of the confidential letters which had been received in confidence and profited from the wrongful use of the ideas, emotions and character described in the letters.

15) The actions of the Defendant in using the letters of the Defendant for the creation of the song, ''Possession'', and the CD ''Fumbling towards Ecstasy'', were done

without the consent of the Plaintiff and in
violation of the duty of confidentiality which
the Defendant was under towards the Plaintiff.

16) In basing the song ''Possession'' and the CD
''Fumbling towards Ecstasy'', on the letters
of the Plaintiff, the Defendant took the
fruits of the Plaintiff's labour, distorted
and modified the work of the Plaintiff and used
the Plaintiff's work in association with the
CD ''Fumbling towards Ecstasy'' in a manner
prejudicial to the honour and reputation of
the Plaintiff, thereby violating the moral
rights of the Plaintiff in the letters which
he sent to the Defendant.

17) The Defendant does not associate the name of
the Plaintiff with or give any credit to the
efforts of the Plaintiff in the creation of
the songs in the collection ''Fumbling towards
Ecstasy'' and in particular the song
''Possession''.

18) The Defendant has made considerable profits
from the sale of the collection of songs in
''Fumbling towards Ecstasy'' and from the song
''Possession''.

The Plaintiff proposes that this action be tried
in the City of Ottawa, in the Judicial
District of Ottawa-Carleton. Date: September
2, 1994

Kenneth Bickley
100 Sparks Street #1000
Ottawa, Ontario, K1P 5B7
(613) 237-6430
Solicitor for the Plaintiff

It is quite true I had intended to let the matter drop there; however, in a parallel — more palpable and plausible — world, sublime serendipity: *FRANK* publishes the following page-six update on Vandrei (13 August 1997):

The Death of Sarah's Stalker . . .
Questions about Obsessed Fan Won't Go Away

Will the trials of burgeoning superstardom ever end for Sarah McLachlan? The Vancouver-based chanteuse is currently embroiled in a nasty lawsuit over songwriting royalties filed by former bandmates, while her record label is busy putting the screws to a freelance journalist writing an unauthorized biography of the star (*FRANK* 250).

And now, just as McLachlan's career takes off with the release of her fourth album, SURFACING, there are renewed questions regarding the death of her most ardent fan.

Uwe Vandrei, a freelance computer programmer from Ottawa, was found dead in the woods near Manotick, ON, on 3 November, 1994 — an apparent suicide by gunshot.

The 34-year old Vandrei had spent the previous three years writing hundreds of obsessive letters to McLachlan, concluding with a lawsuit that claimed she had stolen text from his letters for use in a song about obsessive love.

Vandrei's statement-of-claim demanded $250,000 in punitive damages from McLachlan and her label, Nettwerk Records. He also wanted public credit for co-authorship of the song *Possession*, the break-out hit of McLachlan's best-selling album FUMBLING TOWARDS ECSTASY, as well as a face-to-face meeting with the singer to discuss the origin of the song.

With the history of spooky letter-writing and McLachlan's restraining order against him on the books, the local OPP donut-eaters didn't hesitate to declare Vandrei's demise a suicide.

According to the coroner, on 28 September, Vandrei had driven into the woods, climbed into the back of his pick-up truck, and blasted himself with a shotgun. The decomposing body was discovered by campers five days later.

Now there is speculation whether Vandrei may have visited McLachlan's recording studio in the Laurentians, an hour away from where his body was discovered. There is a strange suggestion that Vandrei may have visited the Morin Heights studio where McLachlan often recorded. Her producer, Pierre Marchand, lives nearby, and the area is also home to McLachlan's secret cabin retreat.

If Vandrei had successfully proven in court that *Possession* was lifted from his letters and amounted to a breach of of copyright, Nettwerk would have been forced to pay out big cake in royalties and punitive awards. With FUMBLING TOWARDS ECSTASY selling 2.6 million copies, damages could have charted in the hundreds of thousands.

Nettwerk and its two-fisted supremo, Terry McBride, have long been known to exert obsessive control over the label's artists. Typical of McBride was his interference in McLachlan's 1995 interview with *Chatelaine* magazine.

During a discussion with the reporter, Sarah implied that she may occasionally enjoy a box lunch of sushi.

When McBride learned that this howler would appear in the story, he got on the blower to *Chattlebrain* and insisted that Sarah's remarks were strictly off-the-record. A menacing lawyer's letter from Nettwerk followed and *Chattlebrain* was forced to spike the story. It eventually ran a softer McLachlan piece almost a year later. (McLachlan has since married the drummer in her band, sensitive soulmate Ash Frood.)

Although Vandrei's suit had been dismissed by Nettwerk management as frivolous harassment, Ottawa legalist Ken Bickley apparently believed there was some substance to the copyright claim even after his client died. Sources close to the family say Bickley pressured Vandrei's parents to continue the legal action on behalf of the estate, but they refused. Bickley won't discuss the case due to client-counsel privilege.

Vandrei's father, Gerhardt, a European immigrant, says he's willing to accept the suicide explanation and doesn't want to make waves. If it wasn't a suicide, he says he'd rather not know about it.

"I don't know what kind of business he was mixed up in. I don't want to get involved." Uwe's sister, Connie, is also reticent to discuss the death. "I'm not interested in finding out why my brother died," she told *FRANK*.

Family members say Vandrei was convinced before he died that he was being followed. There are also rumors that files on his computer were wiped clean after he died.

Conspiracy theorists on the Vandrei beat suggest that the private suicide is totally incongruent with the psycho-narcissistic pathology of obsessive fans. When stalkers cash in their own chips, they usually do so in a most public way to gain the attention of the objects of their desire — not hidden deep in the woods.

The physical details of Vandrei's death are locked away in a coroner's report until his next-of-kin requests its release. With Vandrei's parents unwilling to explore their son's death further, the "suicide" will remain case-closed.

Some dozen days later, *Maclean's* provides its cross-country readership with a mainstream perspective. In an unconsciously jaundiced fashion, its reporter injects a touch of the macabre into the otherwise party-line patter, leading into it by comparing the Fumblers with the Grateful Dead's devoted Deadheads "who follow their idol from venue to venue. But McLachlan seems unperturbed by the presence of those camp followers," reports Nicholas Jennings, "even though past experience might give her cause to fear such intense attention.

"For three years, McLachlan was stalked by an obsessed fan who followed her to Vancouver from his Ottawa home. Eventually, after receiving hundreds of letters from computer programmer Uwe Vandrei, McLachlan obtained a restraining order against him. She wrote about the experience in her hit song, *Possession*, prompting a bizarre lawsuit from Vandrei claiming 'breach of confidence' because McLachlan had used his correspondence as the basis for the song. Nothing came of the suit and Vandrei subsequently committed suicide in December 1994."

Naturally, I contact Textor Communications' CEO, web-wizard Lavina Galbraith, the cyber-designer who conceived and created several gorgeous sites scattered throughout Cyberia — including my own — on a question of Netiquette: "How," I ask, "does one go about retrieving messages from a dead man's mailbox?" In the same e-note, I wonder if she might also know how one goes about locating the Fumblers' archives for September 1994 or thereabouts.

Galbraith re-mails me a quarter-hour later with an applications program by the name of MacGzip and the address where the Fumblers' archives are stored. She also explains the protocol involved when one wishes to access another's e-mail account: "You contact the System Administrator and make a formal written request which must include authorization from the deceased's next-of-kin."

"Consider it done," I e-reply, "Connie Vandrei put the letter in the mail Xpress Post today. She also authorizes me to close down Uwe's account," I add, a kind of anti-morbid side note (for accuracy's sake on the Internet).

"Holy shit," she e-flashes back, "how in the hell did you do that?"

"Conn/ections."

```
Subject: [listserv@yoyo.cc.monash.edu.au: Output
of your job]
Date: Tue, 19 Aug 1997 15:35:01 -0400 (EDT)
From: ae064@freenet.carleton.ca (spare)
Reply-To: ae064@freenet.carleton.ca
To: fitz@onlink.net


============ Begin forwarded message
================

From: listserv@yoyo.cc.monash.edu.au (Listserv
v3.0.3)
To: ae064@freenet.carleton.ca (Uwe Vandrei)
Subject: Output of your job
Date: Tue, 06 Dec (1994)



> unsubscribe fumbling-towards-ecstasy
You have been removed from the list.
Command executed.
```

"You're lucky you got hold of me."

"Why's that?" I ask Connie, sole surviving sibling in the Vandrei family.

"Well, if you had talked to my parents," she sighs, "they won't talk to you at all."

"That's okay," I say, "I'm getting used to it."

"This is really weird because, I just wrote a letter to Sarah McLachlan and now, you! You call me out of the blue. I can't believe it."

"It's okay, Connie. This happens to me all the time."

"What's your sign?"

"Scorpio."

"Oh, God, no! Me, too!"

"There you go," I say, "we were meant to meet telephonically like this. How often do you visit your folks?"

"Once a year, in the summer, that's all I can afford."

"And, where are your parents now?"

Connie explains their absence and adds that I'm the first person who's ever called her about Uwe. She also describes the contents of the letter she'd sent McLachlan at Nettwerk Productions:

"I didn't say much, just that I was sorry. I read another article in the paper; and, she mentioned a rabid fan who'd ending up killing himself and I thought she was speaking of my brother. So, I just wrote her a letter saying, 'Correct me if I'm wrong; but, this stalker you keep speaking of, it sounds like you're talking about my brother'; and then, I just said I was sorry she was having so much trouble with fans. I couldn't live with that. And, I heard she just got married — so, I wanted to congratulate her. That's about it. That's all. It was a nice letter. I don't know if she'll even get it. Doubt it."

See, I'd called Connie's parents and, since both were elsewhere, Connie had answered. As I was to discover much later, she spoke truthfully when she averred I was lucky I'd reached her. During that first conversation, however, I simply established contact with her and tried to determine her attitude towards the apparent suicide of her older brother, an attitude, I would soon discover, which veered drastically from the message-track.

At her parents', Connie felt uncomfortable discussing the details surrounding Uwe's death. Both parents, she'd told me, had profoundly suffered the devastating effects of losing their only son, each in his or her own way. Anita Vandrei, always on good terms with Uwe and a friend to whom he looked for advice, suffered no less than Gerhardt, Uwe's father (whose final conversation with his 34-year-old son, unfortunately, had ended on an argumentative note).

Judith Fitzgerald: Before we begin, it's important that you understand I'm writing an unauthorized biography of Sarah McLachlan.

Connie Vandrei: Yeah, right. I know that.

No, I mean, for the record, I have to establish that fact with you so the playing field's level, you know? These are the rules; I have both an ethical and legal obligation to tell you what I'm doing and to make certain you understand the implications of that.

Yeah, I understand. You're recording these conversations and you're going to quote me.

Right. Unless you tell me something you consider off-the-record; then, you just say so. Did you read the articles and stuff I sent you?

Yeah.

Okay, I'm going to refer to the information in those articles and ask you to give your opinion or verification or correction, okay?

Okay. Geez, *Maclean's*! I can't believe they can write those lies and get away with it because my brother's dead.

Apparently, there's nothing you can do, according to a professional I asked, an expert in libel and stuff . . .

You mean, anybody can write whatever in the hell they feel like writing about a dead person?

Technically, it sounds like that.

Even if it's all a bunch of lies?

Looks like. I'm sorry. I wish I had another answer. I don't; but, you do. You can tell me the truth, your truth, the truth about your brother. Do you believe Uwe Vandrei committed suicide?

Am I in danger?

Not as far as I can tell, why?

Why? I don't want to end up dead is why.

What makes you think you will?

Well, it doesn't take a brain surgeon to figure out if Uwe didn't commit suicide; then, you know . . . I'm worried about my parents. My mom can't handle any of this; and, I think that's why my dad isn't doing anything, because of my mother. I'm scared it's going to be the death of her, you know?

Yeah, I know. You sure you want to do this?

Yeah, I mean, he's my brother. He's their son. I was always suspicious. You're lucky you got me; I only visit my parents once a year, in July. If you'd got my mom or dad . . . My parents wouldn't have talked to you. It's so weird that you'd called when they were out and I was the only one there to answer the 'phone . . .

You don't think either of them would speak with me?

No way.

Did anybody ever contact you or speak with you about Uwe's death?

No, never. Nobody did. Not until you called me at my parents.

Were you and your brother close?

Yes and no, you know? We're very close in age and we grew up together. You know, normal brother and sister stuff. We were always in contact, one way or another though, until he died. . . . It's hard to explain. When I say we weren't really close, what I mean is we'd both grown up and followed different paths and lived in different cities and stuff. We didn't have a lot in common. He was into things that didn't interest me in the slightest and vice versa. He was highly intelligent and that kind of got on my nerves, sometimes. He always had his nose in the books. If he wanted to play with anything, it would be like getting out a science kit or something. He tried reading the encyclopedia from A-Z. I remember all this because, at the time, I thought, God, how boring. And, when we were at LaSalle — LaSalle High School in Kingston — I always got bothered because people would come up to me and say, 'Your brother is so intelligent; what's your problem?'

Was he a loner in high school?

Get out! Uwe had friends — lots of them — friends like him. They were really into computers and being the best they could be. They weren't into drinking or going out drinking and partying; they never did any of that. They were into expanding their minds — all of them, the people he hung out with. And, a lot of them did go into the military.

Did Uwe go to university?

He didn't go right into university because he went into the military. He went after that, though; but he was in the military for years and he was gone a lot. As soon as he got out of high school he took off and went into the military and he was all over the place with them. He worked in Quebec for a while before he quit.

What kind of work?

He was working on radar stuff at the airport; he was in the tower monitoring their computers; he was full-time employed with the army for a long time.

Did he tell you why he quit?

Yeah, they were going to ship him to the Northwest Territories. No way he wanted to go there. That's when he decided he wanted out, when they were going to send him there. He didn't want to be that far away from everybody; so, he decided to go out on his own, to go freelance. He only did that for the last little while.

In Vanier? Ottawa?

Yeah, he lived in Vanier and he had jobs with the government there, freelance jobs, I think. I mean, I'm not into computers and stuff so, he wouldn't tell me a whole lot about what he was doing because I wouldn't know what he was talking about anyway, right?

Right. Did he have girlfriends that you recall?

Yeah, he had girlfriends. I met a few of them over the years; and, he actually lived with a girl once, when he was in the military, for a while. But, he said, 'Oh, I can't stand it. She's always in my way. She's always over my shoulder. I can't live with her'. I could see that. I could see him saying that. He could never live with anybody, anyway, I don't think. I couldn't see it.

Was he in debt? Did he have investments going sour?

No, he wasn't in debt. He didn't have financial problems; he didn't have bad investments that I'm aware of. He had tons of computer and music stuff and a motorcycle he could have sold. His rent was paid for three years in advance, eh?

What did he look like? Can you describe him for me, physically?

He was almost completely bald. He was taller than me — I'm 163 cm and he was about 10 or so cm taller — He wore glasses, always wire-rimmed glasses. He had problems with his eyes; he always had glasses in school. He didn't smoke. He didn't drink or do drugs. Uwe was real clean-cut; he was very strong and healthy; he was a health nut! He was right into exercizing and working out, he was. And, he loved driving his motorcycle, a really good one. But, he was straight. Didn't have a criminal record, anything like that. He was the kind of guy who followed the rules, law-abiding. He even paid his parking tickets.

What else did he drive?

His truck, a black one.

A Mazda?

Yeah, I think so . . . I think it was a Mazda, a black Mazda.

When was the last time you talked to him?

That spring or summer. We didn't talk all that much; but we did keep in touch by writing letters. Uwe preferred it that way. He said it helped him think more clearly. We corresponded by letters. I'd written him a letter saying I was scared he was going to do something because he was so obsessed with her and that. He sent me a letter back saying, 'Don't be silly; I'm not going to do anything stupid over Sarah. Life goes on, with her or without her, *c'est la vie*, whatever'. It sounded to me like he really didn't care; he knew there was a chance he was never going to be with her. His letters were beautiful. They were like poetry.

Did you keep them?

I have them; I keep them together in a big envelope.

Can you send them to me?

I can send you some stuff, some of his poems.

Can you read one or two of the letters to me so I can hear how they sound?

Yeah, I guess. . . . This one's dated 23 April 1994. I'd just written to him telling him he was nuts, to go get help because he was so obsessed. I mean, you know what he said to me the day after our wedding? He said, 'Well, Connie, I didn't really want to come to your wedding' 'cause there was a Sarah McLachlan concert he was going to miss! Idiot! But, that was Uwe; he was very straightforward. He also gave us quite a large sum of money for a wedding present, though, you should know that, too. But, this letter, it's dated 23 April? It was one of the last letters I ever got from him. It's really eerie, reading them. He said he was going to write more; but, he never did.

You don't have to, you know?

I know, I know. In my heart, I still don't know if he committed suicide. Until it is positively proved to me, I can't accept that, I guess. I'm having a lot of trouble sleeping. It's been hard, a little. It wouldn't do them any good, though — Would it? — to harm me? I mean, I hope it wouldn't do them any good to harm me. . . . Or you. . . .

Who?

Them.

Who are they?

I don't know. I can't say for sure.

What does the letter say? Can you read it now?

Where's your sense of wonder, magic and romance? I keep trying to find the starting point to all the things my first letter did not cover, to all the things that have happened to me to cause me to arrive at this world view. That starting point is just a human being. [Because I'd said to him, 'Sarah's just a human being'. I told him he couldn't just put another person on a pedestal.] Thank you for your candid letter for it gives me a perspective as to your world view and offers a challenge of my own view. I will start a series of letters with the goal of learning to love you. I prefer this format because it gives me time to reflect, organize thoughts and gives you a record upon which you can contemplate. Your only responsibility is to write back candidly, honestly challenge anything I tell you. 'Just a human being.' I have come to understand that we are programmed and conditioned by society to meet its mediocre goals, to limit our true potential. Someone else has failed — or never even dared — and then tells you that it can't be done. We must keep people dependent for the consumer market. Perms, dyes, come out ... The turning point came when I started to throw off the programming. I questioned every thing I did, every habit, everything I'd been taught to accept as normal. I looked inside without expectation, open to whatever would arrive and boy did I get a surprise. Some of them are very difficult to deal with. Very time-consuming; but, so what? What more important thing did I have to do but let myself become all I can be? I want to send you some reading material; and, I will, when I come across the right book [He never did send me anything.] So on to your concerns. I can, in fact, prove to you — line by line — where those lyrics come from; but, I'm not one to kiss and tell. Believe me, I tried very hard to find another interpretation. The references and sentiments are just too specific to be mistaken. If anyone has a problem, it is Sarah, for being so touched and inspired by my expressions of love and not realizing that she is, in fact, emotionally involved with me. Yes, this is an obsession for me. Consider. I imagined her before I discovered her; that is, I built a woman of very specific sentiments, emotions, expressions. Consider the shock to discover that such a creature actually exists. Yes, I do know her. That is one reason the letters had such a profound effect. Imagine someone sending you letters telling you your deepest secrets. It's all pretty metaphysical Twilight-Zone stuff. As to what I am going to do about it? Nothing drastic. The occasional love letter or gift when I am so inspired. This leads me to another point. We each have a path to walk and lessons to learn. Some paths are more unique than others — mine has become unique because I have opened myself to it. My current lesson is to accept that even if I have touched Sarah so profoundly, she chooses to keep her distance. So be it. Life goes on, but never like before. Imagine if Jon Bon Jovi had put your love letters to songs, played them on national television, and didn't even bother to call and thank you. Anyway, tell me, Connie, where are your limitations, frustrations? Any victories lately? The good news is you have far more potential than you are aware of. Let me show it to you. It just now occurred to me that we might be connected; that is, the things that have happened to me may yet happen to you. What are those things? They are the realization that everything you've been taught is wrong, that nothing is as it seems; and, that most of the world's crazy. [The whole letter's done on computer and he just signs it *Uwe*].

How old was he when he died?

Thirty-four; he would have been 35 on 28 February 1995.

How old are you?

I'm going to be 34 in November. How old are you?

Forty-four. I'm going to be 45 in November. You're a kid.

So was Uwe.

Yeah. McLachlan says somewhere she figures kids grow up when they're about 19 to 23. I don't think most kids ever grow up, really. We just grow older, you know what I mean?

Older or wrinklier.

Yeah, maybe. Life certainly gets wrinklier. Did Uwe ever seek professional help, that you know of?

He did. He told me he had. He said he felt like the person was patronizing him instead of listening to him; so, he gave up on it.

Did anybody ever give him a name for his obsessive behavior?

Yes. It was a complicated name; but, he knew what it was.

Was it Obsessive Compulsive Disorder?

I think it might have been. I can't say for sure.

Was he taking any medications for it? Did he have any other obsessions, to your knowledge?

No, I don't think so. Not that he told me about, anyway. And, I don't think he had any other obsessions. He had this thing about Sarah; but it had started to fade away, too, you know? He was more interested in music. He wanted to make his own music. I had tons of musical equipment that I had to sell of his after. His basement was full of recording equipment and stuff; he was really into it. There were synthesizers and old guitars, all kinds of stuff. He wasn't just into Sarah's music; he was into a lot of other stuff. Liona Boyd, Sade, all kinds. He loved music. He wanted to make music. That was the biggest passion in his life. . . .

Nobody's perfect (or everybody is). Did he ever mention something called the Fumbling-Towards-Ecstasy List on the Internet? Did he ever mention a guy by the name of David Dalton to you, a guy on this List?

Not that I recall. Did David Dalton kill him?

God, no. Nothing like that. David Dalton told him to go to another List on the Internet — alt.support.depression — for help. The Internet's got a group for just about anything and everything that ails you or twizzes your nix, from Angels to Druids to Wicca to Zen. You name it, you'll find it there somewhere. And, the people on the 'Net form communities, you know, tiny villages — I call 'em cybertribes — in the virtual global village. Anyway, Dalton's famous, listed right below your brother in the Q & A thing I mentioned, the FAQ. Interesting individual. But, do you think you can walk me through everything you remember that may or may not apply to Uwe's death?

I can try. It'll be three years next month. I try not to think about it, usually . . .

Don't blame you, Connie. It's not something that bears too much dwelling upon. Like, if you have to hang up or do something else, just let me know. I think it's important, though, to just go over every little thing you thought or saw or noticed or heard or read or whatever. Take your time; we can do this in stages, okay? We don't have to do it all today. We can take as long as you need, okay?

Okay. Well, I think Uwe fell in love with her — got obsessed with her — around the fall of 1991. Why? Because I remember Uwe, years and years ago, saying something about Sarah and he couldn't understand how they let her do that. He didn't like the way they were portraying Sarah. He hated the image they were creating. In one of the videos, she was naked and covered in mud or something. He didn't think it was right. Also, I say it was around then because I had just gotten married and he was talking about going to see her in concerts and stuff like that, then.

Did he say where?

Not usually. Mostly places he could drive to; and, I think, he'd rigged up the mattress in the back of his truck so he could get some sleep before driving back home the next morning. He was very careful about stuff like that.

Is that why he lived in Vanier, in Ottawa?

Partially, maybe; but, no, mostly it was because that's where he could most easily find work, after he left the army.

And, what did he tell you about his obsession?

Not a lot. He said he'd sent a couple of letters, some poems and a few gifts — a scarf, some perfume, a piece of jewellery, flowers, things like that. And, when I was going through the stuff? I found a beautiful beautiful jewelry box with Sarah McLachlan's name engraved on it. I don't know whether that was a gift for her or what. I wanted it; but my parents have it on their shelf now. Mom wanted it. He talked more about it with Mom, really. And, even my mom said, 'You know, it is possible that he did write it' because, you know, she had been close to my brother and my brother had sworn up and down, 'Mom, I did. That song is from my letter. That song was taken from my letter to her'; and, Uwe didn't lie. He didn't invent things. He didn't imagine things. But, Mom said, 'I couldn't go through court and prove that, though. I don't want to do it; I don't even want to think about it'.

This is a little more difficult, Connie. I want you to take a few deep breaths; and, if you don't understand or need a break or whatever, say so, okay? We've got all the time in the world. I've got to take my own deep breaths, anyway. Okay. You mentioned your parents received first a letter and a little bit after, a package from Uwe, right?

Right.

When was that?

It was, I think, after the letter he'd sent where he said he had absolutely no doubt that those were his words and he could prove it to me but he wasn't one to kiss and tell. And, you know what? Those words keep sticking in my mind, 'Kiss and tell. Kiss and tell'. Is that a hint? Is there something in that? Is it written down somewhere? Is it on one of the computers? Is there a file called "Kiss and Tell" or what? Anyway, Uwe did say, in this letter to my parents, that he was going to go public with it and release it to the press or whatever. And, we just thought, 'Yeah, right'. He said we'd probably read about it in the papers; but we never heard anything until you called. That's the first time anybody tried to contact us about it or anything. . . .

And, the package? When did Uwe send the package?

July 1994. I know because I always visit them around the middle of July; and we found out later that year he had died. He'd sent us this big package. I was visiting, then. I said to my Dad, 'Why is he sending us all this stuff?'

What was in that package? Did he send another one like it to anybody else?

There was a whole bunch of stuff, letters and stuff. A lot of it, though, was just articles about her in the paper and that. He'd circled stuff; I don't know exactly what the reason was for everything he highlighted. No, he didn't send it to anybody else. He sent another package of stuff to the press, I think; but not this stuff. This was very private. We thought he might have been frightened or something. I sat down with the package and read through everything very carefully, all of it. I couldn't quite figure out some of the underlined and circled stuff; but, then, I didn't know the whole story (and, to tell you the truth, I'm not a fan of her music. I prefer hip-hop and stuff like that, okay?).

Okay by me. Music's another word for joy in my dictionary, Connie. If we all liked exactly the same music all the time, we'd all be bored silly, right?

Variety's the spice of life.

You got it, Pontiac. Anything else in the stuff Uwe sent you remember?

Uwe wrote to my parents that they'd told Sarah a story about how he was an ex-con in for rape. I don't know how he knew that; but he said he'd talked to somebody who'd told him that and he was horrified. Uwe was obsessed, Judith. We all knew that; but, he wasn't psycho or anything. He didn't follow her around or go to Vancouver and hang in her windows like they said he did.

Who said he did?

Uwe said that's what they'd said about him. Uwe sent her letters and gifts. He went to as many concerts as he could go to. That's all he did. He didn't even telephone her. He was very careful about not stepping over the line. I know that about him. He was not the type of person who didn't know the difference between right and wrong; and, he knew very well what he could do according to the law and what he couldn't do. He didn't do anything illegal. We thought he was crazy; but he was never violent or anything. He had a psychological problem; but he was never the type of person who would want to hurt anyone, ever. He couldn't hurt others. It just wasn't part of his personality; and, if he hadn't had that disorder, he would've probably recognised what he was doing. He loved her. He couldn't see how it could be upsetting, to be loved by him. That's all. And, I just kept thinking, she must've had another somebody bugging her because this stuff was so unreal and so unlike Uwe.

Looks like she did; but it wasn't your brother.

Who was it, then?

Did Uwe ever go to Vancouver?

No. I don't think he did.

Well, a source in the media (among others) corroborates that another person, in Vancouver, spotted McLachlan at a coffee shop about two blocks from her home and took it upon themselves to escort her there, apparently after waiting several days to do so. And according to a report in Maclean's . . .

P-f-f-t! Who's gonna believe *them?*

Same reporter, too. H-m-m . . . Anyway, according to this report I read dated 28 March 1994 — wait a minute, I'll read it to you: "McLachlan's fans include some intense letter writers — a few of whom have developed elaborate fantasies about the singer. One such follower, who believed her songs were written specifically for him, even moved to Vancouver to be close to the object of his obsession. McLachlan felt so threatened that in 1992 she had a police restraining order placed on the man."

No way it was Uwe, then. Uwe had just started writing her around the time I got married. And, he sure as hell wasn't living in Vancouver in 1992. So, there goes that bullshit theory. . . .

Looks like. That's the one they apparently ringed in with the restrainer. And, I heard — but it's just a rumor — the guy was a student or intern or something. Anyway, according to one of my sources, McLachlan makes a point of telling certain select media people "about TWO guys who stalked her" (and, she told my source this when she interviewed her in Vancouver so, I corroborated the story about McLachlan's birth mother was true 'cause I'm the one who found her in Halifax and she corroborated McLachlan was still telling media she had "two stalkers").

Uwe never stalked her, ever. And, he never had a restraining order against him. Uwe never followed her around or anything. I had heard there was; but, the police told my dad there never was. My dad clearly remembers that. I was sure there was; but, my dad said, 'No, the police said there wasn't!' It upsets him to think people even think that. By the way, did I tell you? I got my letter back from Nettwerk today; they didn't even open it. They just sent it right back.

Uwe mentions, in one of his letters he sent in the media package, that Nettwerk put up a mail screen. I think that's one of the letters he also copied to Pierre Marchand, her producer. Did Uwe ever talk to you about his dealings with Kenneth J. Bickley, the lawyer he hired to draw up his Statement of Claim?

No. I didn't know about it until much later, after the police told us they'd found Uwe.

What happened to the lawsuit?

Dad let it go. The lawyer asked my dad; and, he said, 'No, forget it'. He didn't want to do it.

So, it was ended?

It was ended as soon as my brother died.

When was that?

The day they found him, we got a call. It was 3 November; I know it was because it was the day before my birthday. We got the call that they'd found him; but, the police said he'd already been dead a couple of months. I've been thinking. Wouldn't Uwe's lawyer have a copy of the letter that proves or whatever that what he says is true? Like, wouldn't he have anything that had to do with that song?

He would have everything that has to do with that song. Why?

Because of the break-in.

The break-in?

Yeah, we didn't think anything of it at the time; we didn't even think to check Uwe's package. My parents come up for Christmas here each year. They always come up at Christmas. I always go to Kingston in July. When my parents got back, there had been a break-in. A door had been smashed in; but, it was, like, right around Christmas or just before or whatever. It was December 1995. They took all of Uwe's jewelry for some reason. Mom can't figure that out; it was just cheap stuff. And, they took a VCR and something from Mom's jewelry. It's not like she's got a huge collection, eh? What's weird is my dad's office. They never even went in there. Whoever it was, they didn't go in there; I don't even know why; and, that would make the most sense to us. . . .

Did they report it? Is there an incident number?

Yes, they reported it. There's a record of it; they reported it to the Kingston police . . .

What kind of jewelry did Uwe have?

Cheap stuff. Nothing worth anything . . .

Can you describe it, generally, like, was it beads or what?

It was all silver. With some stones in it and weird designs; kind of ugly; we never did figure out what. . . .

When the book's published, check out the jewelry okay? Take a look at the pictures; and, then tell me if it looked like that or not.

Okay. But, I started thinking, right? Just after you called that day. Wow, did they take something out of there? That stuff was just sitting in a cabinet in the living room. It wouldn't be hard to find. And, my heart started pounding really fast. I just got this creepy feeling. I went and sat down to read Uwe's package and it was gone. The letter with the words of that song, the one he'd written to her in March 1992. It was gone. I swear to God I saw it the first time; and then, after you called me, I sat down and went through everything and I didn't see it. Then, I started thinking, where the hell did I see it? And then, I thought, maybe my dad stashed it somewhere else and he's not telling me. I don't know. Like, maybe because you called.

Did you ask him?

No. You don't question my dad. . . . He has his view and that's that. Uwe was like that, too, eh? But, I love my parents; and, I don't want you to give the wrong impression about them. They worked hard all their lives. My dad worked in the Kingston Pen before he retired. He's really glad to be retired. We're just ordinary Canadians, you know? Except Uwe. Uwe wasn't, completely; he was brilliant. And, very bossy, too. You know what he did one time? This was at my parents' home, right? Mom and Dad had some people over to play cards this one time; and, Uwe was down in the basement or something. Okay, it's our parents' house, right? Uwe comes up and says to my parents and their friends, 'Do you people realize just how much noise you're making?'. This was to *our* parents, in *their* house, having fun with *their* friends!

No kidding. Pretty uppity for a kid.

That was Uwe. He's very sure of himself. Always. Like, the black car that showed up on his street? I thought it might be the police; he didn't. He thought he was being watched; I thought it might be somebody else on the street. He didn't. He said he'd done several tests, just to make sure he wasn't being paranoid. And then, this is so weird, he said he'd almost been run down by a Bell-Canada van; and, I thought he was exaggerating. He said, 'No, it didn't look like Bell-Canada guys; but it looked like it was a Bell-Canada van, though.' But, he couldn't be sure. I mean, he was very worried. He even called *me* to talk about it. I think that's when he thought he should get a licence for a gun. He got the form; but he never even filled it out.

I did try calling your brother's lawyer, right? Several times. He never returned a single call. Not a one. I even explained to his assistant that I didn't want to talk about the lawsuit; I would appreciate it if he could just describe Uwe's state of mind, etc. when he filed the Statement of Claim. He must have seen him a couple of times before 2 September that year; it's a complicated action; and, since Bickley believed his case had merit enough to file a Statement of Claim, he'd want to be pretty damned sure to get the details right on this particular one. Never returned a call. Zip. Zero. Nada. Big fat booming silence.

Well, that's probably because my dad told him he wasn't interested in pursuing it at all.

Well, Bickley will have all that documentation in his files . . . So, the police contacted your dad for the first time on 3 November, the day before your birthday?

Yeah, that's why I will never forget it. And, they positively identified my brother on my birthday. They asked my parents for the name of his dentist. They told him it could take two weeks to identify Uwe. The very next day, they phoned my dad and said it was proved who it was and they could get the body and do whatever they wanted with it.

No autopsy?

Don't think so.

No inquest?

No.

What did they tell your family, as best as you can remember?

The way they did contact my parents — it was because of the truck.

Did the truck have a cap on it?

Yeah, I'm pretty sure it did.

Okay, what else do you remember?

He was in the back of the truck, on the makeshift mattress — like a bed — listening to her music with the headphones on. They told us he just asphyxiated himself; he put a vacuum-cleaner hose from the pipe into the back of the truck and taped it all up. That's one thing the police did say. He was very accurate in sealing it up. They said he did an awfully professional job. They said to my dad, 'He really knew what he was doing because he did such an accurate job. A very professional job'.

They didn't say what kind of tape?

No, they didn't say what kind of tape, just that he'd done a really professional job of it. It was sealed up tight. Airtight. And, they'd said he'd made sure that he had lots of gas, like, a full tank. They told my dad he really knew what he was doing. It was all real professional. They said he made himself real comfortable, put the headphones on, closed his eyes and went to sleep.

No suicide note?

No. None. Nothing.

No goodbye?

No. No, they never found a note or tape or received any letters afterwards. Nothing except that one call from somebody who said they were a friend of Uwe's.

When was that, again?

Late November or early December, about a month after the cops told us they'd found Uwe. My mom said she thought the call was suspicious; but she couldn't put her finger on it. Something about what the guy said didn't sit right with her. Besides, he also made a point — two or three times — like really *stressing* the point (or so my mom thought), of saying he'd seen Uwe in October and couldn't believe he was dead. Oh, he kept saying he was so sorry to hear about Uwe's death. But my mom didn't recognize either the guy's voice or his name (and she was closest to Uwe, right?). And, she just let the guy go on and didn't bother to correct him — she knew damned well Uwe had been dead since September. No way, she thought, this guy had seen him in October like he said. But she didn't correct him because something about the call gave her the creeps.

Well, maybe Uwe had a friend who was temporally challenged and couldn't keep track of months and stuff; or, maybe they were just making sure Anita and Gerhardt were your parents?

That crossed her mind. It also crossed her mind they were trying to plant the idea he'd been alive in October; but, you know, they were still in shock over the death. But I remember it because my mom mentioned it when they came for Christmas in '94. But it wasn't until I started telling them the stuff you'd found that they starting going over the stuff they'd put out of their minds.

So, did your parents tell this caller they'd planned to visit with you like every Christmas?

I think so; but, I don't know. I can't say for sure. Anyway, the break-in was the *following* Christmas. . . .

Where did the police say they found the truck?

Out in North Gower, about 20 meters off Dwyer Hill Road. It was Manotick police. I think that's when they said a group of hunters found him.

That makes sense. The truck wouldn't be found right away; that's a fair distance from the road, right? And, that's right around hunting season, too, isn't it?

Dad asked the police if they wanted him to identify the body. The police said it was so badly decomposed, there was no body to look at. I couldn't get those lines out of my head, 'So badly decomposed' and 'skeletal remains' . . . I just couldn't imagine. . . .

I know what you mean. I get it too. I can barely look at his picture.

Well, they told my dad it was being investigated. We didn't know why; but, we figured, well, he's going through court with this thing.

Actually, it's standard procedure, when a death's ruled an "apparent suicide." That means, as one exceptional road warrior told me, "Appears like a suicide. Appears. And we always put that because we're not sure; it could be a homicide."

What's a road warrior?

It's not a "what", it's a "who": Sgt. Michael Brehmer, 20-year vet with the OPP. Likes McLachlan's music. Owns two of her CDs, SOLACE *and* FUMBLING. *He also said it was standard procedure to notify survivors that dental identification can take up to two weeks (so the survivors can prepare themselves if they have to wait).*

Well, the coroner says the cause of death was 'presumed carbon-monoxide poisoning'. It's in the report. I just got it in the mail today.

That's why you're upset, right?

Well, it's . . . gruesome.

It's okay. We can do this later.

No, I'm okay. You've got to hear what else.

What else?

It says Uwe was pronounced dead on 3 November 1994. That's wrong. They had to get the dental records.

Do they list the means?

All it says is, "Undetermined."

What about the date presumed dead?

28 September 1994.

Is the autopsy included in the report?

Yes. It says, "Made upon the body of Vandrei, in the city of Ottawa in the Province of Ontario, on the 4th day of November 1994 at about six-seven weeks after death." And then there's stuff about the time the examination commenced.

"The body was identified to me with a comparison of dental records." And there's a whole page of organs and stuff that's blank 'cause I guess there was nothing left . . . ? And then, on the last page, it describes bone marrow: "In a state of decomposition. No cellular elements . . ."

What does the autopsy give as the cause of death?

"Presumed carbon-monoxide poisoning based on circumstances and evidence only. Skeletal remains." It's dated 7 November 1994.

So, there was an autopsy?

Yeah. They found his body on 3 November; and, the autopsy says "six or seven" weeks. So, he might have been dead as early as 15 September?

Yeah. That's what I'm thinking. I'm also thinking he posted his letter to the F-T-E List on the Internet on 12 September at 9:40 in the morning. And, you know what else? I went and checked his original post to the List and found out a couple of things in the archives. It's all computer-related stuff; but, get this: The letter that everybody reads on the Internet is missing a key piece of information that appears in the post he sent. He wrote it the Friday before, on 9 September, right? You know Uwe, he was very conscientious about that kind of stuff. Right on the original letter he wrote, "From Uwe Vandrei Ottawa, Ont. 9 Sept. 1994"; Uwe also wrote the following paragraph which he had included in his media-package letter but either refrained from posting it or, by the time the post showed up in the archives, it had been edited: "The reason I contest her statements, is because I know where the inspiration for 'Possession' was actually derived. Enclosed you will find a copy of a letter I sent to her in mid-March of 1992. I cannot prove the date of publication. The only person who can do that is the person who currently possesses the letter (presumably Sarah). To give you a little background..." Still, he waited, for some reason, until the following Monday, 12 September, before he actually posted it. It was his one-and-only post to the F-T-E List, ever. Somebody else on the List, a couple months later, mentions the fact Uwe only made that one post to the list.

Weird.

Know what else? After Uwe posted his letter? Later that day on this

List, at 4:36 p.m., Cathy Barrett — she's on the same List as a Nettwerk resource person and she posts tour schedules and upcoming appearances and stuff. So did another guy named Lane, for a while, shortly after all this happened; and people on the List started whining about not hearing anything from Nettwerk about McLachlan's tours and appearances and all the important stuff. Anyway, Barrett sends an e-message to the list asking members if someone can forward their copy of Uwe's message to her because she says her copy of the auto-generated e-mail sent to all Fumblers on the list has been "edited" and she needs to see the whole thing. That doesn't make sense, Con. If a letter is sent through the main computer, it's automatically sent to everybody. No way in this world one of those 300 machine-made messages differed from the 299 or so identical messages. A little later, somebody posts a message telling every other subscriber not to flood Nettwerk's e-mailbox with copies of Uwe's post because this person's already sent a copy of it to "cathy b" (which is how she signs her name on the List). Then, at 5:23 p.m., Nettwerk issues its official statement on Uwe's post to the list. It says something to the effect Nettwerk flat out denies all of your brother's allegations. It's from Nettwerk, not cathy b.

Isn't Cathy Barrett Terry McBride's wife? Didn't Uwe tell me that? Her name was Cathy or Catherine or something, anyway.

Yeah, that's what I've heard, too. Don't know, though. Don't much care, either. Anyway, that happened on the Monday, right after Uwe posted. He waited a whole weekend to send the letter he'd written on Friday. Why? Why didn't he send it when he wrote it? What happened between Friday — and, it had to have been midday-ish Friday because it's quite a long document — and Monday that caused Uwe to tell the whole world about the lawsuit he'd put into motion nine days earlier on 2 September 1994 (which is the date on the Statement of Claim)? More to the point, why'd Uwe write the thing on Friday in the first place? Did somebody call him Friday morning and say something to him that really frightened him? I mean, he knew the situation he was in at the time, judging by what you've heard from Uwe — why would he risk the wrath of God by alerting the world to the fact he was disputing authorship of the song, "Possession" and, worse, he was claiming infringement of his right to reasonably trust his letters addressed to McLachlan would not become public fodder.

Uwe was very careful and methodical. He must have had a reason for what he did; he wasn't the impulsive type.

Obviously not. I have a few theories. You interested?

Yeah.

On 11 September 1994, McLachlan gave a concert in Montreal, about 130 kilometers away from Ottawa. You think Uwe's going to miss it, especially considering the fact he'd know her tour sked and he'd know that, right after she played Montreal, she'd hit the road for points south and overseas for a long long time?

Doubt it. I can't see that. He'd go for sure, seeing as how it was *that* close.

Well, maybe that's why he composed the letter he posted on Friday 9 September. Maybe somebody called him and told him not to show up in Montreal come Sunday 11 September. Maybe he promised he wouldn't but couldn't stay away; or, more likely, maybe somebody called him that Friday to find out if he was going to the concert; and, when he refused to back down, maybe the caller struck a deal with him to meet him at his place and talk this thing over mano à mano? Maybe that's the company he was expecting? Or, what about this? He posts the article on Monday morning after driving back from Montreal because something might have so scared him at the concert, he felt it essential to do so. Likely, if you're under surveillance, you're going to be watched and followed very closely. Or, maybe he'd found a date at the Montreal concert and had invited her over? Or, maybe he met an old friend there? All kinds of things could have happened; but, whatever happened, we do know Uwe was preparing for company, right? As for the rest, who knows? God and Uwe. Just a couple of theories, though, to give you an idea of what might have happened. What do you think?

I think Mom would agree with you.

She would? Why?

She said she thought something like that must've happened; Uwe wasn't a real big entertainer, you know? That's why she thought it was so weird he'd gone to the trouble of tidying up and preparing stuff for visitors.

Smart lady. Get this: Remember the authorization you gave me to close down Uwe's account on the Internet?

Yeah.

Yeah, I did. And, when I did, Sheila Alder — she was great and sends, by the way, genuine condolences to you and your family — she closed down Uwe's account while I was on the telephone with her. She walked me through everything she was doing.

Thank God it's closed down. Tell Sheila we appreciate her condolences and her help shutting it down. Now, those people won't be able to make fun of my brother.

I agree with you, Con. I corresponded with a few of those people. I couldn't believe how heartless, mindless and egomaniacal — megalomaniacal — they were. It made me want to puke. They post this shit; but they don't know shit about shit, let alone any of the facts. It gets them tons of attention at the expense of a dead man (who can't defend himself). Bloody parasitic cowards, going on about how Uwe committed suicide because of the nasty 'flames' he received on the F-T-E List. But, Uwe wasn't a subscriber. And, as Sheila will corroborate, there were only three measly messages in his mailbox. If he were a subscriber, he would have received at least 30 e-mails a day. I received as many as 150 in a 24-hour period during the short time I subscribed to the List. No, Sheila said the rest of the stuff was administrative notices, updates and the like from Carleton Freenet. Two of the e-mails sent Uwe were from private individuals. The third, on 6 December 1994, was from the F-T-E computer, an auto-generated response: "Command executed." It's a piece of machine-generated e-mailery, a response to a command somebody sent to get Uwe off a list he'd posted to only once in his 34 years on the planet. And, since I subscribed and then unsubscribed to the same list — as a test — I know it takes about 24 hours to get off the thing. Uwe, according to both the coroner and pathologist, was dead months before. He never sent an e-mail requesting he be taken off a mailing list I don't believe he was ever on, if you follow me.

Yeah, I follow you.

One of the two e-mails was sent on the 14th; but Carleton Freenet doesn't include the time of day in messages that have a different year on them. The other was sent on 16th September. Just the usual stuff one gets. Uwe, like most of us who depend on the Internet for various reasons, would've checked his mail a couple of times a day. Dalton? He told me he recalled sending Uwe a message after the post about alt.support.depression. That message wasn't there. Dalton was, however, an active participant in the post-post discussion on 12/13 September. Still, that's not the main point. What does matter — at least, to us — is what Sheila Alder told me the day I closed down Uwe's account.

What did she tell you? What?

Uwe logged onto the system for the last time, ever, on 14 September 1994. So, if he logged on for the last time on 14 September, maybe he died that day or the next or the next all the way up to the 22 September? Doesn't the Coroner say 28 September?

Yeah. That's three mistakes. Uwe had a truck, not a van. He didn't die on 28 September. And the date they give for his official death is wrong. Not only that, eh? They spelled our name wrong. They called him Uwe Vagrie or something. Maybe it's like parking tickets. If they don't spell the name right, maybe they've got the wrong person. I don't know. Sometimes, I feel like he hasn't really died.

Oh, God. That's a pretty sad comment, not even spelling . . . You know, I gotta wonder about those errors. The coroner had to have the pathologist's report to file his report. That's standard practice. I tried to contact both the pathologist/doctor and the regional coroner to ask a few questions about procedure and stuff like that. The women in the office were great; and, they said they'd give the regional coroner my message. They also said the pathologist was no longer working with the coroner's office; but, was still in private practice. Well, I waited and waited, called again, waited some more. I'm still waiting. The only people who return calls these days would seem to be the police . . .

The police? Yeah, right! You gotta wonder whether the police . . .

The police, what?

Well, I don't know. Dad said the police went into Uwe's place before he and mom were even allowed to . . .

That's normal, especially in an "apparent suicide." They were playing by the rules. If they had suspicions it could have been a homicide — even one little suspicion — they'd have to investigate; and, if your parents were to go into Uwe's apartment before the police, they could disturb evidence without even knowing they were doing so.

Yeah? Okay, then — why did the police disturb the evidence, then?

Whoa, Girl! What do you mean?

The police went into the apartment and took everything out of there; they went through everything; and they took his main computer — he had a laptop or something else, too — and cleaned it out. I don't know much about computers; but they cleaned out everything. The file names are still there; but the files are all empty. There are files named 'Sarah' and stuff like that; but all the files are blank. That's what bothered us. And it scared us, too. Not only that; but, according to the computer expert, there was another disk drive in his computer and it had been removed, for some reason. It was programmed for two disk drives and there was only one when we got it back. We can't even get the one to work. This guy we hired to work with the computer to get it to work? He goes, "I can't get it to work; I don't know how Uwe had it set up. It was obviously something in his own mind; but, I have no idea how he did it." But he said there was DEFINITELY another disk drive in there; and, it wasn't in there anymore. The guy said, "His computer's been tampered with." And, only the cops went into his place before my parents.

You think? You don't know that for a fact, do you? You talked to the investigating officer; and, did he sound like he was hiding something to you?

Rudy, you mean?

Yeah, Rudy Shaefers. He called you, right?

Yeah, after I called him about getting the investigation report.

And, what did he say?

He told me how to get it; and, he told me, if I wanted to give it to you, I could. But, he couldn't give it to me; and, I couldn't authorize him to give it to you. He gave me the number of Freedom of Information and, he was sorta helpful. Kind of nice. For a cop.

Well, he's going by the book, sounds like. What makes you think he wouldn't have gone by the book during the investigation? Like, he'd know the files will be purged forever on the 6th of November, right? If he didn't want you to see the report, he could've stalled or something or given you a hard time about getting it.

Or, maybe he felt guilty about the lousy investigation?

Or maybe he couldn't go any further?

What do you mean?

Well, if your dad accepted Uwe's death as a suicide, they didn't have a lot of incentive for disputing his acceptance. I mean, that's probably why the coroner didn't worry none too much about the careless mistakes on the report. Just get the job done quickly and file it under "Forgotten, The Sooner The Better."

Yeah. . . . But if the cops didn't screw up Uwe's computer stuff, who did?

Maybe the person or persons he was expecting for company? . . . Did you have a funeral service, a memorial service or something?

No. Nothing. He was cremated 7 November 1994. I keep thinking he needs a proper *something*. My friends say to me, "Uwe's soul will never rest." So, a couple of days ago, I kind of got thinking, you know? Like, I started to write out what should be on his grave and I got to "beloved son and brother" and I couldn't stop crying. It was like in waves. It really physically hurt, almost.

I don't blame you at all. That's grief. I know how that feels. It's indescribably terrifying because you can't believe it's happening because you never believed — never looked at — the fact it happened. It just . . . it just racks right through you, right, and nothing can stop it, not even you . . .

I had to put it away, Judith. I couldn't do it. There was no closure with regard to Uwe; my therapist taught me that much. God, there was no ceremony, no funeral, no memorial service, nothing . . .

Why was that?

That was my dad's idea. We were all in shock. And we couldn't handle anything else. Especially Mom. But Dad was in pretty rough shape, too. When it happened, he didn't even want to go up there. I had to get a couple of my friends to go up there with him. My dad wasn't even going to go.

Up where?

To the Kanata Police Department. All he did was look in the back of the truck. He never saw anything else. We never saw a body. Dad just got rid of the truck. He didn't want to take it. They just trashed it. It stank so bad. It smelled like death. They gave my dad Uwe's watch and wallet and the other stuff — the papers — from the truck. There was a check in his wallet for $4000. There was no cash. When Mom and Dad went to his apartment, Mom said something was really weird. It just didn't make sense to her. She said it looked to her like Uwe was expecting visitors or something. He'd tidied up and bought stuff for company. It was too much for a bachelor. She said it looked like he was expecting something special.

Oh, Sarah

by Uwe Vandrei

Will I ever hold you on that shore?
Or only live it in a dream?
Will I ever tell you of my fears?
Will you ever collect my tears? . . .

Nights she conjures faceless loves
and sweats between the sheets.
Morning light turns her eyes to stone;
her beauty with Medusa could compete.

She covers neck to toe with office veils,
no hint of curve nor desire.
Camouflaged, she spends her day
letting no man see the fire.

I can smell your smoke;
let me be your fan,
expose that burning coal,
prove to you I'm a man.

Five alarms, we're hand in hand.
Tear away the veil; as one we stand:
A towering inferno . . .

Oh, Sarah

Who touched you tonight?
Alone in your melancholy dreams,
clutching lovers
that fade in morning's light.

You see, drunk, I dreamed you, too;
caress your skin.

Where do you go to be yourself;
who sees you in your tears?

Touched by everything; yet, untouched;
passion too much for any man to bear . . .

Do you have any idea what it was like —
waiting for an answer?
Holding something inside
that became a cancer?

We're told to make love,
according to Hite and Ruth.
When all I can do is caress your fire
in truth — or hite-sight . . .

I cower in confession;
not knowing my crime
that should keep me away from you.

You surrender your own reason;
poison your drinking well,
turn friends into enemies
and heaven into hell.

Feelings I never knew;
sentiments that can't exist.
The one consecrated before me
before her parents kissed.

So tell me there's no gold
at the rainbow's end,
that Venus is only a planet,
and Cupid, a myth.

Oh, daughrer of Jupiter and Diane
to yet beget Eros:
Come let us beget Eros unknown.

Forever blind
by the countenance
of your face —
To share bliss
out of time,
out of space.

How about a twist of the plot for the prisoner where the captives are recruited into activities that are meant to subvert them for malicious purposes? Consider the case of an individual who has always been mild and ineffectual, given psychological combat training in order to instill a sense of achievement and power — along with camaraderie — then, putting that power to work towards the ends of the organization involved. Not unlike taking opera and conditioning to the ultimate. The individual is inspired to use these newfound skills despite moral considerations, simply for the joy of being able to exercise the powers they now possess.

— Uwe Vandrei, *A Treatment for a Screenplay*

MUSIC

QUESTIONS ABOUT OBSESSED FAN WON'T GO AWAY...

The death of Sarah's stalker

Will the trials of burgeoning superstardom ever end for **Sarah McLachlan**? The Vancouver-based chanteusse is currently embroiled in a nasty lawsuit over songwriting royalties filed by former bandmates, while her record label is busy putting the screws to a freelance journalist writing an unauthorized biography of the star (FRANK 250).

And now, just as McLachlan's career takes off with the release of her fourth album, *Surfacing*, there are renewed questions regarding the death of her most ardent fan.

Uwe Vandrei, a freelance computer programmer from Ottawa, was found dead in the woods near Manotick, Ontario, on November 3, 1994—an apparent suicide by gunshot.

The 34-year-old Vandrei had spent the previous three years writing hundreds of obsessive letters to McLachlan, concluding with a law suit that claimed she had stolen text from his letters for use in a song about obsessive love.

Vandrei's statement-of-claim demanded $250,000 in punitive damages from McLachlan and her label Nettwerk Records. He also wanted public credit for co-authorship of the song *Possession*, the break-out hit of McLachlan's best-selling album *Fumbling Towards Ecstasy*, as well as a face-to-face meeting with the singer to discuss the origins of the song.

With the history of spooky letter writing and McLachlan's restraining order against him on the books, the local donut-eaters didn't hesitate to declare Vandrei's demise a suicide.

According to the coroner, on September 28, Vandrei had driven into the woods, climbed into the back of his pick-up truck, and blasted himself with a shotgun. The decomposing body was discovered by canoeists five days later.

Now there is speculation whether Vandrei may have visited McLachlan's recording studio in the Laurentians, an

KEEP BACK: Sarah received hundreds of letters from Uwe

hour away from where his body was discovered. There is a strange suggestion that Vandrei may have visited the studio where McLachlan often recorded. Her producer **Pierre Marchand**, lives nearby, and the area is also home to McLachlan's secret cabin.

off-the-record. A menacing lawyer's letter from Nettwerk followed and Chattlebrain was forced to spike the story. They eventually ran a softer McLachlan piece almost a year later. (McLachlan has since married the drummer in her band, sensitive soulmate **Ash Frood**.)

Although Vandrei's suit had been dismissed by Nettwerk management as frivolous harassment, Ottawa legalist **Ken Bickley** apparently believed there was some substance to the copyright claim even after his client died. Sources close to the family say Bickley pressured Vandrei's parents to continue the legal action on behalf of the estate, but they refused. Bickely won't discuss the case due to client-counsel privilege.

Vandrei's father **Gerhard**, a European immigrant, says he's willing to accept the suicide explanation and doesn't want to make waves. If it wasn't a suicide, he says he'd rather not know about it.

"I don't know what kind of business he was mixed up in, I don't want to get

6 • FRANK

CITO MUST GO!

FRANK

RACISM, BOOZE & THE JAYS' COLLAPSE

$2.50 • JULY 16, 1997 • ISSUE 250 • EVERY TWO WEEKS

PETEY OVER THE HILL?

CBC pretty boy to replace aging anchor?

He's my heir apparent.

Hair apparent, shurely!

LILITH FOUL!

SARAH MCLACHLAN UNAUTHORIZED

HASLETT CUFF TURFED BY THE GLOBE

PRESTON MANNING'S LIVING

76879 00001 3

(Left) Uwe Vandrei,
22 November 1991

(Below) from Uwe's
"Oh Sarah"

six

LILITH'S FAIR

or Do What You Have To Do

D uring the years between the release of FUMBLING
TOWARDS ECSTASY and SURFACING (15 July 1997), it
became imperative to keep McLachlan's ever-transform-
ing image uppermost in her ever-expanding target market's
minds, as Nettwerk Marketing VP George Maniatis told Jeff
Bateman of *The Record*. "This isn't a circus, and we're not going
out there with balloons. ... As much as Sarah is now becoming
an international superstar, we are developing her as an artist.
Imaging is very important in terms of what goes out and what
surrounds her. You don't want to piss off her fans."

While it is quite true FUMBLING TOWARDS ECSTASY ignited
the career of 'our little diva,' it is equally true McLachlan (and
crew) had not really managed to burn up the world. Truth is,
McLachlan needed a hit, a hit with a bullet attached to it, especially south of the border. Trouble was, hits were hard to come
by, particularly since songs are a such a bitch of a thing to make,
at least for McLachlan. In the interim McLachlan released several cassingles, provided BGVs on a series of recordings made by
her contemporaries in the pop-rock field (Blue Rodeo,

Junkhouse, Ginger, Stephen Fearing, Papa Brittle, Bass Is Base, Delirium), and contributed dozens of songs to a veritable train of compilations and soundtracks right across the spectrum — from Taco Bell (with a *Melrose Place* tie-in) and The Body Shop International to shelters for abused women and animals through big- and small-screen productions (*The Brothers McMullen, Due South*) to a wide range of socially acceptable benefits to — well, you name it (and McLachlan's probably done it).

Interestingly, during her spring 1995 tour, Fumblers began reporting to F-T-E Listers that one of the tunes in litigation, *Ben's Song*, a staple on McLachlan's set-list, had been dropped in favor of a brand-new McLachlan-penned number, *Full Of Grace*, which appears on several cassingles and compilations before it makes its way to RARITIES, B-SIDES & OTHER STUFF (1996) and again resurfaces on SURFACING as its penultimate track. But first came McLachlan's FREEDOM SESSIONS, originally released on 6 December 1995 in Canada, featuring 72 minutes of mostly stripped-down demo (or initial) versions of FUMBLING tracks plus an interpretation of *Ol' 55* by Tom Waits — simple percussion and acoustic instruments complement McLachlan's artfully spare croonings additionally enhanced by a Kurzweil 2000 synthesizer — and including a 34-minute multimedia entry containing video footage, photographs, audio as well as video clips, backstage footage and interviews, all narrated by McLachlan.

Jay Daunheimer produced the interactive sequence, marking the first time a major-recording star had experimented with bringing the new medium, in a viable format, to market. In it, he includes four "hidden" Easter eggs containing goodies ranging from rare footage of McLachlan playing an accordion or singing the *Banjo Song* to a photograph of Nettwerk's three owners (if users click on the company's logo). *Wired's* April issue (3.04), by the way, hit the stands with a full-page ad for the FREEDOM SESSIONS, an intelligent move on the part of Nettwerk, given its cutting-edge leadership in cyber-marketeering and related computeristics.

Andrea Odintz, in her 18 May 1995 *Rolling Stone* review of the FREEDOM SESSIONS, describes the disc's offerings before pretty much panning the release: "Aside from these and a couple of interesting jazz-inflected rhythms, the main purpose of this project seems to be self-indulgence. As talented as McLachlan is, she simply hasn't amassed the body of work to justify a repackaging such as this. The release from which she borrows is less than two years old and still sells consistently on its own merit. . . . The EP will have its audience, though, as evidenced by McLachlan's large and loyal fan base on the Internet. . . . Beyond that, an album of new material would have been a greater investment on the artist's part."

By the summer of 1995, North American sales of FUMBLING had exceeded the 1.5 million mark while FREEDOM SESSIONS had already racked up equally impressive chartings (as the first CD-ROM to make the acquaintance of *Billboard*'s Top 200 Albums) and stats — 250,000 units — for a rehasher embellished with cyber-bells and bongles.

McLachlan, ecstatic, touched down in Toronto for a capacity-crowd appearance that, according to critics covering the show, sends 16,000-plus pairs of ears into sonic bliss. "Given her performance last night at the Molson Amphitheatre," writes *The Toronto Sun*'s Kieran Grant 30 June 1995, "Sarah McLachlan could be considered a contradiction in terms. . . . After she took to the keys for a stark but soulful new track, *Full Of Grace*, the heat was turned up just a notch for the stripped-down cruncher, *Fear* . . . plus a flawless rendition of *Good Enough*. . . . Even though McLachlan's stage patter grew more acerbic towards the end of the show, it was her awkward between-song rambles that showed the less-confident side to a woman who, despite being a self-described 'slave to my artform,' exercised such a heady command over her material."

Over at *The Globe and Mail*, arts-reporter Elizabeth Renzetti, arguably one of the finest entertainment writers on the continent, approaches her subject from a characteristically clear-eyed perspective. "There's a trend circulating in pop music these days that grates on the ears, not to mention the brain. It involves full-grown women, in bands like Veruca Salt and Belly, who sing in such coy whispers that a kitten's mewlings would seem authoritative by contrast. . . . Dressed in silver pants and a black tank top, McLachlan seemed more rock chick than the gauzy ethereal figure of her videos. There was something slightly witchy-woman about her closed-eyed intensity while she sang songs like *Drawn To The Rhythm* and a new one, *Full Of Grace*, her hands making repetitive, almost ritualistic movements, as if she were conducting her own voice. Unfortunately, pretty as many of her songs are, they are often so similar in tempo (the non-technical term is slow) that things started to sag a little in the middle. ...Also, by the end of the concert, McLachlan had received a small queen's ransom in stuffed creatures, books and flowers, the last causing her to draw a deep breath: 'This makes me feel bad for the story I'm about to tell.'

"She then launched into a rambling tale having to do, I think, with men's self-delusions — or at least the deception of one in particular — and women's continuing ability to fall for them anyway. When she opened her mouth to sing *Plenty*, it all became clear. ...As she wound up the show, McLachlan thanked the audience again, saying, 'It's been really, really therapeutic.' "

With *Fumbling* racking up double-plat stats south of the border, McLachlan's 13-track RARITIES, B-SIDES & OTHER STUFF rolled off the assembly line 25 June 1996. "This is," she tells Denise Sheppard at *Jam!*, "a gathering up of the songs that have come out in a number of different places. Some of them are out-of-print; some were never released. This collection is something for the fans. And, it's a brilliant marketing ploy, really, because I'm not going to have a record out for another year!"

Sheppard asks McLachlan to elaborate on the long wait for her next recorded performance. "I'm trying to write. I've got the biggest block ever. I went to Montreal for a month already; and, I didn't get much done so I came back home and am trying to write here. I'll probably go back in August again."

Back home in Vancouver, probably because she misses her latest squeeze, now-fiancé Sood, McLachlan acquires Rex, her puppy — a black Labrador Retriever with a voracious appetite for pig ears — to keep an eye on her two kittens, Shayla and Simba, romping in the backyard of the couple's yupscale house in Vancouver's trendified Dunbar district where, according to those invited to partake of the goddess's glorious baked goods, one may sample an exquisite array of cakes, cookies, pies, brownies, breads, loaves, bars, and scones. (Apparently, McLachlan considers baking the best kind of therapy.)

It was around this time, so the story goes, that McLachlan

cooked up the concept for Lilith Fair, the vulvapaloozan answer to grunge's grease-gropers for guys, citing the fact that female artists can't get no respect in popular-music boys' clubs.

Prior to her return to the studio for a second run at the song mill, the million-miler McLachlan returned to the road, this time test-driving (or, in market-savvy lingo, conducting focus groups on) the brand-new concept she'd apparently conceived in an effort to right the wrongs of women's place in the testosterone-based world of rock and pop. (Lilith, after all, likes to be on top.)

"**E**xcuse me?"
    "Excuse who?"

"Me, Ma'am, Gregg. I was in one of those focus-group audiences. Wouldn't now be a good time to continue my story? I mean, enough about all this on-top stuff, hey? Where's your sense of timing?"

Readers, it's Wagener, the cut-above painter (who, even in e-mail mode, utterly charms yours truly. Not at all like Ron Jeffers, another army guy who responds to my call for comments with a single-word missive, 'Scavenger.' Naturally, I thank him and he gives me absolute permission to reprint his condemnatory — though mercifully brief — utterance).

But, Gregg's story, of course!

. . . In the summer of 1996, Sarah played the Starlight Amphitheater in Burbank with Paula Cole and Suzanne Vega. I tossed a painting of Paula out when she was on stage. She saw it because it wasn't entirely dark yet at the outdoor theater. Paula said, "Thank you."

Later, she stepped on it. She stepped on it again. She stepped on it a third time. Then, she danced on top of it. I think she was just intent on her performance; I don't think she was commenting on its quality. She did take it with her when she left the stage. That's my whole Paula Cole story.

I tossed the painting of Suzanne Vega out when she was onstage; she heard it land; but, she couldn't see it because it was in the dark and she was in the spotlight. She said, 'Goodness! I'll have to see what that was, later." (I tape the paper to foam-core board so the paintings are easy to handle and toss if need be.) This particular toss had made a noticeable thump. A roadie removed the painting from the stage shortly after that. Damn! I didn't get to see her reaction. I'll tell the rest of my Suzanne Vega story some other time.

I had two Sarah paintings for this occasion. I gave one painting a good toss; and, it landed within reach of Sarah. The other hit a cable and stopped short. She saw the first one, picked it up, looked pleased to me and said, "Oh, everyone got one tonight." So, now I knew Suzanne got her painting. It had never occurred to me until that moment the three of them would get together backstage and look at my paintings. I felt really weird about that.

One song later, some people came up, put flowers on the stage and took pictures of Sarah. The flashes got Sarah's attention and this time she saw the other painting. She said, "Oh! There's another one! Thank you." She smiled at those people the way she had smiled at me three years earlier. I guess she thought they were me. Whether they got a picture of that smile or not, those people owe me big time!

McLachlan motored into Motown for the first of her all-women concerts 13 June 1996 but spoke to *The Detroit Free Press* before the "informal inaugural" from her home in Vancouver about this "unusual bill" that included Patti Smith, Lisa Loeb, Paula Cole, and Aimee Mann. "Basically I wanted to do a whole tour with a bunch of women. Not necessarily as a reaction to the Lollapaloozas of the world, but just to prove to everybody that, hey, more than two girls on the same bill will sell tickets, guys!" Post concert she added, "I just put together a wish list of the women I'd love to perform with — including Patti — and I called 'em all up!" McLachlan tells *The Free Press*. "I was thrilled when Patti said yes because she's such a hero of mine." (Perhaps high-punk priestess Smith's 1975 HORSES numbers among those five to ten fulfilling CDs McLachlan mentions earlier?)

"This is sort of my 'girlie goddess' tour," McLachlan told *The Free Press*. "Next summer I want to do a full tour — sort of an anti-Lollapalooza-boys'-club thing. But, right now, I have to focus on my next record. I'm way behind. I should have been in the studio by now. But, so far, I've only got four really good songs. . . . Everything I've been writing lately seems to sound like old Hank Williams. . . . I don't know where it's coming from. I think I'm channelling some old-country soul or something. I've been listening to Emmylou [produced by Daniel Lanois] a lot — maybe she's been inspiring me and bringing up some old ghosts.

"McLachlan's father was a marine biologist whose work frequently took him away from home," *The Free Press* tells us again. "McLachlan's aspiring-academic mother set aside her own dreams to support her husband's education and career travels. As a result, her mother was haunted by feelings of isolation, loneliness, regret and lack of fulfilment. And, McLachlan suffered 'some psychological abuse,' she says, as a child.

"'My poor mom, bless her heart, is still alive; so, I don't want to get into all of that, because I love her. . . . But, God knows, we went through a hard one. . . .'" Good enough, as she has said before.

As is their wont, most stories featuring McLachlan get around to that troublesome business of obsessive fans; although, in this particular article, the writer puts a more imaginative spin on the approach, segueing from her childhood traumas into her adult trials.

"But, when McLachlan was in her early twenties, the leftover emotional and psychic residue propelled her into the kinds of obsessive relationships — and the state of exquisite torment — she details so sympathetically in her songs.

" 'Yeah, I've definitely been through those; and, I do love to bring it on myself. I don't mean to; but, there it is. I mean, I've always been in the great pursuit of happiness and fulfilment — if I get into a hole, I want to get out of it. . . . And, for me, I've found that the best way out is to write about it. This is such a cliché; but writing is really therapeutic for me. After I wrote *Possession*, I wasn't looking over my shoulder every time I left the house anymore. . . . Some of the letters were really over the top, in terms of what they expected and demanded of me. . . . [*Possession*] is written from the point of someone who's so obsessed with another person that they might become violent in order to obtain that person."

Detroit's Pine Knob Music Theater, one of four testing sites for the Lilith concept, goes off with neither hitch nor glitch as McLachlan, Smith, Cole, Mann, and Loeb wrap the crowd around their lovely little fingers. McLachlan — alongside a slightly altered lineup which additionally features Emmylou Harris and Crash Vegas's Michelle McAdorey — also plays dates in Berkeley and Burbank, where the name "Lilith Fair" begins to appear in press coverage. "On Sept. 14, McLachlan will officially unveil the Lilith Fair name with a show featuring Harris, Cole and Lisa Loeb at Vancouver's 10,000-capacity Nat Baily Theater," *The Los Angeles Times* reported on 18 August 1996.

A week later on 26 August 1996, *The Toronto Star*'s Peter Howell picks up the scent and explains a little about the Lilith thing for readers: "Lilith is variously seen as history's first feminist, the first outcast from the Garden of Eden and/or as a vampire who attacks men in their sleep and abducts newborn children. Legend has it she was Adam's first wife, before Eve; but Adam rejected her because she was too headstrong. God complied with Adam's wishes to have Lilith banished from Eden, replacing her with the more compliant Eve. Before He did that, however, God sent three angels to try to reason with Lilith (who had fallen in with demons). This didn't work and Lilith remained outside Eden, assisting the dark side in mayhem and corruption. Or, fighting for the rights of women, if you choose the much more positive view of Lilith held by modern feminists, McLachlan included. Whatever the interpretation, Lilith Fair has the potential to be one of next summer's biggest tours, an interesting twist to the festival idea."

As a footnote to the Lilith definition, *Billboard* reported in October that "the 'Lilith' in the tour's name — suggested by McLachlan's friend, the writer Buffy Childerhose — is derived from a myth about the first independent woman (Adam's first wife), but the fair won't be a political event. 'It's not a feminist platform, and I totally want men involved,' McLachlan says.... 'I want it to be like a family affair.' "

She expanded on this I-don't-hate-guys definition of Lilith during an interview in *Elle*. " 'It's my gig,' McLachlan says simply, 'so I control what comes in. Even pamphlets. Some radical feminist groups are so far out there, they would love to chop every man's dick off.' She looks guilty, gently petting her dog's fresh scar — Rex has just been 'fixed.' 'I don't want to be advocating that. There needs to be boundaries, definitely.' As for the onstage gender boundary she has created, McLachlan insists, 'Lilith is not about excluding men — I don't want them to feel ostracized.' McLachlan has even brainstormed ways for them to participate: 'Maybe as go-go boys, in cages with butt floss,' she suggests. Jokes aside, McLachlan's drummer of six years is, in fact, a man, and he recently became her husband as well. 'Lilith is really just a celebration of sisterhood,' she says. 'There needs to be an alternative to that Lollapalooza cock rock which' — she pauses, belches like a beer-filled frat boy, and continues, somehow, with a straight face — 'in certain moods, I *love*.' "

It was *the* biggest tour of the summer of 1997, a spectacular smash that knocked the socks off both the media and the music industry. Even Alice Cooper quipped, 'I'm pissed off. They didn't invite me to do my two-hour version of *Only Women Bleed*' — or something to that effect.

Lilith Fair began on 5 July 1997 at the Gorge Amphitheater in George, Washington and ended after 35 dates throughout North America on 24 August at the Thunderbird Stadium in McLachlan's hometown of Vancouver, BC. Over 50 other artists performed during the Fair, including (from A to W) Alisha's Attic, Leah Andreone, Fiona Apple, Joy Askew, Autour de Lucie, Mary Black, Meredith Brooks, Tracy Bonham, The Cardigans, Lori Carson, Mary Chapin Carpenter, Tracy Chapman, Holly Cole, Paula Cole, Shawn Colvin, Sheryl Crow, Julia Fordham, Kim Fox, Patty Griffin, Emmylou Harris, Juliana Hatfield, Lauren Hoffman, Susanna Hoffs, Indigo Girls, Jewel, Katell Keineg, Yungchen Lhamo, Mary Jane Lamond, Lhasa, Lisa Loeb, Lovechild, Tara Maclean, Michelle Malon, Dayna Manning, Abra Moore, Mudgirl, Once Blue, Beth Orton, Joan Osborne, Madeleine Peyroux, September 67, Jill Sobule, Garrison Starr, Kinnie Starr, Suzanne Vega, Wild Colonials, Wild Strawberries, Dar Williams, Victoria Williams, Kelly Willis, Cassandra Wilson — to name a memorable couples of few.

Where Lilith ventured, media madness reigned. *Elle, Maclean's, Time, Entertainment Weekly, US Magazine, The Record, RPM, Billboard, Spin, Rolling Stone etc. etc.* all rounded up their hippest scribes to give credence to the new "old" news that women, like never before, were making their presence felt in popular music.

In *Express*, Katherine Monk reports on the series' opener at the Gorge in George: "Originally intended as a way of igniting Sarah McLachlan's songwriting fire last year, Lilith Fair has evolved into the most ambitious female-fronted rock show ever produced. From the kiosks promoting 'voters for choice' and women's shelters to the fact that a dollar-per-head went to a women's charity to the obvious majority of female attendees gave the whole festival a non-testosterone feel. . . ." (Monk overlooks the role of corporate sponsorship which trounces funding for individual artists working beyond the narrow confines of popular fashion in her otherwise thoughtful analysis.)

"Performers would not usually have the chance to play such large venues — let alone headline the bill. In a tradition built on tight pants, loud guitars and macho sensibilities, the word 'feminine' has always been considered a liability. And yet, as the festival's launch and growing list of sold-out venues for the 35-date Lilith tour proves, 'feminine' is not a valid rock concept — it's a marketing success story."

Nicholas Jennings of *Maclean's* caught up with the tour at the next venue in Mountainview, CA, where he chatted up "down-to-earth diva" Sarah McLachlan and interviewed other "sirens" on the show. "Kicking off her sandals and curling up on a couch, the 29-year-old Canadian performer reflected on the high profile that Lilith has suddenly brought her. 'I love how powerful this whole thing makes me feel. . . . Not a selfish power . . . but a strength that's coming from everyone around me. It's a good kind of feeling and a good kind of power.' "

Concerning her self-appointed role as "den mother" to the Lilith artists and "role model for young women across North America," McLachlan responded demurely, "It's a strange path, this celebrity thing. . . . Becoming famous and losing your privacy can mean losing yourself — which is something I've always struggled with. . . . I never used to be comfortable with that . . . because I wasn't very comfortable with myself. I didn't like parts of myself. Girls would tell me how much I meant to them and I'd think, 'Don't look up to me — I'm more messed up than anybody I know.' But I'm fine with it now. . . . I'm feeling really strong at the moment — ready for anything the world throws at me."

For veteran performers like Suzanne Vega and rookies like Vancouver's Kinnie Starr, Lilith took on special significance. "I feel like I'm taking part in something historic," Vega told Jennings, "something that's never been done before." In Starr's words, "It's nice to be around other female players to see what equipment they use and just to talk. . . . When I go into a recording studio and it's only men, I feel intimidated. Here, I feel totally safe and content." Sheryl Crow jumped on the Lilith praise bandwagon, telling James Patrick Herman at *Elle*, "It's a great opportunity to see other female musicians, which I never do, since I'm always touring." In the *Time* feature "Galapalooza!" Fiona Apple commented, "Of all the tours that you do during the summer . . . this is pretty much the coolest one." The Girls' Emily Saliers praised Lilith's founder in *People* magazine: "Her spirit and sensibility are inspiring."

And everyone, it seemed, accepted the party line that Lilith would once and for all redress the injustices women artists experience in the radio market, thanks to its long-standing policy of not playing women back-to-back for fear of boring or alienating its listeners, a party line presented by McLachlan in an interview with Michael Mehle in *Express Magazine*. "Last year's Lollapalooza all but banned anyone with a pair of X chromosomes," writes Mehle, "and that ruled out nearly every artist Sarah McLachlan and her friends wanted to hear."

"Even three years ago, if we would have tried something like this," she told the *Express*er, "promoters would have laughed at us. . . . Back then, radio programmers wouldn't even consider playing two women back-to-back."

James Patrick Herman in *Elle* approached Tom Poleman, program director at Z100, the number-one Top 40 station in Manhattan, for an insider's opinion on this complaint. "Programmers never used to play two female artists back-to-back," he said. "But everyone woke up and realized it was one of those dumb rules we've been following. The more women took the forefront in music, the more that rule became absurd."

If things were bad in radioland, they may have been worse — so the story from Nettwerk goes — in concert land. "Most concert promoters are guys in their 40s and 50s," Terry McBride told Jennings at *Maclean's*, "and some didn't think an all-woman tour offered enough diversity." When McLachlan was asked by *Time*, "Why did you decide to start the Lilith Fair?", she expanded on McBride's story: "I guess first and foremost is I was touring a lot and there was an incredible amount of talent out there, musicians that I loved, and I wasn't getting a chance to see anybody play live. So partly a selfish reason, I guess. Slightly reactionary too — a couple of years ago when I started touring for a record, I wanted to have another woman open for me, and I got a lot of negative response from promoters saying, 'You can't put two women on the same bill. There's not enough audience for that,' I just thought that was a really nasty attitude, and so of course wanted to prove them wrong — and so I did."

Not a few music critics puzzled over the appeal of "Lilith" music, with Christopher John Farley in *Time* elaborating a "coffeehouse pop" theory. "Call the new sound coffeehouse pop. It has a comforting warmth, a topping of sugary froth, and it provides a kind of buzz, like sipping cappuccino in a corner cafe. It is led, mostly, by female singer-songwriters, writing primarily from a feminist point of view. On her hit song *Bitch*, Meredith Brooks declares that she wants to 'reclaim a word that had taken on a really derogatory meaning.' But ideology or no, these women are unafraid to celebrate their own sensuality. On the inside flap of her album, Jewel poses in a sexy yellow swimsuit. . . .

"Coffeehouse pop is gentle but not tame — there is a quiescent anger within it over social issues and matters of the heart. The songs seek to engage life, not shrink from it. 'There was an innocence that prevailed in the '60s that was crushed with the assassination of J.F.K. and King,' says Jewel. 'Our parents have become disillusioned. It is their disillusionment we deal with in many ways; it's a kind of crust we have to break through.' . . .

"But unlike alternative rock, this music is less about stoking cynicism and provoking anger than it is about overcoming both. This is healing music, devoid of irony and flush with optimism and emotion. 'Apathy is boring,' says Cole. 'It takes real courage to have hope, This is music that wants to feel, no matter how much it hurts. Says Jewel: 'People are hungry for emotiveness. They want bare honesty.' "

Grrrls will be grrrls because they're so wow!, thanks in large part to the proliferation of lesbian chic and its attendant mystique, as much driven by *les femmes* as it is by the guys held in thrall of the endlessly mesmerizing image of women going together. Sex sells, one way or t'other. Freud said something to the effect that 92% of everything's about sex; it is estimated that success in the entertainment business issues from 40% image, 40% presentation, and 20% talent. McLachlan's talent, naturally, provides the extra edge which makes the rule.

But, to tell you the truth, I found the whole Lilith affair boring, naïve, and rather insulting to the intelligence of its audiences (who were, I admit, unperturbed by the blandness it championed). It's one thing to shoot your mouth off about the plight of disadvantaged women when one's already pedestalled in sitting-pretty position; it's another to (even inadvertently) ignore the tears, sweat, and inroads of us who came before. As women, we have always fought for our rights; and, as human beings, we dare never forget what our rights constitute. Lilith Fair — and events similar to it — do effect change, if only because they remind a system mired in patriarchal mediocrity it's time to show 'em how it's most successfully done.

It was yours truly, in my capacity as country-music columnist with *The Toronto Star*, who effected the change in programming women artists back-to-back on radio, thanks almost entirely to *Country 59*'s forward-looking station manager and music director, Bill Anderson and Al Campagnola respectively, actually taking the initiative in response to a rant of my own which commenced 16 February 1992 — "Recent developments suggest radical transformations leading to a new egalitarianism and the rise of a kinder, gentler ambience are just around the corner. Not any corner I know. My [unscientific] survey revealed how few women actually do receive airplay. For every three songs by males, country radio plays one by a female. Both *The Record* and *Billboard*'s

Top Ten charts list only one woman among the hits for the week ending 9 February . . ." — and concluded 15 March 1992 with kudos to *Country 59* for being the first "to risk spinning back-to-back recordings by women."

McLachlan and her Lilith cast chant-a-ranted against guys ruling the touring roost and lapping up millions of bucks excluding women from their lineups; meanwhile, back at the farm, female country performers had already become highly successful, with several tours featuring stars the caliber of Pam Tillis, K.T. Oslin, Reba McEntire, Mary Chapin Carpenter and such. Programmers had discovered a demographic shift in their focus groups and target-market surveys — women in their audiences began to equal men; and, more importantly, Mary Chapin Carpenter, Trisha Yearwood, Wynonna, Reba, and Tanya Tucker, among others, were selling discs in the millions, a fact well established by the time the acorn for the Lilith oak had been planted.

Such "package" shows, as they are called, necessarily reflect what's in demand on the network of radio and video shows gracing the airwaves (from the moment they came into existence). So, the savvy-marketeerist simply got with the concept, repackaged it with a women-are-something-special ribbon, and sold it with a package show featuring bows for belles.

There were other dissenting opinions, stated directly or indirectly. As Ben Rayner in *The Ottawa Sun* reported, Kim Shattuck of the Muffs called "that whole Lilith Fair thing . . . incredibly dorky. It's a bunch of folksy, braless ladies. So what? They don't even rock. They're wimpy, boring and mediocre." Rayner himself commented, "So, the all-girl Lilith Fair tour plays its last Canadian date this week and I, for one, am glad. Now perhaps I can open up a newspaper or flip on a video channel without having to endure another fawning piece on founder Sarah McLachlan or the newly potent grrrl-power her brainchild supposedly unleashed across the land." Chicknames for the tour — "Vulvapolooza" (*Rolling Stone*), Estrofest, and Lilith Fairies expressed a lack of respect for the seemingly noble Lilith Fair.

Nevertheless, Lilith Fair did provide both a meeting place and an environment for political and feminist activists of the female persuasion. The big acts — McLachlan, Shawn Colvin, the Indigo Girls, Sheryl Crow, Tracy Chapman, Paula Cole, Joan Osborne, Suzanne Vega — nicely complemented fast-trackers such as Meredith Brooks, Fiona Apple, and Jewel as well as tried-and-truests Emmylou Harris and Mary Chapin Carpenter (plus, its second-stage performers gained a great deal of media exposure as well as attention from constituents of their target audiences).

And Lilith Fair became the image boost Sarah McLachlan needed just as her next CD was surfacing. "I never realized what an amazing platform Lilith would be for my own record," McLachlan told the *The Globe and Mail* on the release of her finest recording.

Lilith Fair made its mark. It turned the trick. It left an indelible impression on advertisers' minds. Lilith Fair was the second highest grossing tour of the summer, outdistanced only by Ozzie Osborne's adventures with heavy-metal nostalgia. Terry McBride of Nettwerk is "confident Lilith Fair can be established as a franchise that will run for five years," *The Record* reports, "with or without McLachlan's participation." From 5 July to 24 August, McLachlan's beatifically glowing image enlivened the covers of virtually every North American magazine and periodical worth its weight in withits. And the myth is being perpetuated. A "Lilith Live" album is scheduled for release in March 1998 on McLachlan's own record label, Temple, and CBC-TV will air a documentary based on the two Toronto Lilith dates before 1997 ends.

Naturally, when the show touched down for those two nights at the Molson Amphitheatre in Toronto, I attended the extravaganza wearing my reviewer's cap, the one I'd donned for *RPM*, the Canadian music-industry's chart Bible these past 30-plus years. (General manager Stan Klees and publisher Walt Grealis, O.C., by the way, may someday write their own tome on the truly "true story" of the Canadian music industry, a book eagerly awaited by all and sundry, particularly since the irreplaceable duo was *there*. Grealis and Klees co-founded the Juno Awards, the Big Country Awards — the precursor to the Canadian Country Music Association's Awards — as well as designing the Cancon label, the distinctive MAPL pie gracing every Canadian-made recording released.)

"Lilith Fair Scores a First for Molson Amphitheatre," the headline reads on the front cover of *RPM's* 25 August 1997 ish, and . . .

"Pardon me, Ma'am; but, I saw Lilith Fair before you did. Fair is fair, right? My story comes before your review. . . . Logic, Ma'am."

Gregg again.

. . . My 'never-say-die' Lilith Fair 1997 story: I meet Sarah! This takes place at the Irvine, CA Lilith Fair 9 July. I arrive around 3:30 and make my way to the entrance. I have five paintings — Sarah McLachlan, Tracy Chapman, Jewel Kilcher, Paula Cole and Suzanne Vega — to give as gifts to the artists. They're all oil on gessoed watercolor paper. At the security checkpoint, they tell me I can't bring my paintings in. The guy gives me some lame excuse about not allowing large bulky items. I think, if I'd chosen a different line or been a little earlier or later, I would've gotten through with the paintings. I consider walking back until I'm out of sight and then try again at a different search line; but, I'd promised myself a long time ago I wouldn't intentionally break any rules and I wouldn't do anything I had been told not to do in order to give these paintings away.

So, I walk back to the car and put the paintings away. By the time I get to the theater, the extra set Paula Cole does at the second stage is over. Damn! :o(

I speak with some of the security people and end up at the V-I-P gate. Allegedly, someone from the production staff might come escort me to my car in order to bring back the paintings. I leave my name and seat number with one of the guards; but I'm sure they've said that just to get rid of me. I go back, check with the guard a few times? No news. After the concert's over, I wait until the crowd thins out and then hang around at the V-I-P gate for a few minutes. It's clear they'll be busy shuttling handicapped people to the parking lot for a long time; so, I decide to give up and leave.

I get to my car? It's completely boxed in. I wait for two minutes and not a single car moves anywhere in sight. I decide I'll take the paintings and walk towards the theater until they stop me and send me back. That way, I can say I tried everything within reason. I'm the only one walking uphill; but, I pass several security people walking downhill. Not one of them challenges me. I reach the V-I-P gate? It's wide open and unattended. The V-I-P lawn area's empty. There's a security barrier with an opening to pass vehicles about 30 meters from the gate. I enter the gate and feel quite guilty because I had just broken a rule. The ends don't justify the means. I was wrong. I am scum. It'll never happen again! I swear! I continue towards the security barrier and the two guards completely ignore me. I could have gone right past them; but I have way too much bad karma already. So, I stop at the security barrier in the open area. There's a half-dozen or so young women standing around. Then, I see Sarah's dog, Rex (a.k.a. Lilith); so, I figure Sarah must be close by. I see a woman in the shadows apparently giving autographs to two of the young women. Just then, one of the guards asks me a question — I forget what. "No," I answer, "I'm just trying to give the performers presents." I show him one of the paintings. He says he thinks all of the performers have gone already. The woman in the shadows comes into the light; and, it's none other than Sarah McLachlan.

I say, "Isn't that McLachlan there?" and try to see around him.

He says, "No, that's the head of security."

What kind of fool does this guy take me for?

I say, "Oh, okay."

I certainly don't want a scene; so, I back off and head towards where there's a barrier between me and Sarah. I pull out the painting of her and hold it up. Sarah and some of the young women are playing with Rex less than ten metres away from me. I'm afraid she'll duck into one of the buses close by. I don't want to shout at her. I keep holding the painting up. Finally! It catches her eye and she takes a couple of hesitant steps in my direction.

"I have a present for you."

"It's very nice."

"Thank you."

"Would you be so kind as to autograph a picture of the painting for me?"

"Oh, sure."

I hand her the picture and a marker pen. She struggles with the dog's leash, painting and marker. One of the young women offers to take the leash. Sarah refuses and insists she needs to practise her domineering-bitch voice — Oooh. Baaad pun. She orders Rex to lie down and praises her when she does. She signs the back of the picture and writes a peace sign. She starts to excuse herself to leave and I interrupt.

"I have presents for the other performers, too!" I show her the other paintings.

I show her Paula.

"Oh!"

Jewel and Tracy?

"Oh, wow."

I show her Suzanne.

"This is VERY nice. . . . They're all very nice."

"Thank you very much."

"Would you like me to give them to them?" (I'm really glad I don't have to suggest she help me.)

"If you would be so kind, I would be very grateful." (I know, I know. That's incredibly geeky; but, it sounds much better in my head before I say it.)

"I'm sure they will appreciate the gifts."

"Thank you."

"What's your name?"

"Gregg."

"I'll tell them Gregg did these."

"My name is on the back of each."

This adds credibility to Sarah's claim she's really going to give my paintings to the other women (not that I doubt her honesty).

"Goodbye."

"Goodbye."

I leave. I have mixed feelings about parting with those paintings because I had picked out the perfect spots on the walls of my house where I was going to hang them while I'd walked to the V-I-P gate; and, for the first time, I'd begun to think of them as mine and not gifts.

She'd smiled a lot during our conversation and was remarkably friendly. I wish I'd thought to tell her that I'd given paintings to her before.

I guess, under pressure, I just choked.

Thank you, Gregg. You can write a story for my book anytime; and, you're right, you saw Lilith first plus, well, she did give *you* the time of day, eh?

Lilith Fair Scores a First for Molson Amphitheatre

Where else but at a festival aptly named Lilith Fair does one get an earful of Shawn Colvin, Indigo Girls, Jewel, and Sarah McLachlan on top of an eyeful of the way in which benevolent corporations sponsor music festivals?

After all, McLachlan and her people had *pooh-pooed* automakers, *Vanity Fair* and suchlike when hunting for acceptable patrons of the performing arts (ubiquitously and annoyingly "present" throughout the carnival-like venue).

Molson's Amphitheatre, flanked with ginormous banners and a backdrop containing much in the line of loosely labelled art of the new-age aesthetic — princes, vamps, steeds and demons cavorting with carnally mythic figures — tended to interfere with the music presented, particularly since strategically placed video terminals additionally spewed endless repeats of three or four ads for booze and Bryan Adams.

The human view proved far more interesting, at least in demographic terms. Not surprisingly, single nubbie friskies from sandal-and-sneakerdom politely mingled with a representative raft of wallflowers and a high percentage of same-sex couples in a sea of white middle-class festival-flockers.

Given its advance billing among high-end hawkers the calibre of all the usual media suspects, the anti-climactic show, minimally marred by rivers of rain and muck, provided ticket holders with adequate and predictable second-stage performances from Lhasa and Wild Strawberries before Dayna "Half The Man" Manning managed to snag the audience's attention with her distinctive vocal attack.

Roots-oriented singer-songwriter Shawn Colvin came on with a vengeance and delivered a well-paced set of outstanding compositions topped off with an impeccable rendition of "Sunny Came Home" (*A Few Small Repairs*) while Indigo Girls Amy Ray and Emily Saliers captivated the crowd by doing fine justice to a variety of tunes culled from the duo's recent efforts, most noticeably *Shaming Of The Sun*.

Meredith Brooks? The bitch? One can only speculate the rain damp-ened Brooks's edge-blurring spirit or, on a more catty-claws' note, one might further suggest Brooks developed an allergic reaction to what she dubs the "fucking cosmic woo-woos," especially during her alter-ego hit which, for a combination of (mostly) technical reasons, sounded eerily effective.

In fact, throughout the afternoon and evening sets, the sound system inexplicably kicked into murk overdrive far too often for a show appar-ently building its rep on its sensitive-artist handling and top-flight enter-tainment values.

Accordingly, techno-gremlins all but destroyed Jewel's *Foolish Games*, the heart-stopping acoustic ballad with No. 1 hit written all over it currently darting up the chart as I write this.

Jewel oozed music, spontaneously cutting loose with an electrifying lead-guitar solo while her riveting vocals soared along melismatic peaks and showcased an extraordinary instrument on a first-name basis with excel-lence. "You Were Meant For Me," the cathartic highlight of the fair, carved sonic contours and dramatically created theatrical epiphanies reminiscent of Marlene Dietrich in her heyday.

Show-closer McLachlan did not, Saturday August 16 in Toronto, man-age to turn her act into show-stopper stuff, at least not the way Indigo Girls, Colvin or Jewel did. The regally radiant vocalist got by on good enough (which still thrilled the transported audience eating out of her rather mannequinned hands).

Clearly a little road-weary, McLachlan delivered competent versions of *Hold On, Possession* and *Angel* alongside a sampling of her trademark (and soon-to-be) hits including the countrified *Building A Mystery* from her fourth studio release in a decade.

Throughout her set, she graciously thanked and re-thanked her ador-ing audience; but, she ultimately failed to connect with her fervent fol-lowers in any meaningful way, most likely because the nature of her material almost demands a more intimate setting.

Still, despite both techno-glitches and the festival's stagy feel, the evening produced a series of memorable moments which culminated in Jewel's show-stealing appearance just prior to McLachlan's too-brief solo set which climaxed with encores *Ice Cream* and a spirited full-chorus reinterpretation of Can-American Joni Mitchell's *Big Yellow Taxi*.

J ust prior to (the off-limits-to-me) Lilith Fair and the release of SURFACING, McLachlan got together with *Mondo 2000*'s Megan Olden mere days or weeks before she married Sood in a private ceremony in the Caribbean (upon which her significant other had commented: "It was great. We were naked in the ocean before the ceremony; a half-hour later, we were married and naked in the ocean").

It's my favorite online McLachlan interview. (My favorite McLachlan feature, "Fair Maiden," pitched on its cover as "The Suddenly Perfect World of Sarah McLachlan," appears in September 1997's *Vancouver* magazine under the byline of Jeff Bateman, a guy who — I hear through the 'vine — is likewise developing a collection of lawyerly "communications".)

At any rate, Olden asks McLachlan about her work on the new album due in stores 15 July: "Basically, at this point, everything's taken precedence over writing. I've kind of done that on purpose — I just needed to have a little bit of a life, a normal life after two years on the road. In many ways, touring feels like suspended reality in that so much goes by you and you can't focus on it because you're moving in this whirlwind."

"So," asks Olden, "performing isn't your favorite part of the process?"

"Oh, quite the opposite. I adore it. I love playing live. It's the 22 other hours of the day that are in suspended reality. Not that being up on stage and being put on the pedestal and somewhat idolized is not a suspension of reality — because it certainly is — but, that's not the reason I do it. I simply love playing." (So did Glenn Gould.)

Talk turns to differences in reality on and off the road before McLachlan fields a query concerning the content of her work. "People," she explains, "often ask why do I lay my heart on my sleeve, as it were. I have this huge separation between me and my music even though when I'm writing it, it's very personal. I'm right in the middle of it and very involved in it. It's almost like I'm two people. In one verse, I'm talking about me; in another verse, I'm talking about someone else. But because I'm talking in the first person, it always seems like me. Half of the experiences in the song aren't mine — they're me putting myself in other people's shoes. How would I feel if . . . ?

And then, there's creative license, too." (Creative licence? I thought it was *poetic* licence. Did somebody steal my licence? And, another thing, a writer doesn't talk in one verse, a singer does; a writer writes in the first person, not a talker.)

A few weeks before the release of SURFACING, McLachlan returned to this "whirlwind" theme when describing the genesis of the album to Betsy Powell at *The Toronto Star*. "For SURFACING," Powell reports, "she headed to Quebec to a tiny cabin in the mountains free of distractions — something McLachlan says she's highly susceptible to. 'Give me a distraction and, boy, I'll take it.' She spent eight months there — with a nine-day timeout to elope with her drummer, Ashwin Sood, in Jamaica last February — but after weeks of attempts she grew frustrated with the songwriting process."

"I was writing this horrible victim (expletive) whine, whine, whine," she told Powell. "I needed to do that to realize, 'Wow I got to get out of this.'"

"She was able to exorcize her demons with the help of a polarity therapist," Powell reports. "The whole world should have one," McLachlan said. "She'd feel your stomach and know exactly what's going on in your mind."

Three days before the new CD surfaced, Chris Dafoe of *The Globe and Mail* interviewed McLachlan in her new home (where it seems she now entertains her favorite interviewers) to find out what was going on in her mind while recording SURFACING. "There were so many psychological blocks in making this record. . . . The first and biggest one was: Finishing record equals touring, therefore, never finish record. . . . It was the last thing I wanted to do . . . but I was so wrapped up in everybody else's needs. You know — 'must write song.' All that came out was total drivel. Pierre just told me to go home."

Nevertheless, she somehow found the inspiration to compose a set of songs she calls "*ridiculously* autobiographical and had I even thought about it, I don't think I could have written these songs. . . . Usually, it's been really joyful to make music, and this time, it wasn't. It was really hard work, because I was dealing with things in myself that I didn't like."

Taking up this autobiographical theme, Dafoe writes; "SUR-FACING is more nakedly emotional and more musically direct than anything McLachlan has previously released. . . . What's most striking about SURFACING is the way it strips away some of the levels of artifice that McLachlan used in her earlier work, such as the use of characters and murky metaphors. She obliquely comments on that earlier style in the first single, *Building A Mystery*. In the song, co-written by Marchand, she sings of a man 'who lives in a church/And sleeps with voodoo dolls' and wears 'a cross from a faith that died/before Jesus came.' It sounds like a gentle swipe at the elaborate exoticism of teenage Goths, but McLachlan insists that it's about her. 'It's about being insecure and creating a facade that's more interesting than you think you are,' she said, laughing. 'That's me. That's most of the people I know. . . .' "

Hm-m-m. Like, McLachlan knows, person-to-personally, the repulsive subject of *Building A Mystery*? Perhaps that's why SUR-FACING hints, heavily, at the sort of calamity from which — if one possesses dignity and human fealty — one never recovers (evidenced in the high quotient of songs exploring the capriciousness of fate and human fallibility alongside issues surrounding the good, the bad, the bullshit and such).

The disc's lead-off cut, *BAM*, hits listeners over the head with the arresting violence of its imagery augmented by a thwangy acoustic/electric guitar mix. "You come out at night," McLachlan sardonically but melodically rasp warbles. Meantimes, the strident and rhythmic insistence of the track's front-and-center acoustic instruments complements the electric backwash; so, by the time "you live in a church" gets the full vocal treatment, the echo effect dominates, a well-crafted sonic segue where sound and sense collide.

It's a catchy kind of retroactive shuffleduster, a quarter-note shy of country, if only because its vampiric implications ain't gonna wash with the folks back home. And then, there's all that heavy-handed hush-hush on the titillating black-magic stuff. A touch of Lilith, the mistress of dark-lore. Oh, well. What the hell. It's tough work (but somebody's got to do it):

You live in a church
Where you sleep with voodoo dolls
And you won't give up the search
For the ghosts in the halls
You wear sandals in the snow
And a smile that won't wash away ·
Can you look out the window
Without your shadow getting in the way
'Cause you're working
Building a mystery
Holding on and holding it in
Yeah, you're working
Building a mystery
And choosing so carefully . . .
You're a beautiful, a beautiful fucked-up man
You're setting up your razor-wire shrine
'Cause you're working . . .

— from *Building A Mystery*

An intriguing aspect additionally propels SURFACING's most uptempo number. By its third and final verse, Marchand's low and slow emergence singing in the farground of McLachlan's background vocals — combined with an aggressive, almost ritualistic bass-high-hat-snare affair on drums — produces a rather obvious Greek-chorus effect; but it does convey both a sense of moral urgency and an opportunity for catharsis, particularly when the subject, "with an edge and charm," wakes up "screaming aloud."

Many of the compositions comprising SURFACING's song cycle address similar issues or explore thematic concerns directly related to the disc's prologue (which subtly introduces the cast of leading characters grappling with elementary pairs of opposites along the lines of good versus evil, hope versus despair and calm versus chaos on *Black & White*, itself another clue to the mystery at the hole and heart of the disc's conundrum).

Angel, a ballad as sumptuous as *I Love You* (particularly in the production department), was one of the first songs McLachlan penned post-therapy. "It was a real joyous occasion," she told

CMJ New Music's Kurt B. Reighley, who suggests the tune "deals with why people in the limelight turn to drugs for solace."

McLachlan, who doesn't smoke marijuana because it makes her paranoid, mildly disagrees: "I hate to pinpoint it like that. . . . [I did read] a series of *Rolling Stone* articles over the past year and a half, typically about heroin in the music industry, and all these people who, one by one, are getting picked off by it. And I just felt a really great empathy in some way for these people. I've been in that place where you're so fucked up and you're so lost that you don't know who you are anymore, and you're miserable — and here's this escape route. I've never done heroin, but I've done plenty of other things to escape."

> *What ravages of spirit*
> *Conjured this temptuous rage*
> *Created you a monster*
> *Broken by the rules of love*
> *And fate has led you through it*
> *You do what you have to do*

> — from *Do What You Have To Do*

Colleen Wolstenholme (the silvercaster) co-wrote *Do What You Have To Do* with McLachlan. It features elegantly spare piano fill superbly interwoven with Barenaked Ladies' Jim Creeggan's adroit fingerworks on upright bass. Elegiac, mournful, soulful — the works at work contain the key which unlocks the door to now or never again.

It's universally true. You do what you have to do — otherwise, why bother?

> *You are pulled from the wreckage*
> *Of your silent reverie*
> *You're in the arms of the angel*
> *May you find some comfort here*

> — from *Angel*

CANADIAN EDITION / JULY 21, 1997. $3.95

TIME

TEEN CRIME
MEXICO'S NAFTA GENERATION

THE GALS TAKE OVER

Macho music is out. Empathy is in. And SARAH McLACHLAN's all-female Lilith Fair is putting rock's hot new sound on the road

Inside 'Scream 2'

Who's That Gay Guy?

PLUS
Hollywood's Strangest Scandal Robert Mitchum

Entertainment WEEKLY

Lollapalooza?
H.O.R.D.E.?
Fugeddaboudit!
The Women Of The
LILITH
Tour Are Now
Summer's Hot Ticket

music

the rocking girls of summer

It's not Lollapalooza, but it's not trying to be. It's Lilith Fair, and if Sarah McLachlan gets her way, it will be the music event of the year. By James Patrick Herman

sn't this great!" Marla Maples Trump squeals over the roar of guitar feedback as flashbulbs explode all around her. She leans forward on three-inch heels, gesturing toward a wall of posters emblazoned with the words GIRLS RULE and gives the paparazzi two big, glamorously manicured thumbs-up. "It's just like a KISS concert" she says with a laugh.

Except the lineup of tonight's sold-out Jingle Ball '96—New York radio station Z100's fourth annual December live-music showcase—is entirely female. And this 20,000-strong Madison Square Garden audience consists primarily of teenage girls. While the cheering crowd's energy level could compete with that of a KISS concert, testosterone is in short supply, particularly for a rock 'n' roll, stadium-site, $35-ticket event. Following an impromptu backstage photo op, Trump, one of Jingle Ball's celebrity MCs, returns to her position just behind an enormous red curtain,

Left: Sarah McLachlan in front of [...] taking plac[...] tional music," she offer[...] earlier, impulsive compa[...] any fireworks going off.

With star power lik[...] Stefani, Tracy Cha[...] McLachlan working t[...] need for schlocky KIS[...] pyrotechnic explosions [...] blood variety. For toni[...] the music appears to [...] enough. "It's about [...] Frederique, another e[...] host watching from the [...] X-chromosome-centr[...] women in music to s[...] and"—the promotio[...] eye—'rule.' Yeah, let them rule"

One woman in particular comes to mind. January 30, 1997, some seven weeks after the Jingle Ball, high on a Montreal mountaintop, folk-pop artist Sarah McLachlan has isolated herself inside of a tiny pine cabin so cold that ice has formed between its logs. A modern-day damsel in distress (though there's no longer any golden hair to let down; she recently hacked off nine years' growth in favor of a boyish pixie), the twenty-nine-year-old Canadian who has sold more than three million albums is suffering from writer's block. And her fourth album for Arista Records must be finished by the "terrifying" deadline of May 12 (six songs down, seven to go). "My fans are not fickle," she rationalizes, stirring the flames of a sluggish fire with a poker, "they'll wait. If I force it, I'll just end up with a crappy record." While McLachlan has always kept one foot firmly planted on the cutting edge (she released one of the first ever multimedia-packed enhanced CDs, her last hit single, "Possession," about an obsessed fan, offset her gorgeous two-and-a-half octave soprano with a hip-hop beat), her current goal is to transcend trends and produce a record of "timeless beauty." But McLachlan's lyrical targets (despite confessional tendencies, she also delivers smart, even hilarious, social commentary) are very of-the-moment. One of her playful new songs teases a certain male music icon who dates groupies half his age; another, called "Angel," viscerally describes the peace that escapism-starved stars find in heroin. She's an acute and frankly honest observer of emotional motivations. Her last and most successful album was titled *Fumbling Toward Ecstasy* and like much of her music, it explored the agony.

"I haven't written a thing in four months >

Volume 65 No. 25 - August 25, 1997
$3.00 ($2.80 plus .20 GST)
Mail Registration No. 1351

Lilith Fair scores a first for Molson Amphitheatre

by Judith Fitzgerald

Where else but at a festival aptly named Lilith Fair does one get an earful of Shawn Colvin, Indigo Girls, Jewel and Sarah McLachlan on top of an eyeful of the way in which benevolent corporations sponsor music festivals?

After all, McLachlan and her people had pooh-poohed automakers, Vanity Fair and suchlike when hunting for acceptable patrons of the performing arts (ubiquitously and annoyingly "present" throughout the carnival-like venue).

The amphitheatre, flanked with ginormous banners and a backdrop containing much in the line of loosely labelled art of the new-age aesthetic -- princes, vamps, steeds, demons cavorting with carnally mythic figures -- tended to interfere with the music presented, particularly since strategically placed video terminals additionally spewed endless repeats of three or four ads for booze and Bryan Adams.

The human view proved far more interesting, at least in demographic terms. Not surprisingly, single nubbie friskies from sandal-and-sneakerdom politely mingled with a representative raft of wallflowers and a high percentage of same-sex couples in a sea of white middle-class festival-flockers.

Given its advance billing among high-end hawkers the calibre of all the usual media suspects, the anti-climactic show, minimally marred by rivers of rain and muck, provided ticket holders with adequate and predictable second-stage performances from Lhasa and Wild Strawberries before Dayna

LILITH continued on page 2

Prior to Lilith Fair, a personable Sarah McLachlan was pictured signing an autograph at a recent HMV in-store downtown Toronto.

During her HMV in-store appearance, Nettwerk recording artist Sarah McLachlan performed four songs to a receptive audience.

NO. 1 ALBUM	NO. 1 HIT	ALBUM PICK	HIT PICK

BACKSTREET BOYS	**BUILDING A MYSTERY**	**JOHN McDERMOTT**	**I AM THE MAN**
Backstreet's Back	Sarah McLachlan	When I Grow Too Old To Dream	The Philosopher kings
41617-2-N	Nettwerk-F	EMI/Angel - 54637-F	Columbia-H

DISCOGRAPHY

TOUCH (Nettwerk 1988)

Out Of The Shadows / Steaming / Strange World / Touch / Vox / Sad Clown / Uphill Battle / Ben's Song / Vox (extended version) / Ben's Song (78 version)

TOUCH (Arista 1989)

Out Of The Shadows / Vox / Strange World / Trust / Touch / Steaming / Sad Clown / Uphill Battle / Ben's Song / Vox (extended version)

Singles:

Vox (1988), *Touch* (1989), *Steaming* (1989)

SOLACE (Nettwerk 1991)

Drawn To The Rhythm / Into The Fire / The Path Of Thorns (Terms) / I Will Not Forget You / Lost / Back Door Man / Shelter / Home / Mercy

SOLACE (Arista 1992)

Drawn To The Rhythm / Into The Fire / The Path Of Thorns (Terms) / I Will Not Forget You / Lost / Back Door Man / Shelter / Black / Home / Mercy / Wear Your Love Like Heaven

Singles:

Into the Fire (1991), Drawn To The Rhythm (1992)

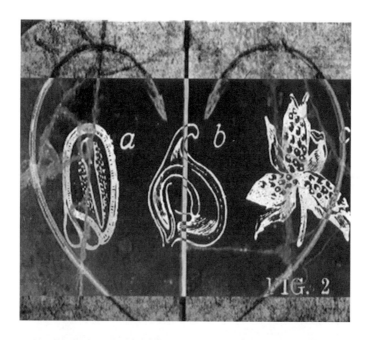

LIVE (Nettwerk 1992)

Drawn To The Rhythm / Back Door Man / Home / Lost / I Will Not Forget You / Black / Ben's Song

FUMBLING TOWARDS ECSTASY (Nettwerk and Arista 1993)

Possession / Wait / Plenty / Good Enough / Mary / Elsewhere / Circle / Ice / Hold On / Ice Cream / Fear / Fumbling Towards Ecstasy / Possession (Piano Version)

Singles:
Possession (1993), *Hold On* (1994), *Good Enough* (1994)

THE FREEDOM SESSIONS (Nettwerk 1994 and Arista 1995)

Elsewhere / Plenty / Mary / Good Enough / Hold On / Ice Cream / Ice / Ol' 55 / Hold On

RARITIES, B-SIDES, AND OTHER STUFF (Nettwerk 1996)

Dear God / I Will Remember You / Fear / Gloomy Sunday / Full of Grace / Song For A Winter's Night / Blue / Drawn To The Rhythm / Shelter / As The End Draws Near / Vox / Into The Fire / Possession

SURFACING (Nettwerk and Arista 1997)

Building A Mystery / I Love You / Sweet Surrender / Adia / Do What You Have To Do / Witness / Angel / Black & White / Full Of Grace

Singles:
Building A Mystery (1997), *Sweet Surrender* (1997)

Videos:
Touch
Steaming
Ben's Song
The Path Of Thorns
Into The Fire
Drawn To The Rhythm
Possession
Hold On
Good Enough
I Will Remember You
Fumbling Towards Ecstasy
Building a Mystery

SELECTED BIBLIOGRAPHY

Ali, Lorraine. "Backstage at Lilith." *Rolling Stone*, 4 September 1997.

anonymous. "AOL Live with Sarah McLachlan." America Online, Inc., 1997.

Anonymous. "By: Women/For: Everyone." *Interview*, July 1997.

Anonymous. "Cockburn and McLachlan Coming to Town." *The Toronto Star*, 10 October 1991.

Anonymous. "Exposed: Regional Reports." *Music Express*, July 1989.

Anonymous. "Exposed: Regional Reports." *Music Express*, September 1989.

Anonymous. "Girlie Goddess Tour Brings Sisters Together in Emotion," *The Detroit Free Press*, 14 June 1996.

Anonymous. "Grapes of Wrath Puts the Squeeze on Four Awards." *The Globe and Mail*, 11 November 1991.

Anonymous. *Maritime Conservatory of Music Convocation Programme*, 1985.

Anonymous. *Maritime Conservatory of Music Convocation Programme*, 1986.

Anonymous. *Maritime Conservatory of Music Convocation Programme*, 1987.

Anonymous. "McLachlan, Blue Rodeo Win . . . Awards." *The Globe and Mail*, 30 September 1994.

Anonymous. "McLachlan Gains Single Eastern Honour." *The Canadian Press*, 18 February 1992.

Anonymous. "Nettwerk Expected to

Sue Duchess of York." (Letters) *FRANK*, 30 July 1997.

Anonymous. "McLachlan on the Rise." *International Musician*, June 1989.

Anonymous. "New Tougher Sound for Sarah McLachlan." *The Vancouver Sun*, 20 November 1993.

Anonymous. "Oh Canada!" *Maclean's*, 1 July 1994.

Anonymous. "Ron Hynes Wins Three East-Coast Awards." *The Globe and Mail*, 15 February 1994.

Anonymous. "Raves." *Rolling Stone*, October 1994.

Anonymous. "Sarah McLachlan Firmed for Hummingbird Date." *RPM Chart Weekly*, 22 September 1997.

Anonymous. "Sarah McLachlan Lawyers Fumble Towards Libel Action." *FRANK*, 16 July 1997.

Anonymous. "Sarah McLachlan Sued Over Song Rights." *FRANK*, 24 May 1995.

Anonymous. "Sarah McLachlan Online Chat." Sprint Communications Company, L.P., 1996.

Anonymous. "Stevie Nicks/Sarah McLachlan." *Interview*, March 1995.

Anonymous. "The Death of Sarah's Stalker: Questions about Obsessed Fan Won't Go Away." *FRANK*, 13 August 1997.

Anonymous. Untitled. *B-Side*, October 1994.

Anonymous. Untitled. *The Indianapolis Star*, 23 January 1995.

Anonymous. Untitled. *L.A. Times*, 9 October 1994.

Anonymous. Untitled. *Seventeen*, October 1994.

Anonymous. Untitled. *The Toronto Star*, 2 April 1965.

Anonymous. Untitled. *World Café*, March 1994.

Arsenault, Tim. "McLachlan Carves into U.S. Market." *The Halifax Chronicle-Herald*, 11 March 1992.

_____. "McLachlan Lightens Up." *The Halifax Chronicle-Herald*, 25 November 1993.

_____. "The Sarah McLachlan Interview." *The Halifax Chronicle-Herald*, 10 July 1997.

_____. "Things Are Moving Quickly as McLachlan Heads South." *The Halifax Chronicle-Herald*, 13 February 1989.

_____. "Touching Début from McLachlan." *The Halifax Chronicle-Herald*, 5 November 1988.

Band, Ira. "Stung by Sting and Lovin' It." *The Toronto Star*, 21 July 1996.

Barnard, Elissa. "Creative Control Provides Solace for McLachlan." *The Halifax Chronicle-Herald*, 13 July 1991.

_____. "Hometown Crowd Awed by Soaring McLachlan Voice." *The Halifax Chronicle-Herald*, 6 May 1989.

Bateman, Jeff. "A Certain Solace for Sarah McLachlan." *The Record*, 1 July 1991.

_____. "Fair Maiden." *Vancouver*, September 1997.

_____. "McLachlan Surfaces at Top with New Tour and Album." *The Record*, 21 July 1997.

Bialis, Michael. "Cool Climate for Songbirds: Sarah McLachlan Latest Canadian to Make Her Mark." *The Denver Post*, 26 September 1994.

Cantin, Paul. "Sarah Comes to the Surface." *The Ottawa Sun*, 13 July 1997.

_____."Fan Sues McLachlan." *The Ottawa Sun*, 16 September 1994.

_____."Fan Sues McLachlan." *The Ottawa Sun*, 16 September 1994.

Chandler, Raymond. *The Simple Art of Murder*. Ballantine/Random, 1934; rpt. 1972.

Charabati, Victoria France. "Suzanne Vega." *Contemporary Musicians*. Gale Research Inc., 1994.

"'Fan Sues McLachlan." *The Ottawa Sun*, 16 September 1994.

Chua-Eoan, Howard. "The Shaping of Jewel." *Time*, 21 July 1997.

Citron, Paula. "Soothing Sounds for Troubled Times." *The Toronto Star*, 29 March 1992.

Clough, Peter. "Songbird Sarah's Story: The Day She Discovered the Woman in the Jewellery Store Was Her Birth Mom." *The Vancouver Province*, 28 August 1997.

_____. "Surfacing Soon: 'Incendiary' Info about Songbird Sarah McLachlan — Courtesy of Author's Hush-Hush X Files." *The Vancouver Province*, 10 August 1997.

Considine, J.D. "McLachlan Album Boasts Band Sound." *The Baltimore Sun*, 24 March 1994.

Cromelin, Richard. "Hysteria and Tears Help Canadian Singer Bring Out the 'Good Stuff.'" *L.A. Times*, 9 August 1992.

Dafoe, Chris. "Female Rock Fest Battles Attitudes." *The Globe and Mail*, 14 September 1996.

_____. "McLachlan Finds Her Musical Touch." *The Globe and Mail*, 3 May 1989.

_____. "Sarah Surfaces." *The Globe and Mail*, 12 July 1997.

Daigle, Richard J. & Lapides, Frederick R. *The Mentor Dictionary of Mythology & the Bible*. New American Library, 1973.

Dalton, Mary. "Medusa and Dracula." *The Time of Icicles*, Breakwater, 1989.

Daly, Steven. "Jewel's Paradise." *Details*, July 1997.

Debord, Guy. *The Society of the Spectacle*. Trns. Donald Nicholson-Smith, Zone, 1994.

Doole, Kerry. "Sarah McLachlan: A Midas Touch." *Music Express*, April 1989.

Droganes, Constance. "Singing It Her Way." *Flare*, June 1991.

Dunn, Jancee. "Cosmic Girl." *Rolling Stone*, 15 May 1997.

Eagleton, Terry. "Awakening from Modernity." *Times Literary Supplement*, 20 February 1987.

Ellul, Jacques. *The Technological Society*. Vintage/Random, 1964.

Farley, Christopher John. "Galapalooza." *Time*, 21 July 1997.

Ferris, Thomas & Stephenson, Calvin *vs* Nettwerk Productions Ltd., Nettoverboard Publishing (a partnership), N.T.W.K. Publishing (a partnership), Nettwerk Productions (a partnership), Mark Jowett, Ric Arboit and Terry McBride.

Supreme Court of British Columbia. *Statement of Claim No. A951231* (Amended), 15 July 1995.

Fitzgerald, Judith. "Canadian Radio Lets Down Our Stars." *The Toronto Star*, 16 February 1992.

_____. "Country 59 a Welcome Addition." *The Toronto Star*, 15 March 1992.

_____. "Lilith Fair Scores a First for Molson Amphithreatre." *RPM Chart Weekly*, 25 August 1997.

Gabereau, Vicki. "An Interview with Sarah McLachlan." *CBC Radio* (Bowden's Transcript Service), 30 May 1997.

Gardner, Elysa. "Fumbling Towards Ecstasy." *Rolling Stone*, 16 June 1994.

_____. "New Faces: Sarah McLachlan: Happy To Be Unhappy." *Rolling Stone*, 6 February 1992.

Glader, Mike & Gordon, Julia. "Sarah McLachlan Radiant at Riverport." *Night Times*, September 1995.

Germovsek, Kim. "McLachlan Brings Refreshing Honesty To Her Songs." *Knight/Ridder Tribune News Service*, 17 March 1994.

Goldberg, Michael, ed. "Lilith Fair Needs a Dose of Punk." *Addicted to Noise*, www.addict.com, 25 July 1997.

_____. "Sarah McLachlan Surfaces on Charts at No. 2." *Addicted to Noise*, www.addict.com, 24 July 1997.

_____. "Sunday Morning: Reflections on the Lilith Fair." *Addicted to Noise*, www.addict.com, 13 July 1997.

Grant, Kieran. "McLachlan Holds Fans Spellbound with Old New Tunes." *The Toronto Sun*, 30 June 1995.

_____. "Shorn Sarah Wows This Benefit Crowd." *The Toronto Sun*, 13 February 1997.

Graves, Robert. *The Greek Myths*. Viking/Penguin, rpt. 1960.

Harrington, Richard. "The Beat Goes On." *The Washington Post*, 6 June 1997.

Harrison, Tom. "Lilith Fair Rocks with a Mellow Vibe." *The Vancouver Province*, 25 August 1997.

Harvey, David. *The Condition of Postmodernity: An Enquiry into the Origins of Cultural Change*. Blackwell, 1990.

Heinrich, Kim. Untitled. *The Vancouver Sun*, 11 August 1992.

Herman, James Patrick. "The Rocking Girls of Summer." *Elle*, June 1997.

Hughes, Kim. "Gifted Singer Uses Classical Roots to Propel Eloquent Pop." *Now*, 11 - 17 July 1991.

Howell, Peter. "McLachlan Busy Fending off Fanatics." *The Toronto Star*, 25 November 1993.

_____. "McLachlan Tour Potential Powerful." *The Toronto Star*, 26 August 1996.

_____. "Oysters Like Their Country with No Bull." *The Toronto Star*, 6 December 1991.

_____. "Rising Star McLachlan Does it Her Way." *The Toronto Star*, 12 July 1991.

_____. "The Wired World of Sarah McLachlan." *The Toronto Star*, 19 June 1995.

_____. "Who's That Girl...?" *The Toronto Star*, 11 November 1993.

Jackson, Rick, ed. "Sarah McLachlan." *Encyclopedia of Canadian Rock, Pop and Folk*, Quarry, 1994.

Jennings, David. Untitled. *Melody Maker*, 13 June 1992.

Jennings, Nicholas. "Heart on Her Sleeve." *Maclean's*, 28 March 1994.

_____. "Front and Centre Stage." *Maclean's*, 28 July 1997.

Johnson, Anne Jannette. "Emmylou Harris." *Contemporary Musicians*. Gale Research Inc., 1994.

_____. "Mary Chapin Carpenter." *Contemporary Musicians*. Gale Research Inc., 1994.

Joyce, Mike. "McLachlan's Fine Fumble." *The Washington Post*, 16 September 1994.

Keeley, Denise. "Sarah Has Cause to Celebrate." *Scene*, 27 August 1997.

Lacey, Liam. " 'I Don't Need to Sell a Million Records to Feel Satisfied.' " *The Globe and Mail*, 15 June 1991.

Lasker, Steven. "Liner Notes." *Billie Holiday: The Complete Decca Recordings*. MCA, 1991.

Lee, Kagin. Untitled. *Mindlink*, www.best.com/~donh/sarah/mindlink.txt, May, 1994.

Lesinski, Jeanne M. "Tracy Chapman." *Contemporary Musicians*. Gale Research Inc., 1994.

Linden, J.J. & Burman, Terry. *Building a Star System in Canada*. RPM Music, 1980.

MacDonald, Ronald Foley. "Sarah McLachlan: Pre-Raphaelite Pop." *Music Express*, November 1988.

Mackie, John. "Down-to-Earth Singer Who Makes Heavenly Music." *The Vancouver Sun*, 13 October 1988.

_____. "McLachlan Gives Heart to Darkness." *The Vancouver Sun*, 28 October 1993.

_____. "McLachlan's Voice Travels Well." *The Vancouver Sun*, 3 July 1992.

_____. "Music to the Touch." *The Vancouver Sun*, 19 August 1991.

Maroff, Diane. "Sarah McLachlan." *Contemporary Musicians*. Gale Research Inc., 1994.

McLachlan, Sarah. "On My Mind." *Network*, February 1993.

_____. *The Sarah McLachlan Songbook*. Hal Leonard/Sony Music Publishing, 1994.

McLuhan, Marshall. *Understanding Media: The Extensions of Man*. McGraw-Hill, 1964.

Meers, Erik Ashok. "Kiosk Connection." *People*, 10 July 1995.

Mehle, Michael. "McLachlan Drives All-Female Festival." *Express Magazine*, 17 July 1997.

Melhuish, Martin. *Oh What a Feeling: A Vital History of Canadian Music*. Quarry, 1996.

Michel, Sia. "Sarah McLachlan: Between Two Worlds." *The New York Times*, 18 August 1997.

Mills, Hilary. *Norman Mailer: A Biography*. Empire, 1982.

Monk, Katherine. " 'Feminine' Rock Concept Marketing Success Story." *Express Magazine*, 17 July 1997.

_____. "Lilith Fair's a Hit, But It Won't Make a Profit." *The Vancouver*

Sun, 23 August 1997.

_____. "Lilith Fair." *The Vancouver Sun*, 23 August 1997.

_____. "Love Pours Down at Lilith Fair." *The Vancouver Sun*, 25 August 1997.

Morse, Steve. "McLachlan Is Making Her Mark." *The Calgary Herald*, 3 August 1989.

Munday, Chris. "Jewel." *US*, August 1997.

Muretich, James. "Beyond Touch." *The Calgary Herald*, 26 January 1989.

_____. "Glimpses of Ecstasy." *The Calgary Herald*, 24 October 1993.

_____. "Growing Up." *The Calgary Herald*, 30 June 1991.

Neudorf, Darryl *vs* Nettoverboard Publishing (a partnership), Mark Jowett, Ric Arboit, Terry McBride and Sarah McLachlan. Supreme Court of British Columbia. *Statement of Claim No. C950847*, 1 February 1995.

Nicholis, Stephen. "Cochrane Rides High After Junos." *The Canadian Press*, 31 March 1992.

Niester, Alan. "Audience Adores Beatific McLachlan." *The Globe and Mail*, 15 April 1994.

_____. "A Voice at the Cutting Edge." *The Globe and Mail*, 28 March 1992.

Odintz, Andrea. Untitled. *Rolling Stone*, 18 May 1995.

Olden, Megan. "The Art of Contradiction." *Mondo 2000*, Winter 1996/Spring 1997.

Ostick, Stephen. "McLachlan Content to Await U.S. Break." *The Winnipeg Free Press*, 15 November 1991.

Pierce, Jennifer. Untitled. *Vogue*, May 1994.

Pittaway, Kim. "Tumbling into Ecstasy." *Chatelaine*, November 1996.

Platt, Trevor. *Physiological Bases of Phytoplankton Ecology*. Canadian Bulletins of Fisheries and Aquatic Sciences Series, 1981.

Postman, Neil. *Amusing Ourselves to Death: Public Discourse in the Age of Show Business*. Viking/Penguin, 1985.

Powell, Betsy. "Hip Picks in the Sticks for Yet Another Roadside Attraction." *The Toronto Star*, 31 July 1997.

_____. "Colvin Heeds Lilith's Call." *The Toronto Star*, 14 August 1997.

_____. "Lilith Fair Tour Knocks Rock's Roll." *The Toronto Star*, 11 August 1997

_____. "Lilith Sings Women's Song." *The Toronto Star*, 16 August 1997.

_____. "McLachlan Resurfaces." *The Toronto Star*, 25 June 1997.

_____. "McLachlan's CD Surfaces Tomorrow," *The Toronto Star*, 14 July 1997.

Powers, Ann. "Sarah McLachlan." *US*, August 1997.

Press, Joy. Untitled. *Spin*. October 1994.

Punter, Jennie. "Sarah McLachlan Spins a Charming Spell." *The Toronto Star*, 28 November 1993.

Pynchon, Thomas. *Mason & Dixon*. Henry Holt, 1997.

Ramstad, Evan. "Music Industry Uses Leftover Space on CDs." *The*

Winnipeg Free Press, 7 May 1995.

Rayner, Ben. "I Am Woman, Hear Me Roar." *The Ottawa Sun*, 30 August 1997.

Reighley, Kurt B. "Sarah McLachlan in The Garden." *CMJ*, August 1997.

Renzetti, Elizabeth. "Sarah McLachlan's Therapy Sends Fans Home Gratified." *The Globe and Mail*, 1 July 1995.

Roberts, David. Untitled. *Q*. November 1994.

Robertson, Robin. *Your Shadow*. A.R.E., 1997.

Robicheau, Paul. "Surfacing." *The Boston Globe*, 7 August 1997.

Ross, Mike. "Dark Angel Delivers Beauty." *JAM! Music*, www.canoe.ca, 19 July 1997.

_____. "Songstress Emerges Victorious from Her Struggle with Celebrity." *Music Express*, 13 July 1997.

Sakamoto, John. "Anti-Lollapalooza Announces Dates." *JAM! Music*, www.canoe.ca, 19 May 1997.

Sawatzky, Jeffrey Charles *vs* Nettwerk Productions Ltd., Nettoverboard Publishing (a partnership), Mark Jowett, Ric Arboit, Terry McBride and Sarah McLachlan. Supreme Court of British Columbia. *Statement of Claim No. C951105*, 1 March 1995.

Scherman, Tony. Untitled. *Entertainment Weekly*, 18 February 1994.

Scribner, Sara. "Into the Light." *Request*, August 1997.

Sheppard, Denise. Untitled. *JAM! Music*, www.canoe.ca, June 1996.

Shulman, Morton. *Coroner*. Fitzhenry & Whiteside, 1975.

Sischy, Ingrid. "Jewel." *Interview*, July 1997.

Slater, Philip. *The Pursuit of Loneliness*. Beacon, 1970.

Smith, Chris. "Paula Cole." *US*, July 1997.

Stevenson, Jane. "Beautiful Women, Beautiful Day." *The Toronto Sun*, 7 July 1997.

_____. "Down to Earth: Sarah McLachlan Doesn't Know How to Be Anything but Honest." *The Toronto Sun*, 3 August 1997.

_____. "Honest, Sarah." *The Toronto Sun*, 26 June 1997.

_____. "Lilith Is Fairest of Them All." *The Toronto Sun*, 16 August 1997.

_____. "Sarah McLachlan Is Down to Earth." *The Toronto Sun*, 3 August 1997.

_____. "Sarah's Surfacing with Her Dark Side." *The Toronto Sun*, 24 June 1997.

_____. "Success Has Drawbacks for Critically Acclaimed Singer Sarah McLachlan." *The Canadian Press*, 17 May 1990.

Stoute, Lenny. "Folkie Sarah McLachlan Looking More Assured." *The Toronto Star*, 14 April 1994.

Styron, William. *Darkness Visible: A Memoir of Madness*. Vintage/Random, 1990.

Tattersall, Jane & Hrynyshyn, James. "Object of Obsession." *Ottawa Xpress*, 18 January 1995.

Tearson, Michael. Untitled. *Audio*, June 1994.

Thigpen, David. "Joni's Heir." *Time*, 21 March 1994.

Thomas, Elizabeth. "Indigo Girls." *Contemporary Musicians*. Gale Research Inc., 1994.

Vandrei, Uwe vs Sarah McLachlan. Ontario Court (General Division). *Statement of Claim No. 85502/94*, 2 September 1994.

Vandrei, Uwe. *A Treatment for a Screenplay*, 1993. Private collection.

_____. "Oh, Sarah." Judith Fitzgerald, ed., 1992-1994. Private collection.

Varty, Alexander. "Under the Surface." *Georgia Strait*, 14 - 21 August 1997.

Verna, Paul, ed. "Reviews & Previews." *Billboard*, 26 July 1997.

Watson, Dave. "Hungry & Focused." *Vancouver*, December 1989.

Whiting, Don. "Medusa Nickname Post." *Fumbling-Towards-Ecstasy Listserv*, 1994.

Willman, Chris. "The Women of Lilith Fair." *Entertainment Weekly*, 9 May 1997.

Wyatt, Nelson. "McLachlan Sheds Clothes for 'Path Of Thorns' Video." *The Canadian Press*, 20 September 1991.

Zinn, Megan Rubiner. "Shawn Colvin." *Contemporary Musicians*. Gale Research Inc., 1994.

Vital Links and Cyber-vistas

Textor Communications
http://www.textorcom.com/

FRANK
http://www.frankmag.com/

The Sea of Waking Dreams
http://www.aquezada.com/sarah/

Out Of The Shadows: October Game Factoids
http://www.fumbling.com/sarah/october-game.html/

The Quiet Touch of Solace
http://www.interlog.com/~ditko37/sarahmc.html/

Environment Canada Weather
http://www.weatheroffice.com/

Canada 411
http://www.canada411.sympatico.ca/

Yahoo! Canada
http://www.yahoocanada.ca/
Directory of /listserv/fumbling-towards-ecstasy/archive

ftp://yoyo.cc.monash.edu.au/listserv/fumbling-towards-ecstasy/archive/

Uwe Vandrei's [edited] Internet Post to F-T-E http://www.users.compass-works.com/~squid/sarah/oldfaq/

Jam! Sarah McLachlan Database
http://www.canoe.ca/JamMusic SarahMcLachlan/home.html/

The Muse Interview
"A Journey that Led to the Extremes of Human Kindness and Cruelty."

http://www.val.net/
The Official Mondo 2000 Website

http://www.mondo2000.com/
Dalhousie's Department of Biology Home Page

http://is.dal.ca/~sfry/homepage.html

Virtual Nowhere
http://www.onlink.net/~fitz/

ACKNOWLEDGMENTS
and Credits

Permissions
"Sarah McLachlan Sued Over Song Rights" and "The Death of Sarah's Stalker . . . Questions About Obsessed Fan Won't Go Away," copyright by FRANK, reprinted by permission of FRANK. "Medusa and Dracula," copyright by Mary Dalton, from *The Time of Icicles*, reprinted by permission of Mary Dalton and Breakwater. "Lilith Fair Scores a First for Molson Amphitheatre," copyright Judith Fitzgerald, reprinted by permission of *RPM Weekly*. Letters, poems, and screenplay treatment by Uwe Vandrei, copyright by Connie Vandrei, reprinted by permission of Connie Vandrei.

Lyrics
Lyrics quoted from songs from TOUCH published by Tyde Music; on SOLACE published by Tyde Music; on FUMBLING TOWARDS ECSTASY published by Tyde Music, except for *Elsewhere* published by Nettoverboard; on SURFACING published by Tyde Music.

Photographs
Cover photograph by Robin Weiner and frontispiece by Thomas Aoyagi, courtesy of CANAPRESS. Photos on pp. 31 (bottom) and p. 32 by Judith Fitzgerald, copyright Judith Fitzgerald.

Author's Acknowledgments

I am forever indebted to Lavina Galbraith (at Textor Communications) and Maestro GM, tireless devil's advocates who challenged, aided, and fortified me in the search for the truth. Without their vital help, technical expertise, specialized information, good judgment, and soul-sustaining encouragement, this book simply would not exist.

I am indebted, in this life, to Connie Vandrei, Sergeant Michael Brehmer (of the Longsault detachment of the Ontario Provincial Police Regional Headquarters), Constable Rudy Schaefers (of the Manotick detachment of the OPP), The Dollards, Hot Stuff, Judy (Kaines) James, Sheila Alder at Carleton Freenet, and Norman Stein.

Special thanks to Adele & Andrianna at the Kingston Coroner's Office, Chet Atkins, CGP, Ken Anderson, Yildiz Atasoy, Jeff Bateman, Anthony Baxter, Blake Bell, David Berg, Chris Blythe, Sonya and Teri Brandt, Dr. Sheena Brannigan, Tony Brown at MCA/Nashville, Al Campagnola at CISS-FM, Paul Cantin, Caroline & Yvette Corriveau at Freedom of Information, Russell Carter of the Indigo Girls, Ray & Tracy Childerhose, Greg Clark, Peter Clough at *The Vancouver Province*, Connie at 310-BELL (Kingston), Norma Corbett at the Halifax Reference Library, Lynn Crosbie, David Dalton, Linda Dalton, Mary Dalton, Dawn-Marie (1093), The Darcys, Mike & Lorraine Dart at North Bay's Sure Copy Centre, Dave Deeley at Sony Music Canada, Joanna Dines at Warner Music, John Donlan, Julian Che-Way Dunn, Edmund & Eric at Apple Canada, Barry Edwards, Luchina Fischer at *People*, Frank, Josie Galati at SOCAN, Charlie Gall at SOCAN, Gail Gallant at the *Canadian Broadcasting Corporation*, Meliha Gearing at Sprint Canada, George, Scott and The Girls at Sundridge Pharmacy, Brian Gorman at *The Ottawa Sun*, Jane Harnish at the Maritime Conservatory of Music, Marian D. Hebb of The Writers' Union of Canada, Janet Hillier at the Maritime Conservatory of Music, Cheryl Hines at Bowden's Transcript Service, Michael Holmes, Ken Jalowica, Ron Jeffers, Jennie & Dave, Jennifer at ACS, Bryan Jensen at Environment Canada, Autumn Johnson at Almaguin Automotive, Brian D. Johnson at *Maclean's*, Nancy Keating at the Maritime Conservatory of Music, David Kershaw, Shirley King at SOCAN, Jack Kirchhoff at *The Globe and Mail*, Ann & Bill Lang at Lang & Black, Anita Locs, Liz Locs, Carol McIntyre at the Sundridge Post Office, Paul McKenna, Dorice McLachlan, Mary Dorothy McLachlan, Klaro Mizerit at the Maritime Conservatory of Music, Sarah Murdoch at *The Globe and Mail*, Vel Omazic at Sony Music Canada, Patty at Muskoka Delivery Service, Paula & Jennifer, Rob Payne, Dr. Dan Pessoto, Joan Primeau at *The Toronto Star*, Mr. & Mrs. Jack Quick at Almaguin Automotive, Sandy Radecki at Environment Canada, Don Richardson at Stan Darling Real Estate, Dr. Robin Robertson, Rod at Halifax's Boutelliers, Patrick Roscoe, Sprugeon (Spud) Roscoe, Brad Saltzberg, Sandra, Betty Semple, Sharleen and Paul at Sundridge's One Stop, Jane Sharp & Leah Toth at Sundridge's Royal Bank, Lisa Shepherd at 1-800-56-FRANK, Jonathan Simkin, Dan Smith at *The Toronto Star*, Wayne Snow at the Sundridge Post Office, Mr. & Mrs. John Standing, Jim Sutherland at *Vancouver*, Gregg Wagener, Gail Wahamaa, Bug Walsh, Steve Waxman at Warner Music Canada, Jennifer L. White, Don Whiting, Ulrica Wihlborg at *People*, and Rob Wills at North Bay's Neil Communications & Computer Store, as well as the Writers' Development Trust Fund.

To my cherished friends who understood my long silence (and provided valuable research assistance), especially Ayanna Black, Tom Dilworth, Donn & Bob, Avrum Fenson, Peter Goddard, Jan & Ken Harvey, Ronn & Angela Jefferies, Dick & Lenore Langs, Adam & Martin Levin, The Oasis, John Paul (J.P.) Roberts, Laurie Smith — now, where were we?

To my best friend, tenant-in-common, researcher, nit-picker, editor, proofreader and hero, Dan Jalowica, an eternity's worth of love and *thank you*s.

Thank you, Bob Hilderley and Susan Hannah, *Mystery*'s makers, for understanding and recognizing the possible in the impossible.

Lu thanks Anderson's Do-It Centre, the Berriedale PetroCanners for the doggie biscuits, Penny & Dr. K. A. Euler, Sadie & Sophie Anderson-Galbraith, Jiggs & Jitamo Blythe, Heidi Dart and especially, her best friend, Veronica.

Quarry Press Music Books

□ *Neil Young: Don't Be Denied*
by JOHN EINARSON $19.95 CDN / $14.95 USA

□ *Magic Carpet Ride: The Autobiography of John Kay & Steppenwolf*
by JOHN KAY and JOHN EINARSON $19.95 CDN / $14.95 USA

□ *American Woman: The Story of The Guess Who*
by JOHN EINARSON $19.95 CDN / $14.95 USA

□ *Superman's Song: The Story of Crash Test Dummies*
by STEPHEN OSTICK $19.95 CDN / $14.95 USA

□ *Encyclopedia of Canadian Rock, Pop & Folk Music*
by RICK JACKSON $24.95 CDN / $19.95 USA

□ *Encyclopedia of Canadian Country Music*
by RICK JACKSON $26.95 CDN / $19.95 USA

□ *Some Day Soon: Profiles of Canadian Songwriters*
by DOUGLAS FETHERLING $16.95 CDN / $12.95 USA

□ *Snowbird: The Story of Anne Murray*
by BARRY GRILLS $19.95 CDN / $14.95 USA

□ *The Hawk: The Story of Ronnie Hawkins and The Hawks*
by IAN WALLIS $19.95 CDN / $14.95 USA

□ *Ironic: The Story of Alanis Morissette*
by BARRY GRILLS $18.95 CDN / $14.95 USA

□ *For What It's Worth: The Story of Buffalo Springfield*
by JOHN EINARSON $19.95 CDN / $14.95 USA

□ *Falling Into You: The Story of Céline Dion*
by BARRY GRILLS $19.95 CDN / $14.95 USA

□ *The Legend & The Legacy: The Story of Dick Damron*
by DICK DAMRON $19.95 CDN / $14.95 USA

Available at your favorite bookstore or directly from the publisher:
Quarry Press, P.O. Box 1061, Kingston, ON K7L 4Y5, Canada.
Tel. (613) 548-8429, Fax. (613) 548-1556, E-mail: order@quarrypress.com.

Name _____

Address _____

_____ Postal Code _____ Telephone _____

Visa/Mastercard # _____ Expiry _____

Signature _____ Your books will be shipped with an invoice
enclosed, including shipping costs, payable
within 30 days in Canadian or American currency
(credit card, check, or money order).